FOR THOSE WHO SERVED

WORLD WAR I 1914 - 1918

WORLD WAR II 1939 - 1945

ENCOMPASSING THE GENERAL AREA OF

ALBION, BOLTON, CALEDON EAST, KLEINBERG,

MONO MILLS, MONO ROAD, NASHVILLE, NOBLETON,

ORANGEVILLE, PALGRAVE, SAND HILL and TULLAMORE

National Library of Canada Cataloguing in Publication

Hesp, Murray
     For those who served : World War I, 1914-1918, World War II, 1939-1945 /
Murray Hesp.

ISBN 0-9731724-0-1

     1. Veterans—Ontario—Peel (Regional municipality) 2. World War, 1914-1918—Ontario—
Peel (Regional municipality) 3. World War, 1939-1945—Ontario—Peel (Regional
municipality) 4. Peel (Ont. : Regional municipality)—History, Military—20th century.
I. Caledon East and District Historical Society. II. Title.

UA601.O6H47 2002   305.9'0697'09713535   C2002-904769-2

The Caledon East and District Historical Society gratefully acknowledges the financial
support of the Ontario Trillium Foundation, an agency of the Ministry of Culture. With $100
million in annual funding from Ontario's Charity Casino Initiative, the Foundation provides
grants to eligible charitable and not-for-profit organizations in the arts, culture, sports, recreation, environment and social services sectors.

Care has been taken to trace the ownership of copyright material used in the text. The author
and publisher welcome any information enabling them to correct errors or omissions in
subsequent editions.

Cover design by David Stokes
Edited by Donna Davies
Printed in Canada by Ampersand Printing, Guelph, Ontario

Front Cover: *The two medals shown were awarded to Adam Wallace. The medal on the right is the
Distinguished Conduct Medal. On the left is the Military Medal. The Bolton Cenotaph pictured here is
in the Laurel Hill Cemetery. Both photographs are courtesy Bill Whitbread of The Caledon Enterprise,
Bolton, Ontario. The World War I soldier in the photograph is Adam Wallace and the second photo is
Doris Evans (Porter) of the Canadian Women's Army Corp. Both are from Bolton, Ontario.*

Back Cover: *The First World War is represented by the picture of the Vimy Memorial in France,
courtesy John Stephens of Brampton, Ontario and the soldier pictured representing the Army is Roy
Hesp of Bolton, Ontario. The ship, HMCS Haida, at the Ontario Place dock in Toronto, Ontario,
represents the Navy in the Second World War. The Lancaster bomber from the Canadian Warplane
Heritage Museum in Hamilton, Ontario is an example of the planes flown by the Royal Canadian Air
Force in World War II. Both photos are courtesy Murray Hesp.*

CONTENTS

PREFACE

When I was quite young I remember seeing a newspaper announcing the beginning of World War II. It showed a picture of some men in uniform in a circular formation presenting arms. In my child's mind I interpreted WAR as something that happens when a number of uniformed grownups stand around in a circle and shoot at each other! Obviously, I have since learned that this is not the case. Because war has never been a favourite subject of mine, I must admit I have never really known all that much about what went on from 1939 to 1945, when the Second World War ended. And, I knew even less about World War I. That is, until I met Murray Hesp and became acquainted with his project.

Once I had a chance to look at Murray's research, my knowledge grew by leaps and bounds. I also became convinced immediately that this extensive work had to be published, if only for people like me who knew so little of either of these wars. *For Those Who Served* puts a human face on what happened in those two world wars. True, it illustrates mostly the stories of the men and women from our local area who served, but their stories so parallel the history of the times that it reads like a history text with a personal voice. The book offers an understanding and insights into what the men and women of those times were experiencing and adds knowledge in a manner you would never find in a textbook.

Murray researched the background of the local men and women, their parents, when and where they served and for some, sadly, where they are buried. He spent hours searching for letters written during both wars and ferreting out the experiences of the local people. Without this effort, the stories in *For Those Who Served* would have disappeared along with the people who lived them.

Looking for the right approach to tell their stories, it was decided that the book needed to be structured on a thematic as well as a chronological basis. Thus, Part I covers the First World War while Part II imparts the events of the Second World War. The Introductions to Part I and Part II by Ken Weber are a helpful synopsis of the two world wars. The stories and letters start at the beginning - 1914 and again in 1939 - and work towards peace, in 1918 and 1945. They illustrate what was happening during those years. Casualties and losses and the medals and honours earned are in separate chapters at the end of the two sections. To distinguish Murray's explanations and comments from other elements of the text, we have set them in italics. The letters from the soldiers are in a typeface to simulate handwriting.

I would like to thank the Caledon East and District Historical Society for their support and the Ontario Trillium Foundation for the grant, without which, the book would not have been published. We are indebted to Ken Weber for his interest in this book and his confidence in the project has encouraged us to forge ahead. We have endeavoured to distribute *For Those Who Served* to correspond with Remembrance Day in November 2002 because we feel it is important to keep what we owe these men and women alive in our memories.

Donna Davies
Editor

INTRODUCTION AND ACKNOWLEDGMENTS

When I visited the site of a Canadian War Cemetery in Italy two years ago a deep feeling swept over me. Looking across a massive sea of white stones arranged in neat rows had a profound effect. It brought home the point that these young Canadians had paid dearly to ensure that we at home could continue to live freely in this country we love so much. By the time I left the cemetery I had become inspired with the idea that their sacrifices should not be forgotten, and what better way than to publish a book about their experiences.

For Those Who Served is dedicated to the Canadian men and women who served in the armed forces to protect this land, allowing us to continue to enjoy the many freedoms which have prevailed throughout the years. To them, full praise and glory is extended for their great contributions. Some gave their lives; many were wounded, physically and emotionally; still others, thankfully, returned home to resume their lives in whatever manner was possible at the time.

Those veterans from the County of Peel, as it was known, before it became the Region of Peel in 1973, can take pride in the part they played in preserving freedom and democracy. In particular, this book comments on the sacrifices and praiseworthy achievements of the servicemen and women from the general area of Albion, Bolton, Caledon East, Kleinberg, Mono Mills, Mono Road, Nashville, Nobleton, Orangeville, Palgrave, Sand Hill and Tullamore.

For Those Who Served records 1,018 names from the Caledon area in the two world wars. 123 of these gave their lives. There are 586 names of people listed for the World War I period, of which six are women. During this war, 95 of this number lost their lives. In the section on World War II, 432 names are shown. This includes twenty-three servicewomen who served in various capacities. Of the 432 servicemen and women named, 28 lost their lives.

While I have made every effort to include the names of all people from this area who served during World War I and World War II, there may be omissions. In those instances, I extend a sincere apology to anyone affected.

Ten men from this area served in World War I and again in World War II: Private Charles Wilfred Byrne of Bolton, Private Harry Courtney of Schomberg and Toronto, Private John Hanna and Private Frank Hodgson of Mono Road, Sergeant Norman Hutchinson of Caledon East, Lieutenant Colonel Cecil Roy McCort of Albion Township, Major Charles Read of Toronto and Bolton, Captain William Randall Richardson of Barrie and Bolton, Sergeant Adam Wallace of Bolton, and Major Charles Hunter Wilson of St. George and Bolton.

Many people have generously supported this undertaking by supplying names and dates, lending pictures and informing others about the project so they too could furnish useful information. In particular, the following people have been very helpful by supplying data: Anne Allengame, Heather Broadbent, Edith Downey, Jean Gibson, Mary Grogan, Doug Hill, Roberta Linkletter, Gordon Logan, Bill Munro, Doris Porter, Jean Proctor and Betty Ward. A special contribution was made by Captain (Ret'd) Douglas F. Hersey, CD, RC Sigs who provided advice relating to the proper use of military terminology and abbreviations. His helpfulness was of significant value and much appreciated.

A resource of great importance was the Peel Heritage Complex in Brampton, which stores micro-filmed copies of the Bolton Enterprise, and where Diane Allengame-Kuster and Rowena Cooper were always helpful and obliging. Some photos came from a book in the Peel Heritage Complex entitled,

From Brock to Currie - The Military Development And Exploits Of Canadians In General And Of The Men Of Peel In Particular - 1791 to 1930 - by Wm. Perkins Bull - 1935. *The National Archives of Canada provides access to World War I Attestation papers information. Details regarding servicemen and women who lost their lives in the two world wars are available on the Commonwealth War Graves Commission Debt of Honour web site. These were the original source of valuable data, and their support was important and encouraging. Information was also obtained from birth, death and marriage registrations, cemetery transcriptions and census records.*

In addition, the book, They Shall Grow Not Old, *which lists World War II RCAF casualties, provided important details. The Chinguacousy Branch of the Brampton Public Library was another valuable source of information. Records preserved by Denny and Margaret Leavens of Leavens Printers and Publishers Ltd. were of significant value and their assistance contributed prominently in this venture. Bill Whitbread of the* Caledon Enterprise *was also very helpful by granting permission to review and to use portions of earlier editions of the* Bolton Enterprise.

It is unfortunate that this record was not produced many years ago when more of our veterans were here to review the pages, add their personal stories, and receive some measure of enjoyment. However, with this publication we can at least preserve whatever can be gleaned from the existing, sometimes contradictory, scattered sources of information. During this entire process, the memories of two servicemen who enlisted in two wars, in two generations have been very prevalent. They are my dad, Private Roy Hesp (1894 -1972) and my brother, Leading Aircraftsman John Hesp (1920-1980). They, along with others, served their country with courage and on them special tribute is bestowed by the publication of this book.

There is no doubt this book would not have been published without the involvement of the Caledon East and District Historical Society headed by its President, Donna Davies. Much credit is due to Donna Davies for her initiative in leading the drive to move this project to a printed conclusion and for her editing expertise. Donna's interest, as well as that of others in the Society, never wavered as the project progressed to the finished stage. Thanks also is extended to Ken Weber for his sincere interest in this book, his interesting introductions to the sections on the two world wars and his suggestions to enhance the final product. I am most grateful to The Ontario Trillium Foundation for their grant, which enabled us to go ahead with the plans for publishing For Those Who Served. *Genuine appreciation is expressed for this essential support.*

Sincere thanks are also extended to all the people who offered encouragement and provided assistance while this account was being compiled. Without such it could not have been completed. To everyone who helped I am indeed grateful.

Murray Hesp
November 2002

⟪⟪ PART 1 ⟫⟫
CANADA IN 'THE GREAT WAR'
1914-1918

At the beginning of the twentieth century, five European countries dominated the world's political horizon, each of them steeped in self-interest, commercial expansion and military might. By the end of the century's first decade, these 'Great Powers', as they were often called – Britain, France, Austria-Hungary, Russia and Germany – had become so caught up in international power politics it was almost inevitable that one day they would face off in a great and bloody war.

The Five 'Great Powers'

In many ways, Britain, sitting at the top of a monolith known as the British Empire, was the biggest of the five. It was at the very peak of its strength; its colonies, Canada among them, spread across the entire globe; and it was a fabulously wealthy commercial giant. Britain's land army was not very large by European standards. At the beginning of the war, the number of infantry divisions Britain put into the field was matched by the little Kingdom of Serbia. But the War Office did not shrink from using that army quite freely, a fact demonstrated frequently in Africa and Asia during the latter half of the nineteenth century. However, it was with the navy that Britain threw its weight around. The Royal Navy was the largest the world had ever known, and the most respected and feared. As a consequence, Britain was used to getting its way, and neither welcomed nor even expected interference.

Across the English channel sat France, no longer the great power it once was – except in the minds of its leaders – yet France still had influence and great strength, for it too had colonies around the world. The country had a centuries-old tradition of deep involvement in European politics and intrigue, and this was never more true than in the years leading up to 1914. A powerful motivation for France in the early twentieth century was her crushing defeat in 1871 in a war with Prussia (Germany). French pride was smarting; the country itched for revenge, and was in a position to seek it for the army had been rebuilt and re-equipped and was once again a formidable force. Ironically, the rebuilding had been carried out entirely on a philosophy of *attack*, a strategy that would lead to horrendous casualty rates in the upcoming trench warfare.

The third power was a curious, fragile – and fractious – mix of countries, duchies and principalities yoked together into the Austro-Hungarian Empire. Powerful only on paper, yet very influential in European matters, the Empire – or 'the Austrians', a term much of Europe used – was inevitably in the middle of everything in the continent, if only because of geography. It was a hotbed of continuing strife, border wars and small rebellions, and much of the political energy in the Austro-Hungarian Empire was spent dealing with these struggles that seemed to pop up everywhere.

Atop Europe sat Russia, the largest country in the world, and one seething with potential for revolution, mismanaged as it was by an autocratic monarchy and a corrupt nobility. Russia's massive military force was outdated, ill-equipped, and badly led – its navy had been trounced in a war with Japan in 1904-5 – and the loyalty of the average Russian citizen was in some doubt. However, the country's sheer size and large population, and its historical involvement with all the machinations in Europe, meant it was bound to be a player in whatever game was afoot.

The newest member of the five-power mix was the German Empire, and in many ways it was Germany that upset the fine balance of bluff and posturing that the other four had found so useful to this point. Germany had not become united into a country under one government until late in the nineteenth century and, as a result, was in a rush to establish new balances. It had only a few colonies and wanted more. That irritated the British and the French. It was building a huge, modern navy and the British saw that as a direct challenge to their conviction that 'Britannia ruled the waves'. Germany's relations with France were delicate at the best of times, and its eastern borders with Russia were often an area of tension. And every leader in Europe was keenly aware that Germany had the best-equipped and best-led land army on the continent.

Other Ingredients in the Mix

Underlying the continuing interplay among these dominant powers were two other factors that helped push the world toward war. For one, there was no country big enough and no mechanism strong enough (like a UN) to interfere with these great powers. Canada, Australia, India – countries with influence today – were mere dots on the political horizon in 1914. Others, like today's Saudi Arabia, Pakistan and Israel, didn't exist. Once powerful countries like Turkey and China were mere shadows, mostly because of internal strife. Japan was still gathering strength, and the United States had declared itself 'isolationist' (a policy it proclaimed but practiced only in regard to Europe. Closer to home, the U.S. was regularly interfering with – and invading – Mexico, Central America and islands in the West Indies). As a consequence, the 'Great Powers' had the table pretty much to themselves.

The second factor was a legacy established almost single-handedly by the former chancellor of Germany, Otto von Bismarck. Throughout the waning years of the nineteenth century, Bismarck had been instrumental in negotiating a series of alliances – open and secret – that were crucial in keeping the European political dance just that: a dance. Although their principal purpose was to protect Germany in both offensive and defensive situations, Bismarck's alliances were quite effective in keeping all the powers in balance and from getting into situations that could lead to war. But they were complicated arrangements and fine tuning them required someone with Bismarck's awesome diplomatic skill. Unfortunately for Europe – and the rest of the world as it turned out – Germany's emperor, Wilhelm II, fired the chancellor in 1890 and decided to run things himself. Wilhelm, like the other royal heads of Europe, was not exactly the brightest bulb in the continental circuit and ultimately, it was the alliances that finally drew everyone into war. All that was needed was a spark.

The War Begins

That came on the 28th of June, 1914, in Bosnia (recently annexed by the Austrians) when the heir to the Austrian throne, Archduke Franz Ferdinand, was assassinated in Sarajevo. Austria, backed by Germany, was convinced that the Kingdom of Serbia next door was responsible, and imposed rigorous terms on that small Balkan country. Even though Serbia met most of the demands, Austria declared war on July 28, and almost immediately the alliances began to click in. When Russia (ally of Serbia) and France (ally of Russia) ignored Germany's request to stay out of the matter Germany declared war on both of them. Then Germany invaded Belgium in order to get at France, and because Britain had treaty obligations to Belgium, it declared war on Germany.

By mid-August, Austria (allied to Germany) declared war on both Russia and France, and Britain (allied to Russia and France) declared war on Austria. Serbia and Montenegro declared war on Germany. Then Turkey came in on the German side (a natural choice in any case for Turkey since it was a long-time foe of Russia, now one of Germany's enemies). And so the war spread. Bulgaria, with designs on territory in the Balkans, came in on the German side in 1915. In 1916, Italy came in on the side of the Allies while Germany declared war on Portugal.

A European War Becomes a World War

Ironically, despite all the declarations and counter-declarations, the entire affair might have remained a purely European conflict in the beginning were it not for the colonies. Canada, although it was called a 'Dominion', was essentially a colony in 1914. Like India, Australia, and other British "possessions" on every continent, it was immediately drawn into the conflict almost willy-nilly, as were the colonies of France and Germany, especially in Africa. Thus by the end of August 1914, the participation of the colonies made the war worldwide. By war's end in 1918, much of the rest of the world had been drawn in too. The USA declared war in 1917, although its troops were only on the battle lines in very large numbers for the final five months or so. Both China and Japan eventually joined in, and even Cuba and Honduras (all on the Allied side).

In 1914, the only colony with an army of any consequence was India, in large part because Britain had trained and equipped Indian units for her many little wars in Asia. Canada joined in with its citizens in full support of the "mother country", but it was not remotely prepared for conflict. The army had only 3,000 regulars, soon to be equipped with a rifle that was next to useless (the infamous Ross rifle). The navy consisted of two training cruisers: the *Rainbow* out of Vancouver, and the *Niobe* out of Halifax. (The latter leaked so badly it could never go far from port.) There were no airplanes and thus no air force; in fact, the first powered flight in Canada had taken place only five years before.

Canada Gets Into It

Yet it didn't take long for duty and loyalty to turn into military reality. By October 1914, Canada's first contingent (30,000 men) sailed for England. After the briefest of training at Valcartier, Quebec, the troops boarded a convoy of thirty ships stretching some thirty-four kilometers, and crossed the Atlantic Ocean. Before going to France, Canadian troops got further training in the mud and rain at Salisbury Plain, southwest of London. (In letters recorded in this book, Canadian servicemen share the experiences of their time here before sailing for France.) By December 1914, just four months after the assassination of Crown Prince Ferdinand, the Princess Patricia's Light Infantry, the first Canadian troops to fight in the war, arrived in France.

World War I battles were fought in the Dardanelles, in Italy, in the Balkans, in Russia, in Africa, in the Middle East, on three oceans and of course, in France and Belgium. It was in the latter two countries where almost all the Canadian forces did their fighting. When the 1st Canadian Division reached France in February 1915 (having been recruited and organized essentially from scratch after August the year before) they were given control of a four-mile stretch in the Armentières (France) sector. Joined there by the Princess Patricia's, who had already seen action at places like St. Eloi and Polygan Wood, the Canadians were then posted on the Allied line inside the Belgian border, near the city of Ypres. It was to prove an auspicious decision by the Allied command for just weeks later, Canadian troops were instrumental in altering the outcome of the war.

Trench Warfare

After a series of rapid successes in 1914, the German advance into Belgium and France had bogged down in the face of counterattacks from the Allies. In the process, the two sides had discovered a horrible truth. The modern weapons carried by both armies were capable of killing and destruction on a mass scale that no one had ever imagined. Yet the tactics employed by both sides were essentially the same ones used in the Napoleonic wars over a hundred years before: troops were marched toward the enemy in close formation over open ground. In the face of machine gun fire and barrages from massed artillery, they were mowed down like grass. As a consequence, both armies began to dig in. They each built a series of trenches, miles and miles of them along what became known as the Western Front, all the way from Ypres in the north to well south of Verdun in France. The area between the trenches, varying from a few hundred yards to over a mile wide, was called 'no-man's-land', a barren swath of mud and shell holes in which artillery had obliterated every tree, every blade of grass, every farmhouse and even, in a few unfortunate cases, whole villages.

Unfortunately, the generals on both sides were unable to adapt their strategy very much beyond that one measure, so that now, instead of marching in formation to their deaths, their troops were sent "over the top": over the top of their own trench toward the opposite trench in bayonet charges. Both sides rained artillery shells down on the other's trenches and on no-man's-land in between. The result of these tactics was vast numbers of casualties and deaths, statistics made even worse by shockingly large numbers of men who would remain forever "missing in action". (The huge military cemeteries in Belgium and France display row upon row of crosses and tombstones on which, instead of a name, is written "Known unto God". Many of these are Canadian. Not until the end of the war did most soldiers carry identification tags. Since many were literally blown to bits by artillery, or were wounded and then disappeared into the quagmire of no-man's-land – the Western Front experienced unusually heavy rainfall all through the war – no one knew what became of them.)

The Canadians at Ypres

Over the course of the war, the trench lines of the Western Front changed very little – the Ypres area was typical – and for four years, commanders on both sides continued to send their men "over the top". In what passed for strategy here, the Allies were trying to drive the German forces back to Germany. The Germans, at the south end of the Front, were trying to push into France toward Paris. At the north end, near Ypres, they were trying to drive to the sea just a few miles behind the Allied line, where they could then get control of the channel ports. Had they succeeded, the war might have turned out somewhat differently. That's why the line at Ypres was so important.

There were three "battles of Ypres" in World War I, each continuing for an extended period, and each an extremely bloody affair (and all contributing to the total obliteration of that beautiful medieval city). The first of these lasted from October 14, 1914 to November 22, 1914. There were thousands of casualties and basically nothing changed. The second battle of Ypres began on April 21, 1915, and changed the course of warfare forever. Canadian troops, British and French were in the line that morning and as dawn broke, sentries were the first to notice a greenish-yellow fog creeping toward them across no-man's-land. Seconds after this seemingly harmless mist reached them, their skin began to blister; some became blind; and all were gasping for breath as their lungs literally burned up. The strange fog was chlorine gas.

All along the line, troops broke and ran in bewilderment and terror – except at one point. The Canadian 1st Division held, the only Allied troops to do so. What might have turned into a huge rout, giving the German army the clear road to the sea that it so desperately wanted, was stopped in its tracks by soldiers from Canada. And they did it again in a second gas attack on April 24 – at great cost though. The second battle of Ypres lasted a month, until May 25. By the end of the first eighteen days, the 1st Division had lost one-third, about 3,500, of its men.

Historians generally agree that for its size '2nd Ypres' was one of the most murderous battles of the entire war. But that didn't prevent a third. On July 16, 1917, the third battle of Ypres, also known as 'Passchendaele', began and continued until November 10 of that year. Like the first two, it was vicious, bloody, and inconclusive, ending with both sides exhausted and inundated with awesome casualty numbers, all for tiny pieces of territory that barely mattered. By this time, 1917, the ordinary soldiers in both armies on the Ypres front were committed enemies, somewhat of a contrast to the early days of the war. On Christmas Eve in 1914, a dramatic example of what might have happened had ordinary soldiers been in command of world politics took place in no-man's-land. Near midnight, an unofficial truce was declared in the trenches and both Allied and German soldiers left their posts to sing carols in the moonlight, exchange little presents, and even have an impromptu soccer game. The next day, the High Command on both sides made sure this never happened again.

In the Thick of It

Although Canadian troops were involved in a long list of separate engagements from 1915 to 1918, several stand out. A particularly bloody affair was the battle at Hill 60 in Belgium in 1915. Another was at Festubert in 1916, where 2,468 Canadians died. A further 400 lost their lives at Givenchy that year. Also in 1916, Canadians were part of the famous Battle of the Somme, a gruesome affair that achieved almost nothing and recorded over 620,000 casualties, the largest number in British military history. Of those 24,029 were Canadians. Included among these was the commanding officer of the 3rd Canadian Division, Major-General Malcolm Smith Mercer, who was killed by shrapnel June 3, 1916, while visiting the front line.

Canadian troops fought in many battles in the Great War and ultimately emerged with a reputation as the British Empire's best soldiers on the Western Front. This reputation makes for an interesting background when one reads the letters these "best soldiers" sent home. They were forbidden to describe the fighting to the folks back home for the most part, but their letters offer vivid vignettes of life in the trenches that became their quarters, their protection, and sadly for many of them, their last home on earth.

The Battle of Vimy Ridge

Perhaps the most famous battle of the war for Canadians was the taking of Vimy Ridge in 1917. Vimy, occupied by German forces, had been an objective of the Allied command almost from the beginning of the war because it was such an important strategic position. Even though the Allies had tried unsuccessfully to take it several times, the German position at Vimy was thought to be pretty much impregnable – by *both* sides. Thus Vimy Ridge was a watershed point of the war for Canada for a number of reasons. It was a remarkable battle, not just because it was entirely planned and fought – and won – by Canadians, the first colonial troops to do so, but because it set a new standard for strategy and employment of troops among the Allies. It was the first time all four divisions of the Canadian Corps, under the command of General Julian Byng, moved forward together and fought shoulder to shoulder. After Vimy, both sides imitated Canadian tactics. The battle led to a new attitude of respect for the Canadian forces on the Allied and German sides. (It was at Vimy too that fighter pilot Billy Bishop won a Military Cross.) Yet this battle cost Canada 3,598 dead and 6,464 wounded.

Fighting continued on all fronts with casualty rates mounting ever higher. Yet very little territory changed until late in 1918 when by September of that year, the Allies were making advances in every sector. By then, Canadian troops had captured

Vimy Ridge Memorial, painted by A. Snelleman in 1968.
COURTESY ROYAL CANADIAN LEGION, BOLTON BRANCH 371

Cambrai and fought their way through Valenciennes and Mount Houy. They reached Mons in central Belgium on the day the Armistice was signed. On that day, November 11, 1918, the Great War finally stumbled to its end. Russia had left the war in March that year to cope with the revolution that would soon turn it into the USSR. Austria had surrendered on November 3, and Germany, after a revolution in Berlin that brought about the abdication of Wilhelm II, signed an armistice on November 11.

An Ending? Or a Beginning?

Sadly, at the end of this war, seeds of conflict were already being sown that would germinate and grow through the rest of the twentieth century. France, especially, pushed for terms of peace on Germany that Adolf Hitler would use to his advantage only a few years later. Most German people felt they had not really been defeated in the field and did not deserve the harsh treaty imposed on them. The Austro-Hungarian Empire was dismantled, creating a number of newly independent but very weak and unstable countries. (Interestingly, Turkey was the only defeated country that actually negotiated its treaty.) France and Belgium had been pummeled into insignificance. The British Empire was done for, with Britain itself utterly used and exhausted, its citizens wanting nothing to do with war ever again. The United States turned its back on involvement and again retreated into its policy of isolationism. Japan invaded Siberia in late 1918, tasting the fruits of imperial expansion for the first time. In the Balkans, Serbia, Croatia and Slovenia formed an uneasy coalition called the Kingdom of Yugoslavia. In the Middle East, with the Turks thrown out of Jerusalem, Britain was assuring Jewish people across the world of a homeland of their own in Palestine, despite the fact that the Arab people – who had helped defeat the Turks – were already living there and believed it was theirs. Even in Canada, the joy of victory had left some bad taste for conscription had created an open split between Quebec and the rest of the country.

Canada in a New World Role

Of all the countries involved in the Great War, however, Canada seemed to come through the conflict with a number of major accomplishments to its credit. In a little over four years, Canada had changed from a large but insignificant colony into a country that mattered. By the end of the war, the German Imperial Staff held Canadian forces in such high regard that they would actually plan strategy based on whether their troops would have to face Canadians. The Canadian army had grown from 3,000 regulars to four divisions, of approximately 10,000 men each, under our own command. By 1917, Canada was participating in anti-U-boat patrols. In the air, Canadian pilots were the principal 'aces' on the Allied side. We also led in war production, for example, putting out 1,900 "Canucks", the JN-4, a two-seater biplane, between 1916 and 1918. About 619,000 Canadians, from all walks of life, served in the armed forces, many of whom were women. (There were 3,141 nursing sisters of whom 2,500 attended to the wounded on all fronts and 46 died while doing so.) Of all the Canadians who went overseas, 66,655 did not return at the end of the war. Canadian casualties totalled over 200,000. The population of Canada was approximately 8.4 million at that time.

Because of our heroic local servicemen and women, like the ones mentioned in this book, Canada became a country that the world came to know and respect. On June 28, 1919, at the Palace of Versailles in France, where the treaty was signed, Canada had its own seat at the table. The country had earned that right and it had done so because quiet, hitherto unassuming Canadians, like the ones you'll read about here, hitched up their belts and joined the fray. We owe them so much. Hopefully, their stories on the following pages will help us all to know them a bit better, help us to treasure their memories and help us respect them and be grateful for what they have done.

Ken Weber

≪≪ Chapter One ≫≫
– 1914 –
World War I Begins

The first mention of the war in the Bolton Enterprise appeared on Friday August 7, 1914 under the heading -

The War

The latest news is that a general European war has commenced. Germany, Great Britain, France, Serbia and Russia are involved. The German and English fleets are expected to clash at any hour. The Belgians have been successful in checking the advance guard of the German army, which is trying to go through Belgium territory in order to reach Paris.

The Canadian Government has purchased two submarines from Chile. An army division of 20,000 men is being recruited to go to the aid of the mother country. The canals and cable stations are being guarded by troops. British reservists are reporting for duty and the militia regiments have been notified to be ready for instant service.

In the midst of the Canadian government's recruiting process, Western farmers were in desperate need of help. The same edition of the paper states:

Approximately fifteen thousand men from Ontario will be required to help in the great work of harvesting the Western crop, and practically the entire task of transporting this great army of harvesters to the West will fall to the lot of the Canadian Pacific Railway.

Excursions from points in Ontario to Manitoba, Saskatchewan and Alberta will be run, and special trains operated, making the trip in about thirty-six hours and avoiding any change of cars or transfers. This will be a day shorter than any other route.

Going trip west - $12.00 to Winnipeg, Return trip east - $18.00 from Winnipeg.

October 9, 1914 -
Walshaw's Woollen Mill has secured a contract for army blankets which will require some weeks to fill and the staff is working overtime at present.

December 18, 1914 -
A carload of German and Austrians under an armed guard passed through here on Tuesday morning on their way to a detention camp where they will remain until the war is over.

Local Men Sign Up (Horses Too)

According to the August 2l, 1914 edition of the Bolton Enterprise:

Frank S. Rutherford, BA Sc., has been called to Toronto to drill preparatory to going into active service. He is attached to the Second Field Company of Canadian Engineers, which with other corps will mobilize at Val Cartier, Quebec. It is expected that 25,000 men of the different corps will be at Val Cartier by the end of the week.

Stanley Rutledge will likely go to the war. He has offered his services in the army medical corps and has been accepted. He made a flying trip to his parents, Mr. & Mrs. John Rutledge of this place on Saturday night and is now in camp preparing for the front.

The August 28, 1914 edition of the same paper states:
Major McDougall and Colonel Hall, representing the Militia Department, and James Fallis, MPP, were in Bolton on Wednesday buying horses. A large number were offered, thirty being purchased. The prices ranged from $125. to $175. After being tried out the horses were branded and placed in the Queen's Hotel stables and shipped on Thursday. The last horse inspected threw the rider who was badly shaken up. Whitney Byrne got too near the heels of one of the army horses and was kicked. His arm was fractured.

An advertisement in the same paper stated "Military Horses Wanted" and that purchasing Officers would be at the Queen's Hotel to secure a number of artillery and remounts.
Horses must be from 14.2 to 16 hands, weigh from 1050 to 1400 pounds, 5 to 6 years old. (No greys or whites) All horses must be sound, of good conformation, free from blemishes and broken to harness and saddle.

◇

Lieutenant Alexander, of the Canadian Veterinary Corps, of Mono Road, left on Saturday evening for Toronto en route to Val Cartier, Quebec where he will join the regiments on their way to the front.

Bolton Enterprise - September 14, 1914
Sidney Jackson has enlisted with the 36th Regiment for foreign service. Sidney has been employed in the woollen mills here for some years.
      Others who joined early in the war included Albert Armstrong, Whitney Byrne and Charlie Clow.

A typical recruitment poster.
COURTESY NATIONAL ARCHIVES

Bolton Enterprise - July 16, 1915
Mono Road -
      Mr. Sam Judge, son of the late James Judge, has enlisted for the front with a Toronto contingent.

◇

Captain Dr. John Graham has joined the overseas Army Medical Corps and is now on active duty.

◇

      Lance Corporal Selwyn Judge writes of his voyage across the Atlantic.
      They were detained by fog for three days, but he says the ocean was as calm as a millpond and the moonlight on the waters was a brilliant sight. Daily drills in the use of the boats and life belts, also in gunnery made them fairly proficient. When the war zone was reached everything was in readiness for the gravest emergency. "Our platoon was on guard one night," he writes, "when away off in the distance lights suddenly flashed on the horizon and as quickly disappeared. About 15 minutes later two long low objects suddenly appeared as if they arose out of the dark waters and floated like dark shadows one on each side of the ship. Alternately they would dash to the bow of the ship. They were torpedo boat destroyers and in the morning light their rakish, vicious appearance foreboded

disaster to any submarine that came in their way." Incidentally, he relates that he was not seasick and that the food was much superior to the fare which they got at the different drill camps in Canada.

Bolton Enterprise - August 27, 1915
Animated by the principles of true patriotism, Adam Wallace has enlisted with the Queen's Own for overseas service and has gone into training with his regiment. Adam, who is only eighteen years of age, is the second son of Mr. & Mrs. R.J. Wallace of this place and has been anxious for some time to get away to the front. For some years he has been active in the Boy Scouts and held the position of Assistant Scout Master of the local troop for some time. "Ad" has many fine qualities that we all admire, and this answer he has made to the call of his King and country has raised him still higher in our estimation. He will do his bit.

A recruitment postcard from 1914.
COURTESY DIANE ALLENGAME-KUSTER

Bolton Enterprise - September 3, 1915
Mr. Charles Snell, son of Mr. & Mrs. William Snell of Albion has enlisted at Kingston with the 34th Battery, and has gone into training for overseas service. Mr. Snell is about 25 years of age and has been in the employ of the T. Eaton Company for about five years.

Bolton Enterprise - October 8, 1915
Freddie Stubbs, an old Bolton boy, has enlisted and is in training at Camp Niagara. "Ginger" was a quick mover on the ice in his hockey days, and will give a good account of himself in the struggle against the Germans.

The following was originally written by Werden Leavens at an earlier date, and reappeared in the Bolton Enterprise - May 4, 1972

Back in 1916 a high pressure recruiting meeting in the Bolton Town hall attracted a "full house" including the youth of the area. Sergeant Major Wrigglesworth, wounded in France, was the speaker and it took little persuasion to bring the boys up front to enlist in the 126th Peel Battalion, which was being organized. Among those volunteering were the Wood boys, sons of Mr. and Mrs. John Wood, Willow and David Street. They were soon in training down in Brampton and youthfulness coupled with their enthusiasm, soon rounded them into "Soldiers of the King", to be proud of.

One of the early chores the newly enlisted 126th boys had to do was come to Bolton to welcome home a local soldier of note. Jim St. John, of North Albion, a soldier who had earlier served in the Cuban War, went overseas in 1914, served in France, and was invalided home due to his age and earlier sabre wounds suffered in the Cuban War. St. John was welcomed in Toronto by Reeve Ted Walshaw. They missed the early train, 6.30 p.m., but managed to catch the train which arrived here about midnight. Jim St. John was by this time in a highly jovial mood. Boys of the 126th, Hubert Corless, Earl Sykes, Albert Kennedy and the Wood boys pulled a cutter bedecked with Union Jacks down to the "city hall". St. John talked and talked and it was with some difficulty the meeting could be ended at 2 o'clock with the singing of God Save The King!

Bill Wood, Earl Sykes and Hubert Corless were killed in action. Eddie Wood is one of the few survivors around to-day. He frequently visits his sister, Mrs. Beatrice Bateman still

34976. FOLKESTONE: UPPER LEAS.

Folkestone – a typical English scene in 1915.   COURTESY BETTY WARD

residing in the family residence here. Until his retirement he worked as a mechanic in Brampton, Bolton and Toronto. Reminiscing about his World War 1 experiences Eddie Wood said:

"I joined the 126th Peel Battalion in Bolton Town Hall at a recruiting meeting along with other Bolton boys, went to Brampton Barracks, also Camp Niagara until fall, 1916. I went all through the war except when I was wounded at Passchendaele in the leg and was in hospital for awhile. I was back again to trenches until I came home in March 1919. Brother Bill was killed at Vimy. Would not like to go through it again, mud to hips, shells bursting around, never knowing if one was going to get you. Some nights we slept standing up in trenches, a hunk of cheese and dry bread with bully beef, but I guess it didn't hurt me too much as I am still here".

Local War Experiences

Douglas Holtby, grandson of Lieutenant J. G. Dennis, DFC, wrote the following account.

Joseph Gordon Dennis enlisted in the 2nd Divisional Ammunition Park, Canadian Army Service Corps, in Toronto, on February 4, 1915. After receiving little more than three months of training he traveled with his unit to Montreal and embarked for England on May 15, 1915 as part of the 2nd Contingent of the Canadian Expeditionary Force. Landing at Plymouth nine days later, the 2nd Division was immediately placed under the command of the Canadian Training Division at Shorncliffe, Kent in preparation to join in the fighting in France and Belgium.

Departing Southampton on September 14, 1915, Private Dennis crossed the English Channel with the 2nd Div. Amm. Park and landed at Rouen, France the following day. Assigned to the Motor Transport Section as a lorry driver, Dennis spent the next twenty-two months stationed at Park bases near the towns of Bailleul, Steenvoord, Poperinghe, Puchevillers, Barlin and Mt. St. Eloi. Transporting ammunition and troops to the front lines, the 2nd Div. Amm. Park supported the Artillery and Infantry Brigades of the 2nd Canadian Division fighting at Somme, Vimy and the Ypres salient. Dennis was appointed the rank of Lance Corporal on June 17, 1916 and promoted to full Corporal on October 18, 1916.

As was his original desire, Dennis applied for transfer to the Royal Flying Corps in August of 1916. Since Canada had no air force at the time, transfer from the Canadian Expeditionary Force to the Royal Flying Corps or Royal Naval Air Service was the only way that Canadians stationed overseas could join the flying services. Officers commanding the CEF units were not eager to lose their men to other services. However by October of 1916, the Canadian Divisions had suffered such severe casualties in battle that a freeze was placed on all transfers to the flying services until the reinforcement needs of the CEF could be met. Dennis's Commanding Officer refused to sign his application.

Corporal Dennis persisted and was finally taken on probation by the Royal Flying Corps in August of 1917, returning to England to commence officers training at the RFC Cadet Wing at Denham, Buckinghamshire and St. Leonards, East Sussex. Upon completion of his course at No. 1 School of Military Aeronautics at Reading, he was commissioned as a 2nd Lieutenant in the Royal Flying Corps on January 20, 1918 and subsequently discharged from the Canadian Forces. He was then posted to No. 6 Training Depot Station at Boscombe Down where he received flight instruction and graduated as a pilot three months later.

On April 1, 1918, the Royal Flying Corps and the Royal Naval Air Service amalgamated to form a single flying service, the Royal Air Force. Plans were being made, as well, for the establishment of a strategic bombing force, to be called the Independent Air Force, conceived to operate independently of the Army Brigades and strike targets "within Germany proper". Casualties were almost catastrophic for the Allied air forces in France at the time and RAF training units could scarcely meet the requirements for replacement air crew considered necessary to bring the Independent Force up to effective strength.

After completing a short course at the No. 1 School of Aerial Fighting and Gunnery at Turberry, 2nd Lieutenant Dennis was considered ready for duty and ordered to report overseas on August 24, 1918. He was assigned to "C" Flight of No. 99 (Day Bombardment) Squadron, one of Major-General Hugh Trenchard's Independent Force squadrons based at Azelot, France.

No. 99 Squadron was equipped with DeHavilland DH9 aircraft. An open cockpit bi-plane, the DH9 was powered by a single Siddley Puma engine that was weak and prone to failure. Each crew consisted of one Pilot and one Observer/Gunner.

At Azelot, Dennis flew on several training flights to learn close formation flying, a tactic utilized by the pilots of the slow, unwieldy bombers to defend themselves against the superior enemy scouts. The following entry from Dennis's journal describes the first of these flights:

"I did my first flight in France on the evening of Aug 29th, which was the second day with the Squadron. The machine was a DH9 with a 200 HP Siddley Puma engine. She was very tail heavy compared with those in the training squadrons at home, & I had rather an uncomfortable time just after leaving the ground until I got used to the machine. I also felt strange after not flying for almost a month. Marshall, the flight commander led, & Warwick & I formed the remainder of the formation. We climbed to about 300 ft. & flew around for almost an hour, when the leader waved us to break up, & we came down. My landing was good, & Marshall said my flying in the formation was fine for the first time flying in such close formation. I was truly thankful for that, as I had only flown one formation of more than two machines before, & knowing how hard it was to keep one's place in formation, I was quite anxious on that point. I was also anxious to do well, so that I would soon be sent on a raid, because I felt that I was not one of the real pilots of the squadron until I had done a few shows. Although I was eager for my first trip over the lines, at the same time I wanted to be able to fly in formation well, so that I would be a valuable asset to the flight & give my leader confidence in me".

The next day's events are described:

"On Aug 30th the Squadron set out in the morning on a raid. It was a thrilling sight to see them take off & I felt a longing to be with them. While they were away I stayed most of the time on the aerodrome, & frequently wondered how they were getting on. One machine came back with engine trouble, & reported the position of the formation when they left it. After leaving the formation they were attacked by two Huns, one bullet going thru their prop. About mid-day all except one machine of our Squadron returned. (The missing one landed on our side of the line with engine trouble). Warwick was the first one to land on the drome, & as

I watched him taxi in I noticed that no observer was visible & I realized what it meant. (He had been shot dead thru the neck). I shall never forget the feeling I had when I realized this, & for a while I must confess that my spirits were dampened by the horror of the whole thing. Still such feelings soon pass off, & I was keen for a show again".

Considered by the Squadron Commanding Officer to be ready for combat, Dennis was detailed for his first "show" on September 8, but the weather was unsuitable and the raid was put off. On the 12th he commenced flying the first of several missions over the lines and was engaged in aerial combat with the enemy.

On September 14, 1918, Lt. Dennis was called as one of the party to carry out a raid on the railway junction at Metz-Sablon. Six DH9's left the ground at Azelot at 7.25 a.m. Unfortunately two were compelled to leave the formation before crossing the lines, owing to engine trouble. The remaining four machines were attacked before reaching Metz by twenty hostile scouts, and one DH9 was shot down. Nevertheless, the remainder of the formation carried on and bombed the objective. When over Metz, Lt. Dennis was seriously wounded by a machine-gun bullet, which passed through his lower back and perforated his intestines in many places. His observer, 2nd Lt. H.G. Ramsay had been badly wounded in the leg and had lost consciousness. A running fight carried on back to the lines but Dennis maintained his position in the formation, brought his machine back over forty miles, and landed safely on their field at Azelot. Still in his aircraft, Dennis collapsed due to the loss of blood from his wounds and was rushed to the 8th Canadian Stationary Hospital at Charmes. His journal entry for that day simply states: *"Called early in the morning & went on show to Metz. Encountered lots of Huns & got wounded. Got back O.K. & went to hospital".*

While he lay in hospital, hovering between life and death, he was awarded the Distinguished Flying Cross, presented in person by General Trenchard, General-Officer-Commanding, Independent Force, in recognition of the extraordinary courage and endurance shown by him in bringing back his machine intact. Thanks to the skillful treatment that he received at Charmes, he was reported as being "out of danger" within a few days.

Lt. Dennis was unable to be moved back to England until October 20, 1918, at which time he was admitted to the 2nd Southern General Hospital, Southmead, Bristol. He was treated there for the next six months, and underwent three operations, as his wound would not heal. He continued to convalesce at the home of his parents near Helston, Cornwall, until he was fit to return to Canada and the girl whom he was coming home to marry.

Arriving back in Canada in July of 1919, Gordon Dennis married Edith Creighton on October 20th of that year. Lt. Dennis was officially presented with the Distinguished Flying Cross at the 1920 Warriors Day Ceremonies at the Canadian National Exhibition, along with four other Canadian airmen, including Lieutenant-Colonel William Avery "Billy" Bishop.

In 1922, on doctor's recommendation, Gordon and Edith purchased a farm on the 3rd Line of Albion, as it was believed that the clean country air would be beneficial to Gordon's health. There, they raised two children, Joseph and Bertha, and ran a dairy operation. Gordon suffered from the effects of his wound for the rest of his life and passed away on June 12, 1957. Edith stayed on the farm, living over sixty years of her life there before moving to Bolton, where she passed away in 1988 at the age of ninety-three.

◇

Lenore Gibson has supplied a copy of an article with respect to her uncle, Flight Lieutenant Charles McKeown, which appeared in the Borden Citizen on June 14, 1989 and is as follows:

When Camp Borden opened in May of 1916, hundreds of young men arrived in the first days to begin the job of cutting trees, clearing land and erecting buildings. They also had to train for the trench warfare of France, and most of them would only be here for a few months

A Curtiss-Jenny plane at the Sandhill Aerodrome, similar to the one flown by Charles McKeown in 1917.

COURTESY PETER ELMS

before departing on troop trains for the east coast, thence to England.

But Charlie McKeown was different. He marched into Borden as a soldier, then won his wings and flew away as a pilot.

"Our first meal (at Borden) consisted of bread and water" he remembers. "The second was a slight improvement. They gave us coffee".

He remembers a curious incident involving one of the units in camp at that time: "Their Colonel took them on a long route march on a very hot day to toughen them up a little. Bear in mind that many of these lads were farm boys like myself, and certainly did not need to be toughened up. On the way back they broke ranks to get a drink from a cold stream. The Colonel ordered them back on the road but they ignored him. He then rode up the stream on his horse, and muddied it up. Some of the boys then dragged him off his horse and threw him in the creek. There was nothing said ... but the entire group was broken up and posted hither and yon over the next few months. There were never any charges laid".

McKeown initially enrolled in the 204th Battalion, and today believes he is the only surviving member of that unit. As a young Sergeant, he was left behind when the Battalion marched off to war, as a physical education trainer, for the next batch to come in. He found these to be somewhat "reluctant volunteers", and did not cherish being stuck with them for any length of time.

At about this time, the Royal Flying Corps, Canada, had set itself up at Borden, and a hangar line was being constructed. In 1917, training of replacements for the squadrons flying over the mud of Flanders had begun in earnest, and McKeown stepped forward. He was accepted, and soon was soaring above the pines and sand in a Curtiss JN-4, sometimes referred to as a "Jenny". This early training biplane was the first production aircraft ever manufactured in Canada.

"Our squadron was well organized under a British Major", he remembers. "In the early stages we used to fly from Borden to Edenvale where we landed and then flew back. There were a lot of accidents and malfunctions; there were almost always one or two planes down along the way".

One day while up flying, McKeown failed to notice that the wind had shifted 180 degrees. He landed with it, instead of into it, and found himself rapidly running out of room. He brought his machine to a halt almost against the perimeter fence.

"The Major had a fit (we were very short of aircraft at the time) and his face was red and he was sputtering away incoherently when I got back to the hangar. Quite an act really. I remember telling him that he must try to control himself or he might have a stroke. He soon did recover his composure and dealt with me appropriately, I suppose".

The casualty rate while training was high, about 40 per cent as McKeown remembers it. One young man, attempting to impress his girlfriend in Barrie, was stunting over Kempenfelt

Bay. He attempted a loop, but couldn't pull out, and crashed into Lake Simcoe before her horrified eyes. It may well be that aircraft is still down there.

"As we advanced in our training, we were permitted to cruise around the area in any direction", McKeown remembers. "I made several trips to the family farm at Sandhill, about 12.3 miles northeast of Brampton. When I started to buzz around the ladies would all dash into the house to dress up a little because they knew that some of the neighbors would soon be calling".

Despite the risks of flying in what would be by to-day's standards incredibly flimsy machines, learning to fly was an exciting adventure in 1917, and it attracted a special type. After their basic flight training was over, the fledgling pilots went to England for advanced schooling, and the dashing young Canadians discovered that they were much sought after by local society hostesses who entertained them lavishly at every opportunity.

However, death struck often in the skies over France, and 70th Squadron, based near Vimy Ridge, was in urgent need of replacements. The half-trained pilots from England were rushed across the Channel, and McKeown found himself in a Sopwith Camel, an unfamiliar type.

By early 1918 it was estimated that a new pilot on the Western Front could expect to last 20 days. McKeown made it to 18, and then he was brought down by a single shot from the ground.

He tried to glide back to his own lines, but ran out of sky and crashed into the mud of No Man's Land. McKeown believes to this day that the Germans could easily have killed him by riddling his crumpled machine as he lay unconscious in the wreckage, but they stayed their hand. When he came to, he surrendered.

He was taken to the Holtzminden infantry barracks in southern Germany, which had been turned into a prisoner-of-war camp. The captured officers were treated with a civility hard to countenance these days. McKeown describes the atmosphere as being like a university residence.

However, escape was not far from anyone's mind. A tunnel was dug, and at the appointed hour the men made their break. Only 40 got out before the roof fell in and of these all but one were rounded up by the Germans, with the help of dogs.

One did get away, however; a wilderness survival type who lay doggo in a pond with a lily pad over his head, breathing through a hollow reed. After several months as a fugitive he made it to Holland just after the war ended.

McKeown is not considered by his family to be one who exaggerates; but another story does seem to test one's credulity. It concerns a British Colonel who had spent some time in Germany before the war and spoke the language perfectly. He is said to have arranged with some of his German friends to bribe the camp commandant, and he walked out the front gate with a special railway pass to Holland. McKeown remembers that the Australians among the prisoners, who had limited tolerance for this sort of upper-class "Pommie" at the best of times, were fit to be tied.

After he was liberated, McKeown returned to the University of Toronto for a degree in chemical engineering. He taught high school for a few years, and later was a student missionary in China. He qualified as a chiropractor and later as a naturopath, gradually finding his way to Abbotsford, where he now resides.

On June 3, Charlie McKeown's family and friends gathered in the British Columbia community to help celebrate his 94th birthday, and to hear more of his recollections about the War to End All Wars.

This article was prepared with information supplied by John Carson of Barrie, nephew of Charlie McKeown. In Chapter Seven, there is a copy of an interesting letter written by Charles McKeown while he was a prisoner of war in Germany.

◇

Like many English immigrants, Mark Allengame of Mono Road answered Great Britain's call for soldiers and enlisted with the 126th (Peel) Battalion, Canadian Expeditionary Force, in December 1915. He spent the winter and spring in training in Toronto and the Niagara Camp and was shipped to England in August 1916. While at Whitley Camp he married his sweetheart Annie Goverd, with whom he had been corresponding since coming to Canada. They were married in their hometown of Bridgwater, England in November 1916.

Mark Allengame and friend Bob Slade. COURTESY DIANE ALLENGAME-KUSTER

Many of the Canadian battalions were broken up to serve as reinforcements for units experiencing heavy losses. Mark was transferred to the 124th Battalion Cdn. Pioneers, a battalion responsible for trenching and building roads and railways. In France he was gassed and wounded, but soldiered on throughout 1917 and 1918. Mark was demobilized in 1919 and returned to Canada. Shortly after, Annie said goodbye to Bridgwater and sailed to Canada and her new home in Mono Road. Neither of them were to see England again.

This information was supplied by Diane Allengame-Kuster, granddaughter of Mark Allengame.

◇

Men from Caledon East who served in the Army. From the left: Reginald "Paddy" Brown, Lawrence Mathews, Wilbert McCaffrey and Arthur Douglas. COURTESY PETER ELMS

When World War I broke out in 1914, twenty-five year old Margaret Black of the Nashville area volunteered as a Nursing Sister with the Canadian Expeditionary Force and sailed for England. She and her cousin Fred Hostrawser, who was killed in action in France, were the first descendants of Flora and John Cameron to return across the Atlantic to Britain. Working at the Aldershot Military Hospital in southern England, Margaret nursed a stream of wounded Canadian boys who survived the brutal trenches of France and Flanders. She recalled her worst experience was actually after the Armistice in 1918, in the winter of 1919, during the terrible influenza epidemic that swept the world. Short-staffed one night because so many nurses were ill, she was the only Nursing Sister on a ward of 30 Canadian soldiers who had survived their wounds but now were wracked with flu. Four young men died in her arms one night.

On her return from overseas, she nursed for a while in Detroit; took a few years off to care for her parents at their home in Nashville, and then began her long career as a Veterans' Nurse. She worked first as a Nursing Sister at the Christie Street Hospital in Toronto and then at the "new" Sunnybrook Hospital on Bayview, caring for "her boys" from World War I, and later the younger veterans from World War II.

This information has been supplied by Jean (Black) Stewart, niece of Margaret Black.

◀◀◀ Chapter Two ▶▶▶
– 1915 –
Letters From the Front

In 1915 some Canadian troops were moved to a bulge in the Allied line near the city of Ypres, France. Wherever they were posted, letters flowed freely to their families at home, describing interesting and sometimes tragic experiences of war.

Bolton Enterprise - March 26, 1915
The following letter has been received by Mrs. S. J. Snell from her son, Major (Dr.) Arthur E. Snell, who went with the first contingent:

France, February 28, 1915

Dear Mother

Well, as you probably know we have arrived in France and as a matter of fact in Belgium. We have been here two weeks to-day and seen the real thing at last. We first came up to our billets about 15 miles from the trenches and had hardly got settled when three of us, Major Beatty, Hardy and myself, and fourteen men and three ambulance wagons were sent up here to work with the English Field Ambulance. We have been here now just a week and our men have been in the trenches four days. The troops go in for four days then out for four days so in that way they get a rest. This No 2 brigade of Canadians with which we are working have been in most of this week as you know and will have heard by the time you get this that we have had some killed and wounded. I guess I was the first one to dress a Canadian wounded – certainly of the second brigade. I was out at the Advance Dressing Station, which is about 900 yards behind the fighting line. The night our fellows went in one Canadian from the 5th battalion from out west came in shot through the cheek bone, then down across through his tongue and lodged in his neck under the angle of his jaw on the opposite side. He was a sorry looking spectacle as his face was much swollen. He ought not to die. Two others the next night were shot through the brain. One dead and the other pretty bad. Our fellows at this time had not learned to keep their heads down.

Another Canadian in the other brigade was shot through the stomach. These are all I have heard of but I believe there have been about 20 wounded. The day before yesterday word came into us here that an engineer officer was felled, by the name of Irving. Well I was quite worked up about it as Tommy Irving I knew was with this Company and we came up with them. I went to the advance dressing station to the funeral and saw Tommy Irving and was quite relieved. The dead man is Lieutenant Bill Irving. It was his first day in the trenches – pretty hard luck – he was shot through the brain.

The first day we arrived was foggy and we went right up to the Regimental H. 2. which is just behind the first line of trenches and perhaps 400 to 500 yards back. Of course bullets are flying there but at present things are very quiet and it is only the snipers who are busy.

There is a funny war as here we are in a fairly good sized town with the people going around and every once in a while shells drop. Of course the Germans are searching out for the guns.

We have a lot of artillery here, and there is an understanding apparently not to shell the billets. The Germans did once and our men gave them a hot time and they have not repeated the dose. We are pretty strong here and especially now that we are here but of course this is only temporary. Our men have done pretty well in the trenches and one of the Generals complimented them. One man who was shot through the head fired 35 rounds through the one loophole and the Germans finally got on to him and he got it. If you did not see the wounded men you would think this just a sham fight, a continual big gun fire and the rattle of the rifles, but do not see anything.

It is rather interesting to hear the officers talk about the retreat in the beginning of the war and then the advance. Things were pretty lively then and I guess we will see something of the same again. Just at present as I write we have an officer from another unit and he is quite a talker, perhaps too much. The officers of this unit are very nice and not too talkative.

Our advance dressing station has had a couple of shells through it right into the dressing rooms. You see the artillery have a battery in the garden and other batteries are a little further off. The day I was out there were twelve shells went over the building and landed in the water. It is surprising how these shells seem to fall in fields. Of course there are any number of houses hit and especially in our street called Plug Street, as it is all shot up. The trip up here is just to get our men used or broken into the smell of blood and powder and give them some idea of what the game is like. I think they have enjoyed it and it will do them good in the way of discipline. They shoot men here for offences that we have let go repeatedly. There is no fooling. A man gets drunk and it is either a shooting or prison for 6 months.

The first night the Canadians went into the trenches a voice in English called out: "Oh, you have the Canadians to help you – well send them over and we will give them hell." How they got to know we cannot understand. They lip each other back and forward across from trench to trench. As far as hardships go just here we have it more comfortable than on Salisbury Plain. You see the people in good many cases have left their houses and the troops simply go in and make use of them as billets. Where I am it is quite a nice house and considerable furniture left in it. The Germans had no time to do much damage here as they were on the run. They blew up all the bridges and our engineers are just now putting new ones up.

I do not know how the Germans are going to be driven out, as it is suicide for either side to get out in the open to charge. I suppose someone will have to be sacrificed when the time comes.

I must close now. Ettie and Evans are settled in Twickenham and are well the last I heard.

In 1917, Colonel A. E. Snell (he was a Colonel by that time) was awarded the Distinguished Service Order for his work tending the wounded behind the trenches in France. He was also awarded the Order of St. Michael and St. George by the King at Buckingham Palace.

The Enterprise has received the following letter from F.S. Rutherford who is in France -

March 2, 1915
It is some time since I have written you and have come through a great many changes since then.

I am writing this letter in a French Estaminet or Public House somewhere within sound of the big guns. We have been up to the firing line for a week and at present are moving to a new position. Our work at the front consisted mainly in assisting the British Royal Engineers to construct the second line trenches and to repair the old front line. We also had some barbed wire entanglement to construct and some wet trenches to reclaim between the firing lines. The work of the Engineers is mostly done at night and under cover of darkness. When a "flare" or "star" is shot up the men have to lie flat until the light drops down and then continue their work. It is when a "flare" is shot up that the snipers get in their work. We were unlucky enough to lose our sandbags along with two R. E. officers superintending the work when a bullet struck him in the head. You may be sure we felt very badly, especially to think that our first loss was an officer and one whom we admired very much.

A soldier's writing paper.

In this neighbourhood both the Germans and the Allies appear to be just holding each other in check until the country dries up enough for an advance. The soil is very wet and it is absolutely impossible to move anything across country except by main roads. We feel quite confident that there will be a great movement when spring comes and that the Allies will not be the losers.

One thing we notice very much is the comparative easiness of the peasants, even within the range of the German guns they will still go about their farming, etc., apparently without any anxiety whatever. On one occasion we were trenching on a man's farm when he began threshing at the barn a hundred yards away and smoke of the engine drew fire from the German guns, we were compelled to take cover hurriedly, several shells hit the barn and house, the shrapnel breaking things in general, but the farmer did not stop work until ordered to do so by a British officer.

Although so near the seat of action we get very little news of the war in general and are always hoping to run across some English papers with some news of events elsewhere than at this particular point.

As for the Engineers we are all quite comfortable, even better than we expected. The mud is pretty deep but no worse than on Salisbury Plains.

No doubt you know that our letters are all censored in order to see that no information, which would be of use to the enemy, leaks out.

Wishing you and all my friends every success,

I am, yours sincerely,
F. S. Rutherford
British Expeditionary Force
1st Canadian Contingent
Division Engineers
2nd Field Company

Bolton Enterprise - April 2, 1915

The following letter was written by Pte. Norman Hutchinson of the 36th Regiment, First Contingent, to relatives at Caledon East. It was dated at the Queen's Canadian Military Hospital, Beachborough Park, Shorncliffe, Kent, England, to which he had been invalided:

Just a line to let you know the set back that I have had. Had to be sent back to England and was transferred into three different hospitals in France and this makes the fourth.

This is a very nice one, only Canadians allowed in it. It is only a small one, a private house belonging to Lady Markham who left it for a hospital during the war. The sisters are all from Toronto and they are very nice to us. We have quite a few visitors to see us.

Well sister, I was most certainly surprised when I got to Armirtreass [sic]. This is a village two miles from the trenches, which the Germans had, but is recaptured and it is as busy as Caledon East without soldiers in it. There are so many soldiers in it you can hardly move, stores are open and business going on the same as in Caledon East and people just as cheery as in Caledon East, and I think a little more so. The Germans shell this town every day with a shell or two and when one hits a place and explodes it makes a noise like the gas explosion that was at Mr. Burrell's in Caledon East a year ago, so you can imagine what the poor French women have to put up with. We slept in a hayloft while in the village and you could hear the rifles firing at the trenches also the big guns right beside us. The first night we could not sleep with the noise of the guns. You can tell the farmers around there that the French are farming and starting to seed two miles from the firing line, but with the rain and snow it is so muddy that it is about six inches deep on the road to the trenches and it makes it very bad going into the trenches and out again. But it is not as bad as I expected in the trenches. We can cook a hot meal and make a cup of tea but you cannot put your head over the trenches or you will get a cuff in the ear that will prevent you from putting it over any more. Well, here I have written this much and have not told you my troubles. It is only an abscess. I am praying that I will soon be better so I can get my old friend Guster (that is what I call rifle) and get back with my old pals in France for you know I'm a happy boy when I get Guster in my arms. I am going to see the boys in the second contingent when I get out of the hospital.

Bolton Enterprise - May 14, 1915
Edward J. Weeks of Macville, who enlisted with the 36th Battalion at the outbreak of war, writes to G. A. Norton from the front as follows:

Here I am in hospital - got a shot through the left leg. The Germans were driven back through, but we lost a lot, including our Colonel-Adjutant and nearly all the officers wounded, in fact I think out of our Company alone at the time I got away from the dressing station, there were 120 killed and wounded. I had some great luck. The stretcher bearers were bringing me in when they set me down to rest. A shrapnel shell burst right over our heads, broke the arm of one of the bearers and also got him in the leg and killed two men right alongside. Then I had to creep in the best way I could - about a half mile. But our boys did well, stuck out like bricks. I expect to be sent across the Channel tomorrow and hope to get back again soon.

Private Mills at Hill 60

Bolton Enterprise - May 28, 1915
Pte. Thomas Mills writes as follows from London, England, to Mrs. Vickery of Macville.

I am pleased to be able to write you a few lines once again, though it seems ages since I wrote you last. You will no doubt be surprised to see that I am in England again, though by the time you receive this and send an answer back I may be back with my battalion at the front.

I was wounded April 23rd near Ypres, at what is called Hill 60. You have I suppose read the news of the fight long before this reaches you. I am glad to say my wound is not serious, though it was in a very awkward place and only missed striking me in the throat by less than an inch. I was struck by a bullet in the nose and it went through my tongue and out under my chin. After being wounded I had a dreadful scramble to safety, bleeding like a stuck pig for some time. The air was full of flying bullets, as the large artillery shells were bursting in all directions. I was showered with earth several times but was fortunate enough to escape being hit with shrapnel. Many of my poor comrades lost their lives that day. We had a very hard task in front of us taking some ground lost by the French the day before. Those of us who came out only wounded thought ourselves very lucky to have come out alive at all.

I have been in England about a week now, and am almost better. Am getting the best of care in England in a country place called Edenbridge. There are several of us here and we are taken out for auto drives nearly every day as well as different places for tea. The people are very kind.

I don't care to write about the war, you likely have plenty of it in the paper. Perhaps you would like to know a little about France and Belgium people. We were in country places most of the time and indeed saw very interesting things when any distance away from the danger zone. The farmer seems to value every inch of ground. There are hardly any fences at all and the ground is in use right into the edge of a ditch or roadway. First thing drew my attention when seeding commenced was to see two elderly men drawing a set of harrows to and fro in a ploughed field. I saw later also women drawing the roller, and again to see a field of wheat being gone over with an extra big hand rake. Dogs have no easy life in France. Every farm that has cows has a treadmill to operate churn and separator, which is run by the dog. Dogs are also seen pulling small carts along the roads with small loads. The old saying "the life of a dog" is fully brought out in that country. Still more interesting scenes came forward when we entered the borders of Belgium and I could not help laughing at the sight. It was a cow drawing a wagon along the road. They are mostly three wheel wagons, one small front wheel and two big rear wheels. This cow I mentioned by looks was a milker. I thought it very unfair she should have to work also but later saw several others in the harness and on one occasion saw a cow harrowing and another pulling a small seed drill. They certainly seem to be very old fashioned. Nearly every farmer has at least one or two real horses and I must say the best I ever did see and horses that any Canadian farmer would be proud to own. These are driven with one rope only. It is amusing to see these sorts of things and most of the time there is neither shafts nor tongue to the wagon.

Then again there is another class of horses, part mule, they sometimes work well and sometimes give trouble. A horse and a mule together make a very odd team. In towns there are lots of donkeys and dog carts. I should like very much to travel these countries in peace times. It would be very interesting. At present the country and towns are in a dreadful state of ruin. We were in many villages and towns that were completely smashed to scrapheaps, large churches crushed into a heap.

The people in both countries will suffer for a time after the war is over. It is much easier to go on fighting knowing that we will find our homes to return to but many of the French and Belgium soldiers will have no homes to return to if they do get through safely. There is a great difference between French and Belgium people. I found the French not altogether too willing to make friends in many cases, but as soon as we got into Belgium the people were so different and gave us a much more friendly welcome and seemed very glad to help us in any way they could. I did meet some nice French people in different places but have not so good an opinion of them as of the others. When going to the country we could not of course speak French so had quite a time to make ourselves understood, but through time I began to learn a few words and quite often when out with a chum or two we would get into some house or other and buy coffee and get talking to the people in a mixed way. No matter where we went it was coffee, they seem to almost live on it. We could not buy tea at any price. Their bread is not of very good quality but has a watery taste and their *butter is even worse. I really don't know how they make it or what they put in it but it is more like lard and has a somewhat greasy taste, salt seems to be something not very much used in any of their eatables.*

With the Canadians at Langemarck

Bolton Enterprise - May 28, 1915
F. S. Rutherford, who is with the Canadian Engineers in France, writes to relatives, in part, as follows:

The Canadians got a severe set back as to casualties but they held firm and did not lose any ground and even retook part of the French lost ground when they were forced to retire owing to the terrible suffocating gas used by the Germans.

We were in our billet and were just preparing to go up to the trenches for our night's work when heavy artillery battle started up on our left. We could see a large yellowish green cloud rising above the hills and trees and slowly rolling towards us. Inside of an hour the air was thick with gas which smelt like chlorine or hydrochloric acid gas and was very suffocating even at a distance of 2 miles where we were. The French were forced to retire and the Germans advanced very quickly and a heavy artillery fire was soon ranged on the retreating French, which caught us. We had to load all our wagons, pontoons, trestles, etc., and abandon our billet. We took up trenches on the canal about one half mile in our rear and mined all the bridges preparatory to destroying them should the Germans threaten to get across. The Canadians by this time were next to the French in the line of trenches and when the French retired it left the Canadians as if it were open and undefended with thousands of Germans besieging them. They held firm. At one time they were surrounded and supposed to be prisoners. They still fought on, however, and in the end took some of their captors prisoners. The Canadian and British reserves were rushed up and recovered part of the ground lost by the French. The shelling all this time was terrible and cannot be understood by anyone who has not experienced it. We stayed in the trenches until noon the next day when we were relieved and had to go around through Ypres and up by St. Julien to reinforce the Canadian left. We saw some terrible sights on this trip and were heavily shelled all the way. We stayed in an old barn until dark and then got up to where we were to work. We had our tools all in wagons, along with barbed wire, etc., for strengthening the position. It was while unloading these that I got hurt and I saw no more, but I understand from reports that our company lost a good many men that night. The hospitals are full of men with wounds and gas poisoning, while the great many of the most serious cases are sent to England.

Life in the Trenches

Bolton Enterprise - June 25, 1915
The following letter was received by Dr. John Graham (before he enlisted) from Donald McKay from Caledon East.

4th Batt., 1st Brigade, France, 1915

Dear Doctor.-
Your letter duly received and I was pleased to receive the same, Most likely you would see by the papers how our battalion suffered at Ypres. Jim Perdue got wounded in the arm, but while he was in the dressing station a shell struck it so he got another one, but I don't know the nature of it at present. However, he was lucky

he did not get killed. We have moved to another position in the line. We went into the trenches on Saturday night, 22nd of May, and came out on the 31st. It is the most advanced point in the trenches, where the Germans have been driven back, that we were in. If there is such a place as hell, it can be found in that trench. However, we stuck to it, we could not advance for we had to get the flanks up first. Poor Harry Hickey got killed on the morning of the 29th. He received a bullet in the neck, which put him right out. A few weeks ago he was made Sergeant. Norman Hutchinson is all right so far. At this game one never knows his luck. One is lucky who only gets slightly wounded. I must say I have been lucky so far. It is nothing to see them drop around you. It is an awful sight to see the dead all over the fields, in some places you cannot bury them for the heavy artillery fire and machine guns, etc. As the warmer weather is here now, they will have to do something or some disease will break out. Since our arrival here we have seen a great deal of France. It is a beautiful country and it is hard lines to see all the homes, etc., that have been wrecked with shellfire. At present we are in billets but expect to move back to (hell) the firing line at any time. We all had a swim in the canal yesterday and I can tell you we required same. By the way I must congratulate you on getting a "Donald" in the family.

I hope this finds you all in the best of health. Lieutenant Blakely is with us now; he came out with the last draft. Remember me to Dan and all the rest of the boys.

With kind regards to all.

Yours truly
Don A.S. McKay

Donald Graham, the son mentioned above, later became Squadron Leader Donald Graham of the RCAF in World War II.

Bolton Enterprise - June 25, 1915

France, June 4th, 1915

No. 2 General Hospital
1st Canadian Contingent
British Expeditionary Force.

Mr. F. N. Leavens,
Bolton, Ont.

Dear Friend,-
Many a time since I left Canada have I intended writing to you but with the whirl and excitement there is in this great campaign one hasn't much time for letter writing.

As you know when we first landed in England we were stationed on Salisbury Plains and any man that can survive a winter like the one we came through there is almost proof against all sorts of weather. When I look back over the past and think of the big strong men who died there it seems like a miracle that I am here to write this letter. The most of our unit was attached for duty to No. 1 General Hospital which operated a number of smaller hospitals all within a radius of about ten miles. While there I was on duty most of the time in the dispensary in the Spinal Meningitis district. That is where every person was on the alert because every time a man was sick his first thought was that Spinal Mac. (As it was termed by a soldier) had got him at last. I was sick for about three weeks myself and as I had every symptom of this terrible disease, I made a desperate fight the first week until I was finally played out and had to go to bed. I didn't mind if a German bullet got the best of me but not getting farther than Salisbury mud was very depressing. However, I recovered all right and as my own unit needed me then they sent for me and I returned to their head quarters at Larington. After spending about a month here our unit was called together again and then the real work started, preparing to leave for France.

From the time we started to load our equipment, which weighed about eight hundred tons, to the present we have surprised ourselves and everybody else by the manner in which we have done the work set before us. Every one of us seemed to be glad to get away from Salisbury Plains and get into the real work that so when we were started at loading goods at the docks in England we certainly rushed it aboard. We crossed the channel in a cattle boat in which I had a first class stall for a berth and neither the rats that were busy running over my feet inside nor the German submarines that were chasing us outside bothered our sleeping abilities in the least. During the night when I would waken up with cold I would take a walk up on deck. It was a beautiful sight crossing the channel that night. The sea was calm and the sky was clear and bright while the huge search-lights on the coast made it as bright as day. The cruiser that was escorting us across seemed very anxious about something though and kept urging our boat all the time to make more speed so the next morning when we arrived at a port in France we learned that a submarine had been on our trail. This was Sunday morning and we commenced unloading. The captain of the boat told us we couldn't have our cargo off at least before eight o'clock that night. Well, just to show him how the Canadians do things we finished it at five. We slept on boxes and bales or any corner we could squeeze into that night and next day loaded our equipment into freight cars which made up two large trains and started on a hundred mile journey through France, arriving at our destination the next afternoon. Here we kept our record breaking pace we had set and had our camp ready in three weeks. It had taken a British unit of the same strength five weeks to do the same work.

Since that time we have been hard at work handling the wounded and doing all we can for the great cause. There are no union hours here and we do our work in the middle of the night as often as we do in the day. This is where you see the awfulness of war. One case that comes to mind just now is of a poor chap that was brought in just a mass of wounds. We tried our utmost to save his life but after taking over fifty pieces of shrapnel from the different parts of his body and amputating his foot, then his leg, he finally died. This is only one of many such cases I could tell you of but I would rather forget them than write about them. I suppose after reading this letter you will think it is mainly one of praise for us. But when you consider the great work of the Canadians and how they have proved themselves to be among the best soldiers in the world and when you hear the British Tommy who has fought with them tell how he might be under sod now if it hadn't been for the dash of our boys, and when our own unit has been three times mentioned in dispatches, I don't think you will blame me for feeling proud that I belong to the Canadian Contingent. I must close now wishing you and all the residents of Bolton and vicinity the best of prosperity.

Yours Sincerely,
34559 Staff Sergt D. Stanley Rutledge

Bolton Enterprise - September 17, 1915
James A. St. John, writing to his mother, Mrs. Thomas St. John of Albion, (August 19) says
they have been on the same line six weeks. He says:

*The Germans don't seem to want to mix up with the Canadians and so they keep quiet
and that gives us a chance to fix up the trenches. We have five lines deep, seven
miles in length. We are never idle, either fighting or working. Been a very wet
season. The day is near at hand when we are going to strike on this west front with
all our might, and God help the Germans when we do for we have both men and
shells to do the job. We have our regiments made up to full strength again. This is
six draughts we have had since we came to France. There are still ninety of the old
boys left and your son is one of them. Oh, am I not the lucky boy. I think this
winter will make a change. I hope so, for I long to be back home for a while. It is
over a year since I put on the khaki and have been in France seven months, and the
longest time I have been off the fighting line is six days at any one time. I was in the
hospital for ten days when I got hit in the leg. It has not got real well yet, but I
wanted to get back with the boys. You see there are so few of us and the new
draughts are no good alone. My address is J.A. St. John, No. 1025, No. 3 Company,
90th Winnipeg Rifles, 8th Canadian Infantry battalion, France.*

Bolton Enterprise - October 1, 1915
The following are extracts from a letter written by Corporal Norman Hutchinson to his sister,
Miss Irene Hutchinson of Albion, dated from Slap Alley, Bombs Retreat, August 21. Corporal
Hutchinson has sent his mother, Mrs. W.J. Hutchinson, some souvenirs in the shape of hand-
kerchiefs sold by the Belgian refugees in the district where he is stationed. He says in part:

A silk postcard from France.
COURTESY DIANE ALLENGAME-KUSTER

*There were loads of thimble berries. We pick them and stewed
them down, but we are a little shy in the sugar line and they
do not get the right flavour. The hazel nuts are just getting
ripe. We eat them green and they are not so bad. After tea we
always have our little band, consisting of an accordion, a
mouth organ and a biscuit tin for a drum. It makes grand
melody. If noise has anything to do with it, the 4th Battalion
is ahead of them all.*

*I will explain a day's work to you as near as I can. We
get up about seven o'clock, get breakfast, perhaps read, clean
our rifle as it is our best friend and we have to look after it
well. Then we have a wash if we have time, then a smoke,
crack a few jokes and do sentry in between times. After dinner
we have sleep, and if we are not sleepy we have a few shots at
Fritz, as we call Germans. Then we have supper. Then we start work for the night,
getting in rations and supplies and other necessary things, which we need, in our
next day's work. We never get any sleep at night - sit around and joke all night. I
am "King of the Barb Wire Gang". We go out in front of our trenches and fix where it
is broken or cut with shell or rifle fire. Of course the Germans watch us very closely,
and they make it very interesting for us sometimes. They generally send up a few
star shells and then a few rounds of rifle fire. But we lie down and kiss the ground
and the shots generally go over the top of our heads and cut the grass all around us.
We have been very lucky so far but don't know how soon they are going to get us.*

*We are looking for a chance to get to England for a rest, but we will not get that
unless we get a bullet in the leg or a flesh wound of some kind.*

On October 4, 1915 Charles Thomas of Vaughan Township wrote a letter to his mother, a copy of which has been supplied by his daughter Betty Ward of Caledon East. It said:

My Dear Mother,
Your letter of September 19 arrived to-day. No, the box has not arrived yet. Did I tell you I had received the papers all right?

Now father must have a very high opinion of the Canadian army. Of course, there are some pretty tough fellows in the divisions. An army picked up as quickly as they were is sure to have a lot of what was the floating element. But the majority are pretty fine fellows. And as for the Christianity of those who are professing Christians, well it is something you can depend on. A little different to those selfish persons who are so frightened that they cannot see beyond the length of their nose. You know, I have always thought there should be more native born Canadians in our contingents instead of leaving it to the "British-born" who so many people profess to despise.

Cannot tell you mother when we shall be back. Expect it will be a hard struggle yet, notwith-standing the victories in the south. Somehow, I have always expected I should come back but even if anything does happen to me, you will know I have done it for two reasons.

A Song for Canadian Soldiers – and Others

Charles Thomas wrote the following poem in the back of his 1915 World War I Diary.

When my King and Country called me and I'm wanted at the front
Where the shrapnel shells are bursting in the air
When the foe in fury charges and we're sent to bear the brunt
And the roll is called for service, I'll be there.

When the roll is called for service, I'll be there.

When the Kaiser's lines are broken and his armies out of France
When the Belgian's desolation we repair
When the final muster's ordered and the bugle sounds advance
May the God of Battles help me to be there.

When the roll is called for service, I'll be there.

When the Allies march thro' Prussia with the foe in full retreat
That our hearts be kept from hatred is our prayer
Where the right of might is ended in a crushing last defeat
And the roll is called in Berlin, I'll be there.

When the roll is called for service, I'll be there.

When for me the Last Post is sounded and I cross the silent ford
I've a Pilot who of mine-fields will beware
When Reveille sounds in Heaven and the Armies of the Lord
Sing the Hallelujah Chorus, I'll be there.

When the roll is called up yonder I'll be there.

Charles Thomas is the Father of Reginald Thomas, Marjorie Murray, Dorothy Thomas, Evelyn Picket and Betty Ward.

One is my love for our Empire which I am glad and proud to know is not now, at least, ruled by self-seeking men, for you know, they would have kept out of it, "and lost their own soul." The other is, I am glad to be able to do my bit on the right side.

Of course, we all wish it was over, but it is a very small minority who would take their discharge at the present time, even if it was offered to them, notwithstanding the Kaiser's success until just lately.

But don't worry about me, I am only one in millions and do expect to see you again before twelve moons at least.

Your affectionate son, Charley

Charles Thomas's pay book. COURTESY BETTY WARD

Bolton Enterprise - October 8, 1915
The following letter was received by Dr. John Graham, M.O. 74th Battalion, C.E.F., from Private Edward Weeks, formerly of Macville.

Dear Dr. Graham: -

I am writing to ask if you could give me any information about Hickey's* parents, their address for instance, as I would like to write to them. I have mentioned to several that he should be recognized for the brave deeds he did in rescuing the wounded at the Battle of Ypres on the 22nd and 23rd of April. I myself saw him bring back two wounded men after he had attended to me, under heavy machine gun fire and high explosives. I have watched the papers and have read where men have received the V.C. (Victoria Cross) and Distinguished Service Medal for much simpler things than he did, but because no one but an N.C.O. and the men whom he brought back and were still alive witnessed his deeds, he gets nothing for it. This was early in the day and I have heard from some of the other boys that he continued his heroic conduct throughout the day. Surely a man like that although dead deserves some distinction.

I have just had a line from Hutchinson. He is still going strong in France. I hope to go back as soon as I can manage the marching but the wound left some fluid on the knee which makes it weak going down hill. Can you recommend anything to make it right again soon? If you could I would be so thankful.

Jim Perdue is still, as far as I know, in Ward 34, Hampstead Military Hospital. Mr. Lindon and I went to see him several times while I was in London. Poor boy; he has had rather a tough time but hear they are going to save his leg. Well now, Sir, I must conclude, trusting you will be able to furnish me with Hickey's parents' address at your earliest convenience.

Yours very truly,
Edward J. Weeks
No. 112996, No. 4 Company
Attached 12th

*Private Weeks was referring to Sergeant Harry Hickey, who came from England and lived in the Caledon East area. He was recommended to receive the Victoria Cross on May 24, 1915, but did not live to receive the honour, if in fact it would have been granted. Sergeant Hickey was killed on May 30, 1915 at Vimy Ridge.

⫷⫷ Chapter Three ⫸⫸
– 1916 –
Recruiting and Fighting Continue

The battle of the Somme occurred in 1916 and Canadians, wearing new steel helmets, played a prominent role. Casualties were high. In thirteen days 1,373 Canadians lost their lives during attacks on the enemy. Fighting continued throughout 1916, and recruitment was intensified.

In an effort to aid recruiting, the February 4, 1916 edition of the Bolton Enterprise states:

Rural recruiting will receive an impetus with the announcement from Brigadier-General Logie in Toronto that farmers and farmers' sons will be given leave to permit them to plough in the spring. This move has been prompted by the difficulties recruiting officers have met in the rural districts in the second divisional area through the great scarcity of farm labour. If the rural recruits are in Canada next fall they will be permitted to go back to their farms to gather in the harvest.

Bolton Enterprise - July 1916
Lawrie Gould, son of Mr. & Mrs. J. Gould of this place, has been attached to the Royal Canadian Band, 250 strong. These men were picked from over three thousand bandsmen, and will be kept together until after the war. They will not be sent to the front. They played before the King at Covent Gardens on the 4th of July and were to play in Paris, France on the 5th. He thinks England a wonderful place, also Scotland where the band spent two weeks. Lawrie is a graduate of the Enterprise office and enlisted at Calgary.

Who's Who in a Battalion
Bolton Enterprise - March 24, 1916
When the recruit enlists he signs on as a Private and his uniform is khaki serge, the tunic fitting close at the neck and fastened with seven buttons. His great coat is of the same, single-breasted. After he has been in a while, if he shows ability and energy, he is promoted to the rank of Lance-Corporal, which entitles him to wear on his right sleeve a chevron or "stripe" – a V shaped piece of braid, worn above the elbow on the tunic or on the cuff of the great coat, with the point turned down. His next step is to Corporal, when he can wear a double chevron or two "stripes".

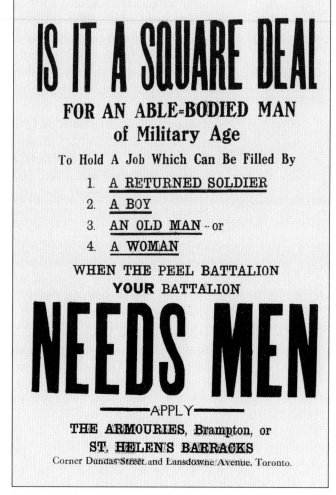

This advertisement was posted during World War 1.

If he is especially smart and keen he will rise to be Company or Battalion Sergeant-Major, the highest rank a man can hold without a commission. His uniform remains the same, but in addition to the stripes he wears a crown placed above the chevrons.

Staff-Sergeants – those on Battalion Staff – are distinguished by different badges worn above the chevrons – Quarter Master-Sergeant, a seven pointed star, Pioneer-Sergeant, cross axes, Farrier-Sergeant, crossed hammer and pincher, and so on. Staff-Sergeant also may wear, instead of three bar chevron, one of four bars, worn on the cuff with the point turned up.

Between non-commissioned and commissioned rank comes "warrant rank", so called because the bearer gets his rank by warrant from Minister of Militia - commissions coming direct from the King. The holder of warrant rank will wear the crown alone on his cuff.

The lowest commissioned rank is that of Lieutenant; and the holder is distinguished by two stars, worn on the shoulder straps in the Canadian Militia, on the cuffs in Imperial Army and overseas forces. The cuff is also trimmed with one band of braid around the sleeve.

Promotion to the rank of Captain entitles the Officer to another star on the shoulder or cuff and another band around the sleeve and discards the stars, substituting a crown. A Lieutenant-Colonel carries a star above the crown and on attaining the rank of Colonel another star is added.

The Brigadier-General's badge is the cross-sword and baton; that of Major-General crossed sword and baton with star above; of Lieutenant-General, crossed sword and baton with crown above; of General, crossed baton and sword above. A Field Marshal wears crossed batons mounted on wreath with crown above.

The uniform of an officer differs from that of a private or a non-commissioned officer in that, besides being made of finer material – the officer has to buy it himself – the tunic has a low collar with lapels and is fastened with four buttons and the great-coat is double-breasted and fastened with five buttons. There are other minor differences.

Presentation to Caledon East Men

The Brampton Conservator - May 18, 1916

On Thursday evening last May 11, the citizens of Caledon East, Mono Road district gathered in Hanton's Hall to do honor to the young men of the 126th who have enlisted from their midst, by presenting to each a handsome wrist watch. There was a short programme, with solos by Miss Smith and Mr. R. Cranston, also addresses by the resident clergyman, Capt. Duncan, chaplain of the Battalion, acting as chairman. The presentation was made by Capt. Duncan on behalf of the Patriotic Committee, who in a few well chosen words explained the object of the gathering and the wish that the recipients of the watches would accept them as a slight token, expressing in a tangible way the feelings of the community towards them for answering the call of country and the 126th Peel Battalion for overseas service. A purse of gold was at the same time presented to Private Rhoebottom who was wounded at Langemarck. Those receiving watches were as follows: Caledon East - L. Mathews, W. McCaffrey, J. McDevitt, W. Smith, J. Smith, A. Douglas, W. Douglas, R. Brown, T. Perdue, T. Warden, Mr. Hensman. Mono Road - Lieutenant McCaughrin, Messrs. Bennett, Bennett, Shepherd, Davis.

In the Front Trenches

Bolton Enterprise - May 26, 1916

Private Adam Wallace of this place writes as follows:

I am now in my dugout in the front line of trenches. We have just finished our little nap and most of the fellows have deserted their dugout for a bask in the sunshine. Some are cleaning their ammunition, others are having a friendly little talk on the war situation, and then there is another very interesting feature for the onlooker and that is a race. In some sunny spot you will see a couple of fellows, bare backed, with their undershirts in their hands, looking for those tiny insects called soldiers' "pets" and seeing who can make the largest catch. Who wouldn't be a soldier?

The other night as we were "standing to" on the firing step the big Claxton horn gave the warning of an expected gas attack so there was a general hustle to get our gas helmets on our heads ready to pull down in an instant. The attack came off but it was some distance on our right and as our men were ready for it Fritz did not get the desired results by his little game of strafe. The artillery opened up on both sides and it was certainly a pretty sight to watch as the flares shot up from both trenches and the heavens almost a sheet of fire, and added to this sharp report of the rifle and bomb, and the boom, boom, boom of the largest guns, presented a spectacle of admiration and at the same time struck terror into the soul of any living person. While this was going on we all stood in readiness for any activity on the part of Fritz but for some reason he didn't seem inclined for a scrap on the frontage covered by us. We all expected it to spread all along the line but dawn broke without any unusual occurrence.

Another little incident happened the morning after this. As we were eating breakfast our sentry noticed a working party climbing back into their trenches from nobody's land and in the dimness of the dawn he mistook them for coming this way, so he gave the alarm of an attack. Our tea and breakfast was thrown down any old place and a rush was made for rifle and bayonet in our different bays with the expectation of receiving Fritz with real Canadian courtesy. We waited anxiously for some time but we waited in vain, so finally we had to go back to our army instead of depending on the hospitality of the enemy for our morning meal. I am keeping fine.

Bolton Enterprise - June 30, 1916

The following is part of a letter received from Pte. Adam Wallace who has been in the front trenches for more than a year and has so far escaped serious injury:

The other night a party of us went to the cinema and saw the battle of the Somme. It was real good and the person who took them deserves credit for the risk he ran in taking them. I could see a few familiar spots but the surroundings were altogether different when the Canadians appeared on the scene in September. In the pictures presented, a person could see any amount of grass but when we went over it would be a big job to find grass of any description from the first ridge until you arrived on the edge of Courcellette, as the ground had been pounded so continually and fierce. The pictures we saw here shows the bringing up of shells, going over the bags, carrying in of the wounded, the big guns in operation, etc.

As we were on the first ridge, a Fritz shell lit in the centre of one of our platoons in the Company, as we went forward in extended order over this shell shattered ground with dead strewn here and there, and A.M.C. men doing their splendid work of carrying in the wounded and all the while shells lighting close by, it was something not to be forgotten in a short while. After passing the first ridge I would judge it to be about a mile and a half before reaching our objective. When within a hundred yards of Courcellette we waited for our own barrage to lift. As soon as the barrage lifted our fellows were given the word to advance and while covering that open space a good many of our fellows were wounded, so by the time I dressed them and rejoined my platoon the work was over, a good haul of Fritzies as souvenirs for their trouble.

In writing this I am trying to give you a little description of what took place, but can't. It would take a Shakespeare or greater than he to do justice to the scene in words. I don't think it is necessary to try and hide the truth from the people at home. They know that on active service it is no picnic, if not by actual experience by reading and a little common sense.

At times there is not as much shelling as at others and I think it is unfair for a person who has just done one trip in the trenches and that at a seemingly quiet part of the line to criticize others who have spent a year and some longer than that midst shells, bullets and mud of Kimmel, St. Eloi, Ypres and the Somme. I haven't the slightest hesitation in saying that the writer of bright news will be playing a different tune and telling another tale and that before many trips in the trenches have gone. All the same, I wish him good luck, and hope that he will have no worse to put up with but I'm a little doubtful if the quietness that he speaks of will prevail.

Many a time have I said my prayers and heaps of others with me before going over on a charge, a raid or in a heavy bombardment, and am not ashamed to say it. Well, Mr. Leavens, I suppose it is time to close, bright news is very scarce. We are enjoying ourselves despite the weather conditions and are not grouching or kicking at our lot in the slightest. We didn't expect that we were going on a summer outing when we hired on with R.L. Borden for a dollar ten. Why should we worry? Laugh and the world laughs with you, grouch and you grouch alone. A cheerful grin will get you in where the grouch is never known. Remember me to Casey when you speak to him. Another British bull has thrown his weight into the fray. Well done, Casey!

Adam Wallace was awarded the Distinguished Conduct Medal and Military Medal and Bar. A park in Bolton will bear his name - the Adam Wallace Memorial Park.

Bolton Enterprise - July 7, 1916
Part of a letter received by Mrs. Purvis from her son at the front, dated June 11th, reads as follows:

You asked me to tell you where I am. I cannot openly do this, but you know that the Canadians are in the hottest part of the British line, and I am quite near the most famous battle ground since the Aisne, namely ...., the place with the odd name and the most tried for (by the Germans) around here. There is nothing left but ruins now. We have a puppy found in the ruined city when it was recaptured. As you doubtless know, we have had a strenuous time of it the last ten days. I am driving a big motor truck on ammunition work, carrying small arms ammunition, bombs, shrapnel and high explosive shells. We were hard pressed when we retook the last positions on Tuesday, working for all the time for three days. It is an interesting thing to be under shellfire. Fritz sends them over quite steadily, and they come with a "whee-ee-ee-ee-izz bang". The screaming of the shells gets on one's nerves, because you can't see them, and when the "whee-ing" stops short in a "zp" you want to duck, because off she goes. If they come on to us with a load on, up we would go. In a heavy bombardment we leave the cars and get into the ditch, shrapnel is the worst. I have some souvenirs of shells, which burst close to me. I cannot tell you very much, not as much as I would like, in writing, because of the censor. The cyclists are all split up. Some are doing traffic control at the intersections. France has a wonderful system of roads. Some of the officers of the cyclists went to the Infantry and some to the trench howitzers of the Artillery.

No. 540094
Pte. C.B. Purvis
3rd Division Canadians
Ammunition, Sub Park, France

Bolton Enterprise - October 13, 1916

Private Adam Wallace writes as follows under date September 23rd to his mother:

I am still in hospital but am almost ready to be out again. My shoulders and left forearm are a little stiff and sore yet. We had just made a successful charge of the enemy's trench and were holding it when a 9.2 shell lit close and threw three of us about ten feet and partly buried us. My case was the slightest; the other two were stretcher cases and had to be carried out to the first dressing station. At first I thought I would try and "stick it" but after awhile as I was feeling rather stiff and sore, asked the Lieutenant if there was any use of me staying and he said "no, you had better beat it for the dressing station" so I made the quickest possible route up and down, out of one shell hole and into one again, and all the time keeping an eye on the places ahead to keep clear if possible of Fritz's "burning iron". The way the ground is torn up is something terrible and what was one time villages is now marked with scattered tile, splinters of timber and stumps of trees. It was no big job taking the trench for the Germans threw up their hands and cried mercy (Kamerod). The trouble was in holding it, and the fighting was against shells which so far neither side have found any method or plan to keep out of their reach although Fritz has made a big attempt. Many of their dugouts are fifty to sixty feet deep and have taken a good while to build. Now that we have them in the open our task of chasing them is a little easier. One old Fritz after he had been captured said, "Me married and got five children, no shoot, mercy, comrade". The majority of them seem quite at home after they have been taken. One fellow came up and handed me two or three field dressings as I was bandaging one of my comrade's wounds. The doctor had just been around looking at his patients and says I will be all right in a short time. I like the Red Cross grub fine; it is a big change from hard tack and bully beef stew. Don't worry, there is nothing seriously wrong.

Back In England

Bolton Enterprise - November 17, 1916

Corporal K. Ross Jaffary, of the 116th Battalion writes to his people at home, and states that the 126th Battalion, of which the boys were all very proud, has been broken up and all the "Peel" boys now belong to the 116th Battalion. Also that the boys are in the pink of condition and have recently gone across to France, most of the officers of the old 126th remaining in England. We understand the Peel boys have been kept together as much as possible which fact their friends at home will hear with pleasure.

Bolton Enterprise - December 1, 1916

Sergeant S.E. Judge writes that his Company is quarantined for measles. He and those of his comrades who are free are visiting the ancient historic buildings in their vicinity.

Lieutenant Dan McCaughrin, of the Canadian Engineers, is camped at Crowboroughs. At weekends he visits the historic buildings in London. He explored the Parliament Buildings and had his already virile Irish disposition renewed and strengthened by sitting in Redmond's and Carson's chairs. He visited Goldsmith's tomb and with hat removed viewed the resting place of the poet whose writings he always so ardently admired.

Captain John Graham, M.D. of the Medical Corps, Bramshott Camp, writes that Private Tomsett, a Mono Road recruit is wounded. He says the rainy weather has set in and Canadian wet weather is badly eclipsed by the brand England hands out. He was medical officer in charge of a Brigade Hospital (20 beds) for two months. Now he is on the Headquarters' staff - a Staff Captain in the office of the Assistant Director of Medical Services.

≪≪≪ Chapter Four ≫≫≫
– 1917-1918 –
The War Goes On

In addition to the battles at Ypres and the Somme, Canadians fought with distinction at Festubert and Givenchy, Vimy, Hill 70 and Lens, Passchendaele, Cambrai and the Battle of Amiens. As the war raged on into 1918, Canadian servicemen contributed greatly to the Allied effort. By September of that year the Allies were advancing in every sector and the war was reaching the final stage. Canadians would soon take their place in the successful march to Mons, where the Armistice was signed on November 11, 1918.

News of the War

Bolton Enterprise -January 5, 1917

> *Mr. Editor - Just a line to let you know I am well, also Jimmie Bolton and Leslie Elliott. I met the two of them over here. They are playing in a brass band and report having a good time. Well they both look the part, for I never saw the boys look as well as they look now. If Leslie Elliott gets any stouter they will have to send him back to Blighty and get a uniform made to order, or send Bob Studholme over to take his measurements, and Leslie Elliott is giving him a hard run on raising a moustache. They both look real cute with their third eyebrows. If they keep on Percy McMurter will have enough hair to make a European pillow. Well, I had my first trip up the line .... They mix things up once in a while, but there is always a quiet time to any of it. I know it is not all sunshine............ I have a wife and mother and I don't want them worrying about me all the time when a few cheerful words might cheer them instead of worry. I have seen a few of the boys from Bolton and around and they are all looking well and standing the game fine. News is scarce out here.*
>
> *Private Albert W. Pilson*

Bolton Enterprise - January 12, 1917

Private James Elliott Bolton, writing to his parents, Mr. & Mrs. J. H. Bolton, from France on December 16, says in part:

> *I hear today we are going to have a great spread for Christmas. I think our Battalion is going to be behind the lines for a month for a rest before they go into action again. I have hopes which I believe to be well founded that we will be home before next summer is over so if this Christmas is not so happy as they have been in the past we will surely enjoy it much more next year and I am looking forward to it now.*
>
> *Just got word through the signalers that the French have taken 6500 prisoners along with artillery and trench mortars and advanced their line. We get news of this kind along the front pretty quick and there is always lots of cheering when the news comes in. There is no getting away from it, we have them just where we want them all over the western front and keep them worried all the time. They could never*

break through our lines in a thousand years and it's only a matter of time until they will have to give way. It seems a slow business to one at home reading the papers I guess. I thought so too when I was in England and sometimes grew pessimistic over the way things were going, but when one gets over here and sees what we have done in such a short time and so handicapped, wonderful is hardly a fit expression.

This was a beautiful clear day and on such days we always have visits from the enemy aeroplanes which come over scouting or trying to bring down our observation balloons of which we have hundreds up all along the line and they stay up all day. Fritz cannot keep up fifteen minutes. There were two or three over this morning. Our anti-aircraft guns were banging away over an hour. One of them was brought down. Leslie Elliott saw it falling but I had just come inside and missed seeing it fall. Thank all the friends for me who have so kindly remembered me this Christmas. Conditions are such that I cannot write to them but you can explain and they will understand.

Private Whitney Byrne writes -

I am feeling all right again and ready to go across again. They need all the men they can get, especially Canadians. They seem to be the only soldiers Fritz is really afraid of. The boys certainly give it to him when they come in contact with him. Often he used to shout over to us what he would do to Canada if he won. So there is nothing left to do but see that he does not win. I don't think it would be fair to the boys whose graves are in Ypres and the Somme to quit fighting now. So here's hoping Canada sends all the boys she can spare. It encourages us very much to know that there are more coming to help us, also to know that you people who can't help directly are helping all in your own power at home.

Bolton Enterprise - February 9, 1917
Private William J. Chamberlain, son of Mr. & Mrs. Wm. Chamberlain, writes from the trenches in France and wishes to thank the members of the Women's Institute, the Ladies Aid and others who sent him boxes at Christmas.

Bolton Enterprise - December 28, 1917
Somewhere in France - November 26, 1917
I thought I would drop you a few lines to let you know I am still in the land of the living. I have had several close calls but luck has been with me so far. The work which I have to do is very dangerous, repairing and keeping up the line of communication. As fast as my mate and I would fix the lines, Fritz would smash them again and it keeps us busy dodging the shells when we are engaged in such work. I have come across several Bolton boys and I am sure glad to meet them. I have lost two of my chums, Willie Woods and Hubey Corless, and I feel the loss of them keenly but you will all have the satisfaction to know that they died as heroes. The other day I came across Ab Pilson. He is the same old Ab, only he has got thin. He and I are going over to see Leslie Elliott and Elliott Bolton tonight. Colonel Sam Sharpe is very kind to us boys and we are sure glad to be in his battalion. We were in Belgium for a while and it is certainly some place, for there is nothing but desolation and we were glad to get back into France again. There is nothing left of Ypres but a rubbish heap. The Germans seem strong yet, but Johnnie Bull with Jack Canuck at his side and the hundred thousand of the R. L. Borden Battalion, which the Union Government will send, will make Emperor Willie sit up.

Wishing all my kind friends in Bolton a very Merry Christmas and a Happy New Year.

E. Lorne Childs

Bolton Enterprise - January 4, 1918
Lieutenant Cross, of Halifax, is spending some holidays with his family here. Lieutenant Cross, who was on a naval training ship at the time of the great explosion, was stripped of his clothing by the force of the concussion, but fortunately escaped injury.

Victory Loan Campaign poster, 1918.
COURTESY PUBLIC ARCHIVES OF CANADA

Bolton Enterprise - January 11, 1918
Byron Leavens left England for France with the 3rd Battalion just before Christmas. Before leaving England he ran across Mercer Hamilton, of Tottenham, who played hockey with the Bolton team a couple of years ago. Mercer is nursing a bullet wound in the shoulder and is getting along fine.

◇

Private Harry Taylor, who met with injuries at the front on November 12th, has had his leg amputated, and says he will be back to help with the harvest next summer. Before enlisting Harry was employed with Mr. James H. Newlove at Macville.

◇

Staff Sergeant S.E. Judge, of the Canadian Corps School, France, writes - "I have just returned from 3 weeks in the battle line. We frequently had some hot work. I voted in the trenches and was scrutineer for our Company. I marked my ballot for the Union Government and judging from the talk of the boys we were all marking the same way.

◇

Private Clifford Judge, son of George Judge, crossed the ocean and is now in England. He belongs to the Forestry Battalion.

◇

Sergeant Norman Hutchinson, son of W.J. Hutchinson, writes of the strenuous times they are having on the battle line. The Sergeant is one of the 1st Contingent and knows what it is to leap the parapet.

Bolton Enterprise - January 18, 1918
Nursing Sister Daisy Dean, of Toronto, is visiting at the home of her uncle, Mr. Alex McCort. Miss Dean spent some time in France and Salonika and is now at the Base Hospital in Toronto.

Bolton Enterprise - January 25, 1918
Private William McKay came to town on Saturday and walked five or six miles through the blizzard to spend his last leave with friends before going overseas. Private McKay has been working with farmers in the district and was given exemption, but decided he would give the Huns a touch of good Irish fighting, so he enlisted and is now away to do what he can to crumple up the German war machine.

Bolton Enterprise - February 22, 1918
Private William E. Berney, son of Mr. & Mrs. George Berney of Caledon East, left Toronto February 16th with a draft of 500 men of the Central Ontario Regiment for Quebec City. It is expected they will be placed on garrison duty for some time before leaving for overseas.

Bolton Enterprise - May 3, 1918
Captain C.R. McCort in writing under the date of April 6th to his sister, Miss Mabel McCort, says in part:

> We have had a great deal of wet weather here this week, and the mud is almost indescribable. No doubt you are reading about the great battle that is going here now. I'm afraid I can't tell you much about what is going on and if I could it would take me a long time to do it. The enemy has gained some ground but the price has been terrible. I was quite surprised to hear Herb Dean was coming back to the farm. However, I think the farm is the best place these days for anyone who can produce food. For after all, food is just as essential for winning the war as shells and out here we get an excellent supply of both.

Bolton Enterprise - May 10, 1918
Seaman Percy Bennett in acknowledging a Red Cross box says he expects to be invalided home. Bennett enlisted in the British Navy about a year ago.

◇

Private E. Lorne Childs, who has been ill for several weeks in France, has now been sent to England to improve his health.

◇

Byron Leavens, writing home from France, broke a long silence by saying
> we were moving around continually from place to place and we got no chance to write at all. The spirit of the troops is excellent. The only thing I have to say is I wish I had been out here earlier on the scene.

◇

Writing to his parents from France, April 12th, Private Adam Wallace, M.M., says in part:

> Last night we kept a gas guard each man doing two hours. When I woke this morning about seven the window was wide open, the sun was shining and the birds were singing away as if there was no war on. It put me in mind of the old home more than ever before coming to France. The hammering of our heavy guns and the demolished houses are the only signs at present of there being a war on. I hear you got my military medal O.K. What is it like and what is on it and is there a ribbon attached to it? A year ago we were on top of Vimy Ridge having secured it from the enemy on the 9th. Terrible weather then, rain followed by snow and as cold as ice. We had nine days' trip of it and believe me we were not sorry the night our relief came in. Our first trip was not so bad as far as artillery fire was concerned - the weather was our worst enemy. Next trip in, however, we had to do some ducking and dodging and more than once we had to shift our residence to keep out of the way of the Krupp works. One of the boys in my old platoon came in yesterday. He was telling us where he was and how he was wounded, ending with - "Gee, I thought a munitions factory had struck me." The doctor and his batman have left for headquarters and I am in charge of the shack.

Unique Meeting at the Battlefront

Bolton Enterprise - April 5, 1918 (copied from the *Hanover Post*)

Horses were also equipped with gas masks.

There are some funny stories told in connection with old chums meeting on the battlefront in France and Belgium, but the following incident is unique. It is the story of how a man and his favorite horse met. In the early part of the war there enlisted in the town of Woodstock, New Brunswick, one Otto F. Gray, of Waterville, a village near Woodstock. He joined a battery draft and duly went to England and thence in the course of time to France. While at home he had worked on his father's farm and one horse was his favorite. Time passed away, and the horse buyers came to Carleton County to buy horses. They visited the home of Charles Gray, the father of Otto, bought a horse from him and it was duly shipped to France. Not long ago Mr. Gray had word from his son that in a shipment of horses for his Battery he discovered the one he had so well liked and whose name was "Queen". Young Gray had become a Sergeant Major and he had influence enough to get his old horse for his special saddle at the front. Just the other day he wrote his father that "Queen", the horse you sold, is still with me. She has been wounded twice but they can't kill her. She knows more than some men, and is tougher than a knot. She has got a great coat of hair now. If this were a part of fiction it would surely be considered overdrawn. But it is a hard, happy fact.

New Call Made for Canadians to Serve

Bolton Enterprise - April 19, 1918

Ottawa, April 12th - The attention of farmers receiving conditional exemption from military service until a fixed date is directed to certain principles which have been laid down by the Central Appeal Judge at Ottawa, which apply to all exempted men in this class.

The need for troops cannot be exaggerated. On the other hand, the necessity for maintaining food production is likewise pressing. The exemption granted farmers is granted solely because of the conviction that they are, or may be, more useful in food production than as troops at the front.

Such exemptions are really in the nature of licenses, and on the condition that the efforts of a person exempted for the purpose of assisting in food production are such as to justify the granting of exemption. All such exemptions are for a fixed period, usually until June 1 or July 1, but in some cases November 1.

In all such cases the person exempted has the privilege of applying for an extension of the exemption period, when it ought to be shown what effort the applicant has made and is making for the greatest production possible.

The application for extension should be sent to the Registrar at least two weeks before the date fixed, accompanied with a statement showing the total number of acres in the farm, the number of acres of arable land, the number of acres in grain, (oats, wheat, barley, peas, etc.), the number of acres in root crop, number of acres in pasture, etc., the number of beef and pork being raised and the amount sold, the number of pounds of milk produced and what is done with same.

If the person is hired help, he must also furnish the name of his employer and the amount of wages paid, and a list of his employer's family living upon the farm, together with any additional help employed.

In the case of a farmer's son, it will be necessary for him to give a list of the members of his family living on the farm, together with any hired help employed.

◇

Ottawa April 16, 1918
Owing to the critical situation which has with some suddenness developed on the western front and which is likely to continue until the allied nations have materially increased the strength of their forces, the Government of Canada, after the most careful consideration of all the circumstances, has reached the decision that it is not only desirable but absolutely essential that substantial reinforcements be secured for the Canadian Expeditionary Force without delay.

In order that the government may have full power to deal with the situation as it may develop from time to time, parliament is asked to approve of the government-in-council being given the necessary authority to call out the men of any age in any class under the Military Service Act and to abolish all exemptions in the cases of any class so called.

The Order removes the exemption now enjoyed by officers and men who have served in the Expeditionary Force, but who did not proceed further than Great Britain and have since returned to Canada and been discharged. They will be required to serve if physically fit when their class is called.

Battle of Amiens

Bolton Enterprise - September 20, 1918
Pte. Jesse McCubbin writes as follows to his parents, Mr. & Mrs. A. J. McCubbin, concerning the recent Canadian offensive in France.

Poster produced for Central Recruiting Committee, No. 2 Military, Toronto. COURTESY PUBLIC ARCHIVES OF CANADA

France, Aug. 18, 1918.
Dear Folks at Home,
I fear my long record of a letter home each week has been broken at last. It could not be avoided though, as you will see from what I have to say. I did send a field card last Sunday, so you were not without word of some sort. I scarcely know where to begin to-day. There seems so much to say I don't know how to start.

On the morning of August 8th I was a short way behind our front line with another Battalion (with which I was attached for duty with our wireless set). We were not the first to meet the Hun, but were close behind and came in contact soon after. One moment before the guns opened everything was quiet; one moment after every gun was throwing great quantities of iron over to Fritz. Around us and behind us the flashes from our guns kept the sky in a constant blaze, while over on Fritz' side the bursting shells did much the same. In a way it was a fine sight, if one can forget the tragedy of lives taken, but as I said at the time, "He wanted war; let him have it".

Soon we were on the march and alongside some tanks we followed the barrage. Fritz sent some our way, but he did not know where to fire so he was out of luck. Our heavy

guns were making it so hot for his gunners that they either "beat it" or were put out of action. For half an hour our party passed through his worst barrage but no one was hit. The shells were cutting off trees among us and throwing mud and earth all around, but we marched on with our load. It was along that spot we met our first prisoners. They were getting out as quickly as possible, too. Some were wounded. I saw one of our boys (wounded) and a wounded Hun marching out side by side, the Hun leaning on Jack's shoulder. Neither had a hat on and both seemed pleased they were able to get out.

For a time while climbing a hill we had things somewhat quiet but going down the other side we were in full view of Heine, who did his best to get us, but the shells could not come near us and his shrapnel was so high it did not trouble anyone. We walked on as though he were not there. We were the advance party at the time. It is unusual for a Battalion H.Q.R.S. Co. to go first but that was the case with us. My partner and I wanted to get our instrument through safely if possible and managed O.K. Soon after this we set up and tried to get in touch with the rear but unfortunately their instrument was out, so we could not make connections.

By this time the other corps had gone on and the guns which did so much trying to get us on the hill, became suddenly silent and the gunners were prisoners or dead Huns. The remainder of the day was more quiet, for any guns he got out, he did not have time to stop and fire, for the cavalry came along and either cut them off or made them travel so fast that they could do no harm.

About noon we stopped and fresh troops carried on past us. I have not been so tired for months and yet the excitement was so great that we did not seem to notice it or complain. As we sat around during the afternoon we saw all branches of the service pass by, moving up to take up their new positions. Every direction one looked we could see troops on foot moving on. Then we could see pack horses and wagons loaded with ammunition for the field guns (the guns and tanks had gone on ahead). Then came Red Cross cars, followed by motor lorries, wagons, staff cars and last, though not least, the observation balloons, tethered to motor trucks, came along. Then gradually the big guns moved up behind us at first, but in a day or two while we rested they passed us. It is a marvelous sight, one I will not soon forget. Everything seemed to move so easily as though it had all been rehearsed many times. Of course it meant incessant work for some of the branches, but under such circumstances everyone seemed to do a double share without a complaint.

In the first two days I only saw one Fritz aeroplane over our lines; he tried to help his artillery, but seemed very nervous and did not linger long with us. For the most part our machines filled the air, bombing, shooting and directing our artillery. Since then, of course, he has been able to muster more courage and machines and pay us more frequent visits. In the line, too, it is not so easy as it was but they are still moving back to the Rhine, or somewhere. I don't know where they are going or don't know if they know. They are not nearly so keen for fight as they used to be. One prisoner taken on the second day said that the Prussian Guards are being sent to this front. He had an idea that would scare us, but they don't thrive any better among our shells than some of the old men and little boys we took at the start.

One square head asked what the "C" meant on one of our boy's collar. He said Canadian, "Mein Gott! Mein Gott!" exclaimed the wretched Hun. They quake at that name. They thought we were up north, as one of their officers said. They left all sorts of junk behind them. I came on an officer's coat out in the open plain. I expect he had shed it in his hurry away. I found a dugout where there was much in the line of eats and mineral water (mostly the latter). I came on a loaf of their bread and of course sampled it. It is heavy and much darker than our brown bread. It smells and tastes sour but is fairly wholesome. I would not like to live on it long.

World War I soldiers from the Albion-Bolton area at Witley Camp, Surrey, England in July 1918. Left to right, front: Patrick Mullin, Roy Hesp. Bottom row: William Berney, Melville Defoe, Delbert Arlow, Oscar Boyce, Albert Boyce, William Proctor, Albert Victor Cole, Vernet Davis, Winston Chapman. Second row: Joseph Reynar, Wardlow Norris, Clinton Martin, Ray Bowes, Leonard Bowes, Charles Norton, Ollie Matson, Jack Martin, George Styles, Harry Courtney. Top row: ?, Robert Henderson, Ernest Patterson, Basil Deacon, Stanley McKinley, Jack Hanna, Dalton Kearns, James Rowley, Robert Bonter, Elgin Speirs, Earl Warwick, James Walsh.

COURTESY MURRAY HESP

There were plenty of souvenirs lying about, but I was so much loaded with our instrument that the only thing I picked up was a small pair of field glasses and a belt. Someone pinched the belt since so I have only the glasses left.

The one fine thing about the whole show is the few casualties on our side. There were very few dead and many of the wounds were only slight. I myself did not get so much as a scratch. Have been in some warm places, too, and had some close calls.

It seems very strange in coming back over the land which only ten days ago was in Fritz's hands. How different it all seems. Things have taken on a different aspect completely. Where there was nothing then, now our men have established themselves and are carrying on as though they had been here a year. One very amusing thing is some prison cages which Fritz had established for the "stupid Englanders", are now occupied by the "boorish Huns". They seem quite contented and as I passed yesterday they were whistling and singing as they ate breakfast. It is now a good deep walk from where we started on the morning of the eighth to where the line is now. The country in between is all idle. Some grain has grown up but it is mostly volunteer grain and I have not seen a good field this side of the river. On our old side the crops are fine and the civies will soon be back again on their farms. There is a fine feeling between the French soldiers and our men. In fact they have given us the title "Foch's Pets". The people, too, back in the settled part will do anything they can for us, at least on this front.

I am so glad to have been here to see this time. I would not have missed it for anything. It is worth all the work and hardship I have gone through to be here to take part in this great advance.

It is too soon to say what effect it will have on the general situation or if it will bring the war to a finish much more quickly. It depends on how far we push him back and the amount of defeat he can stand without giving in. Time will tell and we hope it has a good story.

Jesse

◇

Interesting letters from Ross Jaffary:

France, August 18, 1918.

Dear Mother,

At last I have the time and opportunity of writing you once more and I should be so thankful for there are very few of the old 126th boys left. I expect you will have heard before this reaches you that Ollie Penrice and Les Bowes were both wounded in our big offensive and a number of our old Battalion boys were killed.

I didn't see Les after he was hit but I was fortunate in finding Ollie lying in a wheat field shortly after he had been hit. He was badly, although not seriously wounded, and may consider himself fortunate as some of our boys on each side of him were killed. I soon got Ollie on a stretcher and just then four Fritzies sneaked out from a machine gun post in which they had been hiding and as is the custom I ordered them to carry Ollie to the dressing station. Les wasn't in the scrap that morning but it was in an open fight a few days later that he received his wounds. The attack we made the first day was a great success and we captured numerous machine guns, artillery and prisoners, but best of all, our losses were comparatively light.

Sergeant Nutting, the M.O. and myself all went over the top with the Second Company and all three escaped without a scratch. None of the other M.O's in the Brigade went over with their Battalions. Now our officer is recommended for a medal.

I had a nice letter from Wardlow who is at Witley Camp and in the same reserve as our drafts come from, so it is possible that he may belong to our Battalion some time.

Tell Aunt Edith that I received her parcel and shall write her as soon as possible.

I am sending you a cap, which was worn by a Fritzie artillery Sergeant who with his men and their guns were captured by us. The Privates' caps are the same style only that they have a red band and no peak. The glasses were in a dugout beside the guns so I suppose they are worn when we send over tear gas, or they may possibly be used as a protection against smoke or powder.

I saw Captain Graham a few days ago, but as he was in a hurry we didn't have very long to talk. He is just as lively as ever and is feeling fine and has a much better position than when he was with the Battalion.

◇

August 24th

I expect you are anxiously awaiting another letter. I did plan to send one last week but as you know we have a real war on over here which I will not attempt to describe and are kept so busy that we have not time for writing. I hope the whizz bangs, which I sent out of the line, reached you safely so would know I was well.

We are on the march to-day and are having a rest by the roadside, so we lads are busy writing. The Postie was pretty good to me last week to bring your letters, one from Uncle Ashton, one from Harry Taylor, also your box and a lovely one from the Bolton Red Cross. Everything arrived in perfect condition and we surely enjoyed it all thoroughly. If the ladies could only know what pleasure a box gives us, they would feel amply repaid for all their work. The cake in your box was so good and was as fresh as when made. Some of the other boys got boxes too and we surely had a dandy supper with all the good things. The French lady with whom we were staying made us such a tasty vegetable salad and with it we had sardines and canned chicken. Then followed Scotch brown bread and real home made butter from

Scotland, peaches, strawberry jam, olive butter, cookies, cake and coffee. How is that for a supper? Many thanks for all the good things you and the Red Cross ladies contributed to the feast.

We see lots of Sammies these days and they are all anxious to get a crack at the old Fritz, but I hope the war will be over before they even see him.

It's time to shoulder our kit bags again so hoping you are all as well as I am, with lots of love to all,

Ross

Canadians on the Move

Bolton Enterprise - October 25, 1918

Mrs. James H. Newlove has received a letter from her son, Lieutenant John Newlove, which reads in part as follows:

Grenoble, France
September 28, 1918

Dear Mother:

You will no doubt be surprised to know that I have moved again. This time I believe that I have a permanent location, at least I hope so. This is my first permanent assignment. I am in the southern eastern part of France, about 75 miles south of Geneva, Switzerland, and about 30 miles from the Italian border in the lower Alps. The most beautiful place I have ever been in. This city has 120,000 inhabitants. The altitude of the city is 1800 feet and it is surrounded on all sides by mountain peaks about 5,000 feet above the city. You have heard of Mount Blanc, Switzerland. Well you can see it very plainly from here. These peaks have snow on them all the time. The rivers are pretty and run south to the Mediterranean. In coming here I came around by the Spanish border and the Mediterranean. My office, seven large rooms, is in the centre of the city and is very fine. We'll have a car and an ambulance in a week or two. This is a very nice position and I know I will enjoy the work. The climate is just beautiful at present and this is the playground of France.

I do not suppose I will get to the front at all but one cannot tell. The boys are doing fine work and I think most of us will be home in a year from now. Wish you would write to me as I want to hear from you all.

Love to all,

- Jack
Lieutenant John W. Newlove, M.C.
Grenoble Isere,
A.E.T., France

Air Force Notes and Escapades

Bolton Enterprise - April 21, 1916

It is reported that an aeroplane was seen going in a northeasterly direction by some of the men who attended the League meeting at Salem on Tuesday evening.

Bolton Enterprise - April 26, 1918

The village of Sand Hill is sitting up and taking notice. The Imperial Munitions Board has rented fifty-five acres of land from John Wilson, just east of the village for one year, or for the duration of the war. A force of forty carpenters and labourers has commenced the erection of an aerodrome and other buildings. Three carloads of crushed stone will be used to build a roadway from the Bolton-Sand Hill road past the house to the buildings. The land will be under drained and made suitable for the flying men. The work, which is under the supervi-

Aerodrome built at Sand Hill.   COURTESY EDITH HUTCHINSON/LOIS RUSSELL

sion of Mr. James Duncan of Toronto, will be pushed to completion with all speed. We understand the County Council will be asked to speed up the completion of the highway between the aerodrome and Sand Hill. A private telephone line will be strung between Bolton and the aviator's camp near Sand Hill.

Bolton Enterprise - May 24,1918
Flying Cadet Semple lost his bearings on Friday afternoon and in landing in a field belonging to Mr. Milford Moffatt wrecked his machine. Mr. Thomas Wilson who was working close by, pulled him from the wreck. The plane was badly smashed and Semple was considerably cut, and lost considerable blood. He was put to bed at Mr. Moffatt's and his injuries attended to by Dr. W. Bateman and it was thought he would be required to stay in bed for a time, but not so. The same evening an officer arrived from Camp Borden and, putting the sick man in his machine, started back to camp. It was getting dark by this time however, and the officer also lost his bearings. In attempting to land near Barrie the plane struck a tree and was wrecked. Cadet Semple added a broken nose and other hurts to his injuries of a few hours before, and the officer had his collarbone broken and also sustained other severe injuries. Although Cadet Semple was in his last five hours of training Friday which brought him two wrecks could not by any system of reasoning be considered his lucky day. In fact it was a bad day for fliers in this district. Cadet J. Morren in landing at the aerodrome just at dusk also wrecked his machine.

Bolton Enterprise - December 13, 1918
Walter McCutcheon had a close call while training as an air pilot in England. In his first trip as a passenger the machine got out of the pilot's control and crashed, killing two of the four men aboard.

⫷⫷⫷ Chapter Five ⫸⫸⫸
– 1918 –
Peace at Last

After four long years of wholesale slaughter, in what was called the Great War, there must have been a longing for peace. Canada, as well as other Allied countries, had lost too many of its people. When an end to the fighting was finally realized on November 11, 1918, ships gradually began the journey across the Atlantic Ocean, returning war-weary troops to their homeland. The veterans travelled from their port of entry, mainly by train, reaching their destinations to be greeted by jubilant family members and friends. Huge parades were formed in cities, towns and villages from coast to coast to celebrate the return of these Canadian heroes.

The Brampton Conservator - November 7, 1918

Armistice has been Arranged
Fighting Ceased 2 p.m.

PRAISE GOD

Every man, woman and child, whether in home, shop, factory, office,
on the street, or travelling by land or water, should at once start singing
"Praise God From Whom All Blessings Flow"
Let the allied peoples give thanks to God first;
they can cheer themselves hoarse afterwards.
Let the coming of peace be the occasion for a worldwide demonstration
of thanks to God, and not one of cheering only.
It only requires circulation of this suggestion to make the end of the war
a celebration of our gratitude to the Almighty.

Servicemen Comment on Peace

Bolton Enterprise - December 20, 1918
Extracts from letters written by Private I.O. Matson to his mother and other relatives here:

November 5th 1918
Dear Brother, -
You will doubtless observe by the stationery that writing paper is unobtainable here. I am back in rest after my first trip into the lines where I sure received my baptism of fire. I held an outpost on the extreme edge of a town with Fritz within a few yards of me. My companion was that Scotsman I introduced to you the day I left Toronto and who was a blacksmith by trade. It was night duty all the time and I never had a better time. Every few minutes a regular hail of machine gun bullets would sweep up the street or over us and Scotty would whisper, "This is no a healthy

The Conservator
ARMISTICE IS SIGNED
IS PRACTICALLY UNCONDITIONAL SURRENDER OF ENEMY

Washington --- Announcement made verbally by an official of the State Department in this form :

"Armistice has been signed. It was signed at 5 o'clock a. m. Paris time. Hostilities will cease at 11 o'clock this morning, Paris time."

This means that fighting has now ceased.

"God Save the King and heaven bless the Maple Leaf forever."

THANK GOD

The Brampton Conservator - November 11, 1918

November 13, 1918

Dear Mother -

I suppose there is great rejoicing in Canada over the close of the war. I saw some of it but came off without a scratch. We have just moved to an historic old city in Belgium. We will be here for a few days and then forwarded again, I suppose to let Fritz see that he had better not try to back down on the terms dictated to him. He certainly is a chastened and humbled individual. German officers (with white flags) indicate places where they had had mines laid. Ye gods, how have the mighty fallen.

It seems strange to sit beside a coal fire in a public house with all lights going and everything just as before the war. Caps instead of steel helmets and no gas masks to carry, all enjoying rest and well fed and well contented.

---

place, Ollie; it's no a healthy place, mind you I'm telling ye". Then the big shells would whiz over us and burst within a short distance and I would remark "the present job is far better than horse-shoeing". Scotty's replies were unprintable and to the effect that "where there is nae sense, there is nae fear". Then I would remind him of Premier Borden's speech promising that we would "eat our Christmas dinner in Canada". This never failed to bring the greatest outburst of profanity of all. Scotty's distress was too humorous for words and I laughed (inwardly for safety's sake) until the water ran down my cheeks.

Our day quarters were great. Four of us (including Scotty) cleared out a house a couple of hundred yards from our post and we had stove, cooking utensils, coal, vegetables, dishes, mattresses, etc. I never was more comfortably established in my life. The guns don't disturb your sleep when you get used to them. The four of us were on the mattress when the Corporal came in to tell us that Turkey had quit. Since then we heard that Austria was out, too. Peace with Germany appears to be expected soon. Fritzy is outclassed in men, artillery and gas and realizes it now.

◇

November 10, 1918

Dear Brother, -

Enclosed please find letter of previous date which I was unable to post then as I was *ordered up the line. Got back into this town yesterday for rest and when we halted here, the Kaiser's abdication was announced. This morning while we were shaving, the announcement of the armistice was given us. I'm not sorry for I have seen some ghastly sights in the last few days. Will write full particulars of Hun savageries I witnessed, later on. Am too tired now.*

Enclosed find cap badges I took from two Heinie prisoners (Saxons), also locket affair found in cemetery where we buried dead.

It looks at present as if we would spend Christmas in German cities, but it may be Blighty or I might even be with the Matsons in Ireland. If it is in Germany, to the Heinie I'm billeted with a Christmas goose, believe me, I intend to share it.

I notice that in making a request of Heinie it is never necessary to speak in German. Just point to what you want or want done, then gently test the edge of you bayonet or playfully toss a Mills bomb from hand to hand. It is amazing how quickly the slow-moving Teuton mind grasps the idea and proceeds to execute it. Never argue with Fritzy - just motion.

Tell Dr. Reynar that I have hunted France and Belgium for a pipe suitable for him (even tried several stores to-day), to have poor results so far, but will journey forth into the Rhineland in the hope of a better result.

Am enclosing some tobacco given to me by an ever grateful Frenchman. Either keep it as a souvenir or let the smokers of the family enjoy its delicious flavour and aromatic fragrance.

Bolton Enterprise - December 27, 1918
Private Byron Leavens is recovering from his wounds received at Arras on August 30th at the General Military Hospital, Colchester, England, and writes to his parents in part as follows:

Wrote you about a week ago and explained wounds as best I could. A doctor (Major Davies) has paid special attention to my case and he is more then pleased with the way things have gone. I owe a powerful lot to the nurses and doctors for what they have done for me and I will be a long time in forgetting it, if ever I do.

You were asking me to tell of some of my experiences in France. You have heard of Loos, Lens, Arras and a number of smaller places on the battle front when I was there. Loos village, quite a big place once, is levelled and the church there is just a heap of debris. I had a walk through the civilian churchyard there. The tomb stones and vaults were all destroyed and in many cases the bones were in full view. It made a desolate scene, with the once beautiful trees hewn down by shrapnel. This is the village that the Scotties had such hard fighting in the streets at the early part of the war. In the early stages we lost a great number of men in and around this place. Just in front of here, "Hill 70" was enacted, a drama in which Canadians took part. Arras, once a beautiful place, is now pretty well knocked about. When the Germans made their big push this spring they came quite close to Arras and the civies cleared out, leaving the Canadians with the champagne, etc. The very richest was to be found there. One division paid for their looting by being kept in the line while the others were out resting.

We, another chap and myself, had an S.O.S. station in the front line just south of Arras, at what is called Telegraph Hill. It is known as a funk hole, into which we crawled, just a hole dug in the side of a trench, with no room to stretch out. We had a "D111" phone set on a chunk of chalk and after we had traversed the line for about a half a kilometer back to Company headquarters, mended all breaks in the line, we travelled back to the front line through the mud and water as high as your knees and more. By this time we had communication established and it was our duty to report

S.O.S. It is just a sign for the artillery to open up, that Fritz has attacked. We transmit the word S.O.S back to the Battalion headquarters and then the artillery gets it from there. It isn't much of a job as far as work goes, but you have got to be handy if anything happens.

There were two phones used in France while I was there, the "D111" and "Fuller". Fritzie can pick up the signals from a "D111" phone but not from a "Fuller". So you see a "Fuller" phone is much better. One has to be very careful what is spoken over a "D111" phone. If you are being relieved and you want to know if the relieving party is all in, you would ask, "if the rubber boots are up", or anything to that effect to put Fritzie off his guard. He has men who do nothing but with detectors listen for any information they may get.

I was telling you of being on an S.O.S. station in the front line. Fritzie had the habit of shelling our particular part of the trench with minniewerfers, and putting the candle out. My mate was on duty and I was trying to get a wink of sleep through the noise and concussion of those trench mortar shells. Our candle was going out quite frequently and after one terrific bang (candle out as usual), my mate didn't seem inclined to light up again. After questioning him he said, "They'll only put it out again". We stuck it out for seven days and our relief arrived.

I suppose you are very thankful the war is over, especially those who have sons and relatives in it. It will not be very long till the boys in France come trooping home and as for myself, if all goes well, I hope to be home before they do (fine and dandy). We won't have the German submarines to attack us on the way back as that part of Germany's war machinery is in good hands now.

◇

December 5th

I guess you had quite a time in Bolton when the news arrived of the signing of the armistice. The first information we had of it was the troops cheering and the band playing in the camp close by. In a few minutes the official word came in and then there were three very hearty cheers. I guess you heard how the people celebrated in London. Thank God the thing is over with. I feel sorry for my chums, Hubert Corless, Willie Wood and others who paid the price - to think it is over and they didn't pull through. I expect Adam is alright. I haven't heard from him for some time. I heard from Ross Jaffary in a London hospital. He seems to be getting along well.

We have one Canadian nurse in our ward, Nurse Bennett, from Calgary, and she sticks up for the Canucks alright. Last night we had three little kids come in the ward and sing, then they passed around the hat.

There is a Scotsman in bed on my left; on the other side of him is a Welshman (Taffy), a Londoner on my right and an Irishman across from me, so there is a conglomeration of us. There is a chap who was shot through his right eye. He buys anything we want down town. He certainly has a busy time shopping for the ward, bananas 5d each, apples 9d, so you see we don't buy very much of some things.

Hometown Heroes Honoured

Bolton Enterprise - January 3, 1919

The booklet entitled "Nobleton Heritage 1800-1976" produced by the Nobleton Womens' Institute states in part "In World War 1, there was one girl from the Nobleton district who went overseas, Mary Agar. She spent three years in hospitals there. Two of the boys from this district were killed in action, Mathew Agar and William Chamberlain". Mathew Agar was Mary's brother.

On the return of the soldiers, a celebration was held in Nobleton. A banquet was held for

Mary Agar and the returned boys and their parents in the Hall. Also in the evening, a concert was held in the Old Skating Rink and watches were presented to the returned folks. Mr. Walter McCutcheon was spokesman for the boys.

Beautiful Memorial in Laurel Hill Cemetery

Bolton Enterprise - October 21, 1921

In the presence of a large number of people, including many veterans of the Great War, and with solemn and fitting ceremony the memorial erected in honor of our fallen heroes and of those who carried on in the Great War was unveiled in Laurel Hill Cemetery on Wednesday afternoon. A light rain was falling, which disarranged the plans made by the committee and prevented many from being present at what may easily be considered the most important event in the history of this district. However, the occasion lost none of its solemnity in the minds of those who sought to pay by their presence, the respect and remembrance due to the memory of the men who made the supreme sacrifice during the great world struggle. And that the memorial which was unveiled will also serve as an inspiration to future generations is beyond question.

Constructed of Canadian granite, the memorial, as a whole, is admitted to be a work of art, and conveys a story full of meaning to all who may see it. In front is the cenotaph on which lie a rifle, bayonet, helmet and belt of a private soldier, the whole entwined with laurel leaves. The shaft contains on front and back the names of fifty-six fallen heroes, arranged as far as possible according to the date of their death. The committee has recognized the fact that death has eliminated all distinctions, therefore no rank of the fallen men is recorded. The shaft is supported on each side by the Altar of Sacrifice.

Bolton Cenotaph erected in Laurel Hill Cemetery. COURTESY BILL WHITBREAD

Surmounting this is the full figure of a private soldier in full Canadian uniform, with uncovered head, gun reversed, one arm resting on the Flanders Cross, poppies at his feet, his whole attitude expressive of reverent yet manly courage as he views the bier of his fallen comrade. Around the base is engraved the names of twenty-one battles, from Ypres to Mons.

When all had assembled at the cemetery, the chairman, Reeve D.B. Kennedy, of Bolton called on Rev. R.B. Beynon to open the ceremony with prayer. Mrs. Peter Munro, of Albion, who lost two sons in the war, was then asked to unveil the memorial, and as the ties were released and the large flags fell away, exposing the monument to public gaze, Heggie Herbert, late bugler in the 126th Peel Battalion, sounded the Last Post.

Opportunity was given and several mothers, who had lost their sons in the war, came forward and laid wreaths and flowers on the cenotaph. The school children then marched past in two lines and reverently deposited their bouquets. Among the floral offerings was a beautiful wreath, donated by the Dale Estate of Brampton.

The chairman explained that the committee had seen fit to include among the names on the monument, not only those who were living here at the time of their enlistment, but also the sons of local families who joined the colours at other points as well as a few who had spent their early days amongst us. He also made public the fact that a sealed jar, deposited in the foundation of the memorial, contained the names of all the men from this district who served during the war, also the names of the committee and other data usually recorded in this manner.

An adjournment was made to the rink where speeches were delivered by Rev. P.N. Knight, Anglican minister of Bolton, Samuel Charters, M.P., Major Kennedy, M.P.P., W.J. Lowe, Herbert Taylor, Rev. J.P. Treacy, of Toronto, John Anderson and Wm. N. Riddell, reeve and deputy-reeve respectively, of Albion township.

The speakers, one and all, paid eloquent and sincere tribute to the heroism and patriotism of the men who laid down their lives while fighting on our behalf on the battle fields of Flanders, and complimented the people of the district on erecting the memorial to their memory. Fitting reference was also made to the service rendered our country by the other brave lads who took part in the great struggle but were fortunate enough to return.

The committee which had charge of the erection of the memorial was composed of the following: Robert Smith, chairman; Bert Mellow, secretary-treasurer; T.J. Roe, Thomas Cooke, Anson McCabe, Isaac Steele, Charles H. Rutherford, D.B. Kennedy, George Downey, Emerson Westlake, J.A. Wilkie, John Cairns, Albert Robinson, John Lake and F.N. Leavens.

Among those who were expected to speak at the unveiling but who were prevented by the inclement weather were Rev. Canon Cody, Hon. Edmund Bristol, Hon. R.H. Grant and Hon. Manning Doherty.

The memorial was designed and erected by the Thompson Monument Company, of Toronto.

The Cenotaph was located in an appropriate setting immediately inside the present main entrance to Laurel Hill Cemetery, on the left side of the road, where it remained undisturbed for almost half a century. In 1969 the Cenotaph was moved to the south end of Centennial Drive near Queen Street.

Memories of the End of the War

I remember being told about "Mary", who upon her return to Canada, was walking to her home in the early morning. Young children going to school noticed her and shouted "Mary's home". Storekeepers opening their shops for the day locked the doors and joined the children and other townspeople to celebrate her homecoming. An older gentleman beat a drum leading the group to her parents' home. Her parents met their daughter with tears of joy and sadness. They were happy "Mary" was home but sad because she had lost her left arm during daring risks, as a nurse on the battlefields, to save the lives of servicemen.

"Sam" was a quiet fellow. He arrived in the still of the night and when his family noticed his kit bag in the kitchen the next morning, "Sam" was milking the cows in the barn. The entire household welcomed "Sam" home and was overjoyed he had returned safely and unharmed. His little sister asked him what had happened over there and could he tell her about his experiences? "Sam" said he had nothing to tell her and he had just been doing his job. Later, when his mother was sorting the contents of his kit bag she found a Distinguished Service Order medal among other decorations, as well as a letter recommending him to receive the Victoria Cross. But "Sam" had nothing to say.

Flamboyant "George" or "flaming George", as he was called at home and abroad because a blaze always accompanied him whether on the football field, in the classroom or anywhere he might be, arrived in Montreal. He immediately sent a telegram to his hometown stating his expected time of arrival by rail was 2 p.m. the next day. A large crowd had assembled at the train station the following afternoon as the train steamed along the tracks and slowed to a stop. Three loud whistle toots sounded as "George" appeared on the balcony of the last car waving to the people. "George" did not have a family to welcome him because he had been abandoned as a child, but he had many friends. The parade into town was led by the Reeve driving a Model "T" convertible, which had a habit of coughing, spluttering and stalling regularly. "George" enjoyed the whole affair, especially the antics of the car, as the buggies followed behind in the procession with people marching to the town square. "George" smiled when the car released a loud backfire as he stepped onto the street. A great celebration followed with the local band entertaining all in attendance. "George" contributed with an eloquent speech.

It was said that "Mary" became the owner of a busy medical clinic, "Sam" established himself as a successful farmer and "George" was acclaimed as an outgoing and popular local lawyer.

So peace had finally been restored and life was reaching a state of normalcy. The Great War was over! The world was at peace.

Camp Witley Incident

Not all members of the forces were fortunate in coming home immediately after the armistice was signed. Some Canadian troops were left behind at Camp Witley in England to arrange for the loading and shipment of goods and equipment back to Canada. This was not a happy scene after a period of time. Many thought the British could be assigned this responsibility. As a result of this feeling, which intensified with the passage of time, the soldiers rebelled. Charles Patterson, a soldier from Vaughan Township was there. According to "Erie Patterson's Book of Happenings", Charles witnessed the destruction of the wooden barracks which were levelled to the ground. According to other reports it required some force to bring the situation under control, and in due course, the soldiers joined their comrades back in Canada.

Erie Patterson was the wife of Charles, and their daughter Jean Charlton and niece Adele Caseley made this information available. The following are Charles Patterson's pictures of the incident at Camp Witley.

⟪⟪ Chapter Six ⟫⟫
Casualties and Losses

Memorials to servicemen have been erected in small hamlets, villages, towns and cities throughout the provinces of Canada. They stand, with the National War Memorial in Ottawa, as a symbol of the many thousands of Canadians who served their country well and sacrificed their lives while doing so. For what they represent, all Cenotaphs deserve and receive our respect. These memorials are a chilling reminder of the huge price paid by servicemen and women, defending our liberties and freedoms. This account records the names of ninety-five World War I servicemen from this general area who lost their lives. While some names may not be shown on the Cenotaph listings in this region, they are certainly remembered with the same degree of reverence as the others.

Many servicemen were wounded during these battles and some were taken prisoner by the enemy. Their sacrifices for their country are also noted and remembered.

Bolton Enterprise - June 30, 1916

Word was received by relatives on Monday of the death of Private Robert Stanley McAllister, a young man well known in this district, who has given his life in defence of liberty and freedom. Particulars are contained in a letter from his brother Edgar who was injured at the same time Robert was killed. His first letter was written on the 11th and the second on the 14th, extracts of which we give below:

We left England on May 25th and landed at Havre, the Canadian Base. There we rested for three days and then went on up the line, through Calais, Rouen and Boulogne. Our battalion came out of the line the night we arrived and expected to have been out for some time. On Saturday, June 3rd, we got word that part of our line had been taken and that we were to be ready to go at once. About three o'clock in the afternoon we started. We wended our way slowly toward Ypres. We went forward in sections of about eight with a hundred yards between each section. All the time shells were bursting near us. We went right through Ypres. Every building was completely wrecked. From Ypres we went forward to the line about two o'clock in the morning. I think they saw us coming for we were no sooner near the trench than heavy artillery fire was turned on us. Some of us were in the rear trenches but they did not serve as a cover for the big shells. I was caught in the leg and arm with shrapnel and that laid me out. I lay in a shell hole until four o'clock next afternoon, it being too risky to move out. When I came out I found Bob with three other lads dead in the trench. I stayed there until it got dark again, thinking I would get out and back to the rear under cover of darkness.

As soon as it got dark the Germans started to shell us again. This time I got a nasty cut in the face, right across the nose, and also a gash in my left cheek. Besides this I got cut in the shoulder and several scratches in the back. With the aid of a stretcher-bearer I made my way back to Ypres, fully four miles, about 4 o'clock in the morning. I am now in hospital in London.

Robert S. McAllister was a son of the late Thomas McAllister, of this district, and was in his 26th year. He enlisted at Calgary with the 56th Battalion. While on his way east the brothers, Robert and Edgar, spent a few days with relatives and friends here, leaving for overseas on the 19th of March last. These companions in arms impressed us as being fine young men and soldiers, full of the justice of the cause for which they had enlisted, and while recognizing the seriousness of the situation were yet anxious to do what they could to help right the great wrong which had been done mankind by an over-ambitious monarch. The surviving brothers are James, W. J. and Albert in this district, Edgar at the front, and two sisters, Mrs. Scott and Miss Jean at Innisfail, Alberta.

Bolton Enterprise - February 2, 1917
Some time ago, inquiries were instituted concerning the fate of Private Morley Attwood, a Mono Road recruit who went overseas with the 3rd contingent. The Militia Dept. at Ottawa as a result of these inquiries has sent the following report: "In view of the extreme intensity of this particular battle and as Attwood's name does not appear on the list of prisoners, it is feared there is little chance on his having survived and is now reported missing, believed killed." Sometimes a soldier believed to be killed turns up alive, but, as these occasions are extremely rare, the strong chances are that Morley has made the great sacrifice.

Bolton Enterprise - July 10, 1917
Pte. W. J. Chamberlain Died Hero's Death
Although Mr. and Mrs. Wm. Chamberlain of King have not yet received official notification of the death of their son, Pte. William James Chamberlain, there does not appear to be any doubt but that he has paid the supreme sacrifice on the field in France. His name appears in Tuesday's list of casualties as having died from wounds received in action, and Mrs. Chamberlain has received a letter of sympathy from the Captain and Chaplain of the Battalion in which he was serving.

When the war broke out in 1914, Pte. Chamberlain had just finished the duties on his homestead at Sewell, Man. In answer to the call for men he abandoned his interests there, enlisted with the 46th Battalion and went overseas with the first contingent of the Canadian Army. He was unmarried, 24 years of age, the second son of his parents, and had spent two birthdays in the trenches. The sympathy of all is extended to the bereaved family.

◇

43rd Canadian Batt., B.E.F., France
June 23, 1917
Dear Mrs. Chamberlain:
You of course have been informed by wire of the fact of your son's death. He was killed while in the front line on duty. A bullet or piece of shell struck him in the temple. And caused death within an hour. He, of course, was quite unconscious and died quietly and painlessly. He breathed his last at the dressing station of his Battalion. Everything was done for him that kindness and skill could suggest. Your boy was admired by his officers as a splendid soldier, and was a great favourite among the men who knew him. He lived a clean good life. I buried him about 11 p.m. on June 17th. He was struck about 3 a.m. the same day. His grave is in a little cemetery called Pettit Vimy, Military Map Location S23, D71, near a destroyed village of the same name. He is in a grave by himself marked by a neat white wooden cross, suitably inscribed.

A prayer was said at the grave side for his loved ones at home that they might be given the strength to bear their grief. Half a dozen of his comrades, all that could be spared from the line, were gathered by the grave. They were friendly hands that laid him in his last resting place. May God bless and strengthen you all in your great sorrow is my earnest prayer.

Yours in deepest sympathy,
Geo. C.F. Pringle
Capt. and Chaplain
43rd Battalion

◇

The following is part of a letter to Mrs. Prudence Wood regarding the death of one of her sons:

In the Field, August 5th, 1917
Mrs. Prudence Wood
Bolton, Ontario, Canada

It is my painful duty to inform you that your son, Pte. W.H. Wood died of wounds received in action during an attack ——————— on July 23rd, at 1.00 a.m. The Battalion had received a special order to raid ——————— on a frontage of about 600 yards to a depth of about 400 yards. There were two objectives, and "A" Company, under Captain Gould took the first objective and captured many prisoners. The other objective was captured by "B" and "C" Companies, under Captain Allen and Major Currie respectively. They reached their objective and inflicted much loss on the enemy, bombed their dug-outs and took many prisoners. On the whole we captured about 60 prisoners and the Battalion has received complimentary messages from the Brigadier, Divisional Commander, the Corps Commander and the Commander-in-Chief, but these messages, I am afraid, offer small consolation to the fathers, mothers and relatives of those who have fallen or are missing.

Pte. W.H. Wood had been assigned to me as my personal runner and he accompanied me on all my trips. Consequently I feel a deep sense of loss in his death. He was manly and straightforward and as brave as a lion. He always accompanied me when I visited the front line and during the night of our attack he was with me constantly, part of the time out in No-man's-land, and he assisted in laying the tape for the jumping off line, and in placing the platoons when they were getting in their jumping off positions. He never once flinched and was always ready and willing to do his duty. I do not think we had a better boy in the Battalion. Unfortunately, when we were coming out of the line, he and Lieutenant T.W. Hutchinson were both hit by a shell and they both died of wounds shortly afterwards. I did not think that Pte. Wood was so dangerously wounded, as when I saw him in the Dressing Station he smiled and I shook hands with him, and told him to write to me when he got to the hospital. He displayed great fortitude and you have every reason to be proud of having a son with such a record.

On my personal behalf and on behalf of the Officers, Non-commissioned Officers and men of the Battalion, I desire to convey to you our sincere sympathy in your great loss at this time. Please convey to all friends and members of the family our regret in the loss of such a splendid soldier. We hope that you will take comfort and solace from the consciousness that Will did his full duty to his King and Country and that his loss will be an inspiration to those who come after.

Again extending to you our sincere sympathy, I remain, Madam.

Yours very truly,
Sam Sharpe, Lieutenant Colonel
Commanding 116th (Ontario County) Canadian Infantry Bn.

Bolton Enterprise - December 14, 1917

Just a few lines, hoping you will publish this letter from friends of George Munro. We have parted with our best chum which was the hardest blow we have struck yet. We don't mind fighting for our loved and dear ones, but when it comes to losing a chum it is hard to bear. We stuck together fine and were all looking for the day to come when we would go back together. George was a man of the finest type and proved it many a time. Once, when we made an advance on the 15th of August he was in the front wave. They reached their objective after much hard fighting and all that day the Germans were sniping at our men in the front from a house in "No Man's Land." Just at dusk George went out by himself and went all through the house, but they had beat it. Anyway that house was blown to pieces by artillery fire the next day. George was a scout and he sure was the right man in the right place. He was over in a raid with more of us in March and got wounded but was pleased to get back with his chums again in June. I could write a lot of good that George has done since he came to France. We saw our chum buried, which was a hard thing to see. We know he died a true soldier and did not fear death.

Pte. E.A. Tatum and
Pte. G.T. Stanfield
18th Batt., France

Bolton Enterprise - January 25, 1918

Mr. Abram Moss, of Albion, has been notified that his son, Elmer Abram Moss, has died of wounds while a prisoner of war in Germany. Private Moss enlisted with the 126th (Peel) Battalion, went overseas August 9, 1915, and after training in England for some time went to France in February 1917. Drafted with others into the 116th Battalion he took part in the hard fighting engaged in by that Battalion until six months ago when he was reported as missing. Nothing further was heard until the Germans reported that he had died of wounds while a prisoner of war. Private Moss was unmarried and when the call came for men he rented his 200 acre farm and donned the khaki. He was 23 years of age at the time of his death. The late Private Moss was connected with the Orangemen and a memorial service under the auspices of that Order will be held at the Methodist Church in Palgrave on Sunday February 3rd at 3 o'clock with Rev. Mr. Quaife of Mono Mills to preach.

Bolton Enterprise - March 15, 1918

Mr. J.J. McKeown, of Sand Hill, received a cablegram on Tuesday from the Red Cross Society in Switzerland saying that their son, Flight Lieutenant Charles J.W. McKeown, is a prisoner of war at Karlsruhe, Germany. Lieutenant McKeown was taking part in the flying operations in Belgium and was reported missing on February 18th.

◇

The following article was published by the Brampton Conservator on June 20, 1918, a copy of which was supplied by Mrs. Jack Gibson - Lenore McKeown - a niece of Flight Lieutenant Charles McKeown:
Mr. J.J. McKeown, Sandhill, has received the following letter from his son, 2nd Lieutenant C.J.W. McKeown, who is a prisoner of war at Holzminden, formerly at Landshut, Germany.

April 13, 1918
At last I have arrived at what I expect will be a permanent camp. In place of one day's journey from Landshut, it was two and a half. I rather enjoyed the trip in spite of the fact that we did not get much sleep at nights. The weather was very

beautiful and we came through many interesting and famous old places. The largest ones were Regensburg, Nuremberg, Augsburg, Wurtemburg and Berba. The country where we crossed the Danube was very beautiful. We could see little towns down the valley for miles as far as the eye would carry.

At this camp there are about five hundred officers, principally of the R.F.C. We are quartered in two large buildings very much like the Toronto University residences. In my room there are eleven of us. My bed is right beside the window, from where there is a splendid view of the surrounding country. We have several games, such as football, tennis, baseball, etc. There are also classes in French, German, Spanish, Hebrew, etc. I am taking the French class at present and also intend taking German.

The food which we have had so far is excellent. It comes in parcels and those who are getting the most parcels do all they can for those of us who have not received any grocery parcels yet from the Red Cross. I expect mine to arrive almost any day though. Another chap and myself have our meals together. We have dinner at night and expect to have soup, tea, potted meat, bread, dripping, cheese, rice pudding, milk and sugar, and honey for to-night's dinner. This reminds me that it is time to start preparing dinner. You can see that we shall hardly go to bed hungry to-night at any rate.

I have just been reading the Communiqué, which says that there has been fighting down in Quebec. This looks pretty bad, but I do not think it will amount to much, as there will be any amount of volunteers for a scrap down there.

This afternoon there is a football match on between the "Mugs", as they are called, of the two houses that we live in. The orderlies have a band, which is now playing, and sounds like nothing else on earth.

Yesterday was a very quiet day for a Sunday, where there are a lot of military men. I was at church for the first time since I left England. A football match was announced to come off in the afternoon, but the forces for good seemed to predominate, and it was cancelled. Quite a number of officers of Irish regiments have come here lately. Among these officers is a Major, who is a Chaplain. He seems to be quite a nice chap.

Since coming here I have met quite a number of the officers I trained with in England and one with whom I came over. I am beginning to think that I am extremely fortunate being still alive, since so very many of my pals have been killed.

The weather has been very hazy the last few days. In England the people would attribute it to the intense bombardment that is going on in France. Things certainly seem to be happening now. A German who took us out for a walk yesterday, said he thought the war would be over in three months. Of course none of us have the "foggiest" when it will be over.

Chas. McKeown

Bolton Enterprise - June 28, 1918

Private William Palmer has returned to his home in the Mount Wolfe district bearing the marks of battle, his right leg being about three inches shorter than the other. He had it broken by two machine gun bullets and it was necessary to shorten it in order to get the bones to knit.

◇

Monday's casualties list contained the name of George Mills, who had been accidentally killed in France. Mills worked for a couple of years with Mr. Richard Hutchinson (Sand Hill) before enlisting. He was in the 52nd Battalion, C.F.A., was English of birth and had no relatives in this country. Friends here regret to hear of his death.

Bolton Enterprise - September 13, 1918
Mr. & Mrs. Purvis of this place have been notified that their son, Flight Lieutenant Max Purvis, has been injured in France. Lieutenant Purvis has been engaged in aerial bombing operations of the R.A.F.

◇

Private Thomas Rowley of Palgrave has been wounded. He enlisted with the 198th Battalion.

◇

Word was received on Saturday that Private Byron Leavens had been dangerously wounded and admitted to a casualty clearing station in September. With several other Bolton boys Byron took part in the Canadian offensive which commenced August 8th. He has been in the front lines since going to France on December 22nd.

◇

Mr. & Mrs. Alfred Ireland received word that their son Fred had been wounded at the front.

◇

Mr. James Penrice has received word from his son, Sergeant Ollie Penrice, who was wounded on the field during the first days of what has been called the thirty days' battle. Sergeant Penrice was picked up by Sergeant Ross Jaffary, another Bolton boy, who compelled four German prisoners to carry Penrice to the rear. Sergeant Penrice says he is getting along fine although his injuries are severe.

Bolton Enterprise - September 27th, 1918
Pte. Cuthbert Samuel Pitchford whose death was noted last week was a son of Mr. and Mrs. Samuel Pitchford of Cardwell Junction. He was born on July 25, 1899, while his father was serving in the British army, and before the war broke out had served in the Peel Militia. At the beginning of hostilities he joined Halton Rifles, later transferring to the 176th of Simcoe. He went overseas in 1916, and reached France last February. While in England he held the rank of Corporal and was used as a physical drill and bayonet instructor, reverting to a private in order to get to the front. He was killed in action on September 6th during the big offensive of the Canadians.

In writing to his parents, he said:

We sure have been a busy bunch during the last two weeks and I guess the attack came as a surprise to everybody (especially Fritzie). I have some great stories to relate when I get back but of course they must wait till then. The sad side of the whole thing is the inevitable. I sure have lost some good pals, my special chum was killed three yards in front of me in a charge and we lost the best platoon commander in the battalion. How I got through beats me, but will put it down off hand to good luck. We've had glorious weather for the whole thing, which, of course, has favored us as most of the time the sky has been the only roof we've had. Was pleased to receive your letter of the 23rd about two days ago. Have also received three parcels from you since I last wrote, so you see they have turned up wonderfully at the right time. Am enclosing a few souvenirs. I have many more, including an automatic revolver, but it is impossible to send them. Excuse haste, and cheer up, we've got old Fritzie guessing for sure this time. Just watch the daily news.

Your loving son, Cuthbert

Bolton Enterprise - November 8, 1918
A letter from Captain John Graham states:

I saw Norman Hutchinson this morning, October 8th, and apart from looking a little weary after the strenuous days we have passed through, he is in fine fettle. He did not go to England to qualify for his Lieutenancy as I told you last month. He evidently had no wish to be out of the "big doings". He is one of the outstanding Sergeants in his division. I saw Donald McKay two days ago. Those are the only two from Caledon East apart from one of the Killeen boys, whom I saw two weeks ago, who are in the same division with me. We have been through three of the biggest battles of the war since August 8th, Amiens, Arras and Cambrai. I was sorry to hear of Hilliard Perdue's death, also of young Walker.

◇

LOCAL SERVICEMEN WHO LOST THEIR LIVES IN THE FIRST WORLD WAR

MATHEW AGAR	ERNEST JOHN JACKSON	WILLIAM MCNAIR
ALBERT PERCY ARMSTRONG	SAMUEL JOSEPH JACKSON	JOHN HILLIARD GRAY PERDUE
GEORGE ARMSTRONG	CARL JONES	CUTHBERT SAMUEL PITCHFORD
WILLIAM JOHN ARMSTRONG	WILLIAM JONES	JOHN JAMES PROCTOR
MORLEY A. ATTWOOD	BASIL ROY LEPPER	ROBERT MORRIS RAESIDE
JOHN WILFRED BANKS	CHARLES WILLIAM LILLIE	ALBERT W. RUSTON
JOHN BASS	JOHN LINCE	ELEY SCOTT SCARLETT
HARRY CECIL BISHOP	WILLIAM CHESTER LITTLE	ARTHUR SCOTT
LAMBERT ERNEST STANLEY BOLTON	ARTHUR GIVEN LONG	LEONARD JOHN SEARLE
HENRY BURGESS	DONALD ROSS MACKENZIE	JOHN JOSEPH SHARP
JOSEPH PATRICK BURNS	REGINALD FRANK MAPLES	SIDNEY SHAW
FREDERICK CARDY	EDWARD MASON	THOMAS EDWARD SMITH
WILLIAM JAMES CHAMBERLAIN	LAWRENCE MATHEWS	PATRICK SARSFIELD ARTHUR SMYTH
REGINALD DAN CLIFTON	ARMOUR A. MILLER	ROY MANLEY SPARROW
CHARLES CLOW	HERBERT MILLER	VICTOR SPENCER
CHARLES TREVELLYN CONSTANT	GEORGE MILLS	PHILLIP STEPHENSON
HERBERT ARTHUR COOPER	THOMAS MILLS	EARLE JOSEPH STRONG
HUBERT S. CORLESS	EDWARD MORGAN	ALBERT STRONGE
SYDNEY CHARLES CORNFORTH	JOHN MORGAN	EARL SYKES
WILLIAM VICTOR COWARD	ELMER A. MOSS	WILLIAM THOMPSON
CHARLES WILLIAM CREWE (CREWSE)	GEORGE WATSON MUNRO	JOHN WILLIAM TRIBBLE
GEORGE CHESTER CROZIER	WILLIAM WATSON MUNRO	JAMES RUSSELL TURNER
S. EDGAR DOUGLAS	ROBERT STANLEY MCALLISTER	ALBERT R. WALKER
EDWARD EWART ELLIOTT	WALTER CAMPBELL MCBRIDE	STANLEY ARTHUR WALKER
ISLAND BELLWOOD FISH	WILBERT LAWRENCE MCCAFFREY	JOHN W. WARD
JOHN NORMAN FLEMING	JOHN ARCHIBALD MCCALLUM	STANLEY C. WARRELL
JOHN JOSEPH GROGAN	ELWON DAVID MCDONALD	CHARLES HAROLD WATSON
WILLIAM THOMAS HACKETT	JOHN MCDONALD	J. WEBSTER
JOHN SAMUEL HALBERT	WILLIAM BEATON MCGILLIVRAY	WILLIAM JAMES WELWOOD
CHARLES HASKELL	NEIL MCKAY	FRANK R. WILSON
HENRY WILLIAM HICKEY	THOMAS D. MCMAHON	WILLIAM HENRY WOOD
GEORGE THOMAS HOWARD	EARL N. MCMINN	

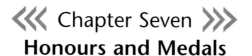

⟨⟨⟨ Chapter Seven ⟩⟩⟩
Honours and Medals

Many Canadian servicemen performed their duties in a most brilliant and heroic manner, risking their lives without thought of their own personal safety. Facing casualties around them, their gallantry and determination saved others on numerous occasions. Records show that medals for heroism and awards for exemplary conduct in battle were presented to a significant number of military personnel. The seventeen distinguished World War I servicemen listed here were, no doubt, among the finest to serve in the Canadian forces.

Honours and Medals

Bolton Enterprise - December 1, 1916
Alex Bowles, son of Isaac Bowles, formerly of Mono Road, has been awarded the Military Cross for gallantry with the machine gun. His Battery played havoc with the Germans and captured 600 of them. When the fight was over, he and five others were left, all the rest of the Battery being killed or wounded.

Bolton Enterprise - January 5, 1917
Signal honour has been paid to an old Bolton boy by the military authorities of the Empire. Temporary Colonel Arthur Evans Snell was among those who at the New Year were awarded the Distinguished Service Order. Colonel Snell is a son of the late S.J. Snell and Mrs. Snell of this place for some years and was attached to the military school at Kingston, Ontario, in the capacity of surgeon. Going with the first contingent to the front he had charge of a dressing station behind the trenches when the Canadians got their first serious cutting up by the enemy. Colonel Snell, with one assistant, passed over three hundred men through his hands in a few hours, and since then he has been in constant service and has nearly sacrificed his own life by his unremitting labours on behalf of the wounded. Much of his work has been done within the shell zone and on several occasions he was nearly caught by bursting shells. Colonel Snell, who is 40 years of age, graduated in medicine at Toronto University in 1899. He joined the permanent Army Medical Corps in 1910 with the rank of Captain and was given his Majority in September last. Colonel Snell's friends here congratulate him upon the great honour, which has been done him.

Bolton Enterprise - January 26, 1917
Colonel Arthur Snell, formerly of this place, who did such good work since the war broke out in France as a surgeon, and whose services have been recognized from time to time by the authorities, has had still more honour paid to him. He was recently summoned to Buckingham Palace where the King conferred upon him the Order of St. Michael and St. George.

Bolton Enterprise - February 2, 1917
Alex Bowles who received the Military Cross is recommended by General Turner for the Victoria Cross.

Bolton Enterprise - August 10, 1917
A signal honour has been done one of our Bolton boys at the front. Private Adam Wallace has been awarded a ribbon and the Military Medal. Private Wallace says very little about the honour done him, barely mentioning the matter in a letter to his parents, Mr. & Mrs. R. J. Wallace. Adam has been in the trenches for nearly seventeen months with the exception of a few weeks while he was in hospital suffering from wounds received when buried with a shell explosion.

Bolton Enterprise - January 11, 1918
About a month ago, Captain (Dr.) James Moore gave an address at Oshawa on his experiences at the front, in which he told the story of the 116th Battalion's famous raid on the German trenches last July, and stated that before Lieutenant Colonel Sharpe, Commanding Officer, allowed his men to advance, he reconnoitered part of the ground in front of the trenches on his hands and knees and at imminent danger to his own life. As a consequence the raid was carried out with few casualties, considering the important stronghold taken. Colonel Sharpe has now been given the Distinguished Service Order, and in all probability the reward came because of his great bravery and care of his men upon this occasion. The Bolton boys and the others from the old 126th Peel Battalion who were drafted into the 116th are loud in praise of their Commanding Officer, Colonel Sharpe, and one would judge from the tenor of their letters that they would be willing to go through anything for their Colonel. The 116th is admittedly one of the best fighting units on the Canadian Front. They have shown dash and spirit in all their actions and that's what wins battles. Colonel Sharpe's name will be a household word in many Peel homes for generations to come.

Bolton Enterprise - January 18, 1918
Mr. & Mrs. Alex McCort, of Albion, have received word that their son, Lieutenant C. Roy McCort, has been promoted to a Captaincy. Captain McCort is in the Heavy Artillery of the Imperial Army.

Bolton Enterprise - March 29, 1918
Mrs. Alfred Ireland recently received a medal from her son, Private Robert H. Ireland, who won the medal for high marks in a shooting competition on the ranges in England. He is credited with being the best marksman in his Company.

Bolton Enterprise - May 3, 1918
Private G.W. Johnston 2022070, well known in the Castlederg and Cedar Mills districts of Albion, has been awarded the Military Medal for his bravery at the front and his friends will be glad to hear of the honour conferred upon him. Private Johnston lived for four years in the home of Mr. C.H. Rutherford before offering his services to his country. The following is a letter from his Commanding Officer to Private Johnston:

February 3, 1918

Headquarters
11th Canadian Infantry Batt.
No. 2022070 Private G.W. Johnston
102nd Canadian Infantry Battalion

My Dear Johnston:

I am very pleased to note that you were awarded the Military Medal for bravery on November 14th near Passchendaele.

The spirit of unselfish devotion you displayed that day in attending to your wounded comrades under the heaviest shellfire is worthy of the highest praise. You lived up to the fine traditions of service of the Battalion stretcher bearers in every respect.

Please accept my heartiest congratulations on your well earned honour.

(Signed)
Victor W. Odlum
Brigadier-General

News of Honours After Peace

Even after peace was declared on November 11, 1918, news continued of honours bestowed on local men and women.

Bolton Enterprise - November 22, 1918
Friends of Corporal Harry Woods, who was a resident of this district when he enlisted, will be pleased to know that he has been awarded the Military Medal for distinguished service on the field. He was with the 20th Canadian Battalion in France. The official record is as follows:

57040, Corporal H. Woods ..... For exceptional resourcefulness and initiative on the night of 14/15th August the above N.C.O. under extremely difficult and trying circumstances made a reconnaissance on foot through an area drenched with gas and subjected to very heavy shell fire. He afterwards guided the Battalion Transport and 61 reinforcements through this area making detours around heavily shelled areas and finally bringing Transport to destination without a single casualty.

Bolton Enterprise - December 13, 1918
An old Bolton boy has had honours bestowed upon him for his services at the front. Dr. Arthur E. Snell, son of the late S.J. Snell and Mrs. Snell, was living at Kingston at the outbreak of the war in 1914, went overseas as a Major in No. 2 Field Ambulance, and from that time until the present he has been a most indefatigable worker in the interests of the men of the Canadian army. His good work has evidently been appreciated as honours have been bestowed upon him from time to time. He is now a Colonel. Some time ago he was called to London where King George bestowed upon him the rank of C.M.G. (Companion of the Order of St. Michael and St. George), the French government decorated him with the Croix de Guerre for his services at the Battle of Amiens, he received the Distinguished Service Order, and he has now been appointed D.D.M.S. of the Canadian Corps. And he deserves all the honours he has received, and more, if one may judge by the letters of praise and commendation which have come through from the front.

Bolton Enterprise - December 13, 1918
Lieutenant Alex C. Bowles who put to flight a whole German Battalion, saving the lines with his machine gun during a counter attack, is coming home. Lieutenant Bowles left Canada in 1915. He was awarded the Military Cross for the above feat and was also recommended for the Victoria Cross by General Turner. Lieutenant Bowles was born at Mono Road and is 26 years of age.

Bolton Enterprise - January 3, 1919
"Corporal Adam Wallace, M.M., 26th Infantry, throughout four days' fighting he displayed coolness and courage in attending to wounded. On several occasions he dressed wounded men under heavy fire, accompanying the medical officer over the fire swept area."

The above is the terse way in which a dispatch from London refers to the fact Corporal Adam Wallace has been awarded the Distinguished Conduct Medal for his bravery at the front.

Corporal Wallace was granted the Military Medal about a year ago for bravery on the field and in September last was given a bar to his medal. Now he has been still further honoured by being awarded the Distinguished Conduct Medal. Corporal Wallace is a son of Mr. & Mrs. Robert J. Wallace of this town, and his parents are being congratulated on the great honour which their son has won on the field of battle.

Corporal Wallace enlisted in the fall of 1915, went overseas almost immediately and reached France early in 1916. He was buried by an exploding shell and injured which gave him a short Blighty, but with this exception he has been in the front line since reaching France. He was 18 years of age when he enlisted. The conferring of this honour on Corporal Wallace recalls his words on the eve of his departure for the war. At a public meeting in the town hall he had been presented with some trinket by Rev. W.S. Westney on behalf of the people of Bolton and in acknowledging the gift the young soldier with characteristic modesty said he "would do what he could to win the war". How well he has kept his word the honours which have been bestowed upon him will testify.

Bolton Enterprise - May 2, 1919 (from *Toronto Telegram* in part)
"Buck" Hutchinson, of Caledon East, Sergeant in the Fourth Battalion, is an "original", holding the D.C.M. and the M.M.. A young fellow, tall and solidly built, he is an athlete all over. He has a slow smile and speaks very quietly. He is very popular.

"I'm sorry, I haven't any story I can give you", he said to the Telegram. He was perfectly willing to talk, but "really I couldn't think of anything of interest".

The story of how Hutchinson won his D.C.M. was told by Colonel Nelles. "While the fight was raging round Abancourt at the end of last September, Hutchinson found two German "75" field guns. He had seen guns fired but there his knowledge of them ended. Lugging them round, he pointed them at the town of Abancourt. He did not know how to sight them, so propping up the tail, he looked down the barrel until he had them trained on the mark. Then he opened fire. At first, thinking the Canadians were going to enter the town, he did not fire any gas shells, but later when he discovered that they were not going to attack, he opened fire with some gas shells the Germans had left near the guns. One hundred and fifty shells, at a range of 1200 yards, were sent by Hutchinson into the town. So great was the damage done that the Germans opened up a barrage all around him, but he went on firing as if nothing had happened. And he only came away when a Company commander forced him to, because he was drawing so much fire on our men, said Colonel Nelles. Our guns were firing very badly that day, and I honestly think that "Buck" alone did more damage than all our Batteries did together".

Bolton Enterprise - July 4, 1919
Nursing Sister Daisy Dean, formerly of Sand Hill, had the honour bestowed upon her of being promoted to the position of Matron with rank and pay of Chaplain in Central Military Hospital, Toronto. Miss Dean was one of the first nurses to go overseas and served in England, France and Salonica, returning to Toronto about a year ago.

WORLD WAR I MEDALS AWARDED LOCAL SERVICEMEN FOR DISTINGUISHED SERVICE

IN ORDER OF AWARD STANDING

Colonel Arthur Evans Snell	Croix de Guerre Order of St. Michael and St. George Distinguished Service Order Mention-In-Despatches - four times	Woodbridge - Bolton
Lieutenant Henry Alvin Whitmore	Distinguished Service Order	Vaughan Twp.
Captain David Luther Burgess	Member of the Order of the British Empire Military Cross	Vaughan Twp.
Lieutenant Alex Clarence Bowles	Military Cross	Albion Twp.- Sand Hill
Lieutenant John W. Newlove	Military Cross	Albion Twp.- Macville
Captain Charles E. Read	Military Cross	Toronto - Bolton
2nd Lieutenant Joseph Gordon Dennis	Distinguished Flying Cross	Albion Twp. - Macville
Sergeant Adam Wallace	Distinguished Conduct Medal Military Medal and Bar	Bolton
Sergeant Norman Hutchinson	Distinguished Conduct Medal Military Medal	Caledon East
Private Albert Godbehere	Military Medal	Albion Twp.
Private George Williamson Johnston	Military Medal	Albion Twp.- Castlederg
Corporal Thomas D. McMahon	Military Medal	King Twp.
Private John Joseph Sharp	Military Medal	Vaughan Twp.
Sergeant Charles E. Snell	Military Medal	Albion Twp.- Macville
Sergeant John O. Wolfe	Military Medal	Albion Twp.
Sergeant Harry Wheeler Woods	Military Medal	Mono Road
Captain John Graham	Mention-In-Despatches	Mono Road

Croix de Guerre | Order of St. Michael and St. George | Distinguished Service Order | Member of the Order of the British Empire | Military Cross | Distinguished Flying Cross | Distinguished Conduct Medal | Military Medal

"While no medal was issued for Mention-In-Despatches, it is highly regarded in military circles as it signified exemplary conduct in battle. In some cases an oak leaf emblem was awarded for Mention-In-Despatches, to be worn on a medal previously issued to the individual," as quoted from information supplied by Captain (Ret'd) Douglas F. Hersey, CD, RC Sigs.

ALPHABETICAL LIST OF
THOSE WHO SERVED IN WORLD WAR I

Where available, this list includes the following information in order:
Rank, Name, Decorations, Reg.#, Service Branch, Enlistment/Discharge Dates.

Albert Acreman, 778495
employed in Lloydtown area, son of Mary Acreman, Somerset, England

Leonard Norman Acreman, 778494, 127th York Rangers, Jan 24 1916
employed in Lloydtown area, son of Mary Acreman, Somerset, England

Sapper, **Joseph Mathew Agar**, A4002, Canadian Engineers, Apr 8 1915
son of Joseph Agar & Eliza Ann Kitson, Nobleton
killed in France June 14 1916
grave - panel 10, Ypres (Menin Gate) Memorial, Ieper, West-Vlaanderen, Belgium

Nursing Sister, **Mary Agar**, CAMC
daughter of Joseph Agar & Eliza Ann Kitson, Nobleton, June 4 1917

Bandsman, **Albert Victor Ainsworth**, 766974, 123rd Battalion, Dec 27 1915
son of Betsy Ainsworth, Lance, England
employed by Orland Henry Downey, Albion Twp.

Lieutenant, **James G. Alexander,** (veterinary surgeon), Governor-General's Body Guards
son of James Alexander & Mary Irvin, Mono Road
"although, in his 65th year when the Great War broke out, Dr. Alexander presented himself for military service and was attached to the Military Transport, first at Fort Niagara and later at Val Cartier. In recognition of his service he was made a Lieutenant in the Governor-General's Body Guards." - quoted from the April 16, 1937 edition of the *Bolton Enterprise* at the time of Dr. Alexander's death.

Lieutenant, **James Lindsey Alexander,** Royal Canadian Engineers, Veterinary Corps, May 16 1918
son of Dr. James G. Alexander & Olivia Ann Lindsey, Mono Road

Captain, **Robert Oliver Alexander,** 118th Battalion, Mar 4 1916
son of Robert Alexander & Eliza Duncan, Bolton

Robert Garbutt Allan, 3037301, 1st Central Ontario Regiment, May 11 1918
son of Robert Allan & Elizabeth Anne Garbutt, Vaughan Twp.

William Allan, 75th Battalion, Caledon Twp.

Sapper, **Mark Allengame,** 775004, 124th Battalion, Dec 27 1915- May 2 1919
son of Alfred Allengame & Ellen Hooper, Caledon East
awarded Good Conduct Badge May 7 1918

Nathaniel Andrews, 136447, 37th Battalion, Oct 22 1915
born at Tunbridge Wells, Kent England - employed by Charles H.Rutherford
Albion Twp. - brother of Caroline Andrews, Peterborough

Private, **Delbert Arlow,** 3037127, 1st Central Ontario Regiment, May 10 1918
son of Thomas James Arlow & Mary Alice Kidd, Mono Mills

Private, **Percy Arlow,** 663137, 164th Battalion, Dec 23 1915
son of Thomas James Arlow & Mary Alice Kidd, Mono Mills

Private, **Roy Arlow,** 3317770, 2nd Central Ontario Regiment, Nov 1 1917
son of Robert Arlow & Sarah E. Kidd, Mono Mills

Private, **Albert Percy Armstrong**, 20292, bomb thrower, 10th Battalion Canadian Infantry, Alberta Regiment, Sept 22 1914
son of Ebenezer Amstrong & Margaret Anderson, Albion Twp.
killed Apr 22 1915, grave – Panel 24-28-30, Ypres (Menin Gate) Memorial, Ieper, West-Vlaanderen, Belgium

Private, **George Armstrong**, 135092, 2nd Canadain Mounted Rifles, British Columbia Regiment, July 29 1915
son of William Armstrong & Mary Fodon, Birmingham, England
husband of Florence Edwards, father of Eric & Lillian, Albion Twp.
killed Sept 30 1916, Vimy Memorial, Pas de Calais, France

Corpoal, **Samuel Joseph Armstrong**, 766118, 19th Battalion, Dec 16 1915
son of George Armstrong & Marcella Thornton, King Twp.

Lance Corporal, **William John Armstrong**, 412992, Canadian Machine Gun Corps, Mar 24 1915
of Albion Twp., son of John Armstrong, Dundonald, Ireland
killed Aug 4 1916, grave V11.D.21., Lijssenthoek Military Cemetery, Poperinge, West-Vlaanderen, Belgium

Clarence Wilford Arthurs
son of William Arthurs & Georgina E. Bradley, Bolton

Frederick William Ascott, 166284, 2nd Canadian Pioneer Battalion, Oct 16 1915
born in London, England, son of Elizabeth Ascott, London, England
employed in Nobleton area of King Twp.

Gunner, **John Leonard Atkinson**, 341199, 70th Battery, Mar 26 1917
son of Solomon Atkinson & Isabella Sheardown, King Twp.

Private, **Morley Abraham Attwood**, 406902, 4th Canadian Mounted Rifles, Central Ontario Regiment, Apr 16 1915
born in Bristol, England, son of Joseph & Emma Attwood, England
brother of Mrs. Radford, Bristol England, lived in Caledon East area
killed June 2 1916
grave - Panel 30 & 32, Ypres (Menin Gate) Memorial, Ieper, West-Vlaanderen, Belgium

William Charles Atwell, 501265, Engineers
son of Maria Atwell, Poole, Dorset, England, lived in Caledon East area, Nov 1 1915

William Bailey

Sapper, **Anthony George Bainbridge**, 778659, 127th York Rangers, Feb 7 1916
born in India, lived in Nobleton area
brother of Edith Mitchell, London, England

Private, **Fred Ballard**, 775023, 126th Battalion, Jan 11 1916
son of Thomas Ballard & Elizabeth Corless, Bolton

Corporal, **John Wilfred Banks**, 140010, 3rd Battalion, July 28 1915
son of Alexander Banks & Ann Jane Corless, Bolton
husband of Mary Alice Banks, Toronto, killed in France Sept 2 1918
Vimy Memorial, Pas de Calais, France

William Henry Barmby, 892171, 190th Battalion, Apr 20 1916
son of Joseph Barmby & Mary Carr, Caledon East

Edward Russell Barons, 3037309 1st Depot Battalion, May 11 1918
son of Mary Barons, Nashville

Private, **William Leonard Barry**, 3034175 1st Central Ontario Regiment, Mar 18 1918
son of John Barry & Rozella Ewart, Albion Twp.

Private, **John Bass**, 406252, Canadian Infantry, Western Ontario Regiment, Apr 16 1915
born in England, employed in Mono Road area
son of Mrs. A.B. Bass, Hitching Herts, England
killed Mar 2 1916
grave 11.J.6., Ridge Wood Military Cemetery, Heuvelland, West-Vlaanderen, Belgium

Private, **Harry Bellchamber**, 775438 & 2251050, 126th Battalion, Dec 7 1915
born in Paddington, London, England, husband of Agnes Frances Hunt
father of Clarence, George, Joffre & Frances, Bolton
"Private Bellchamber served in France with the Railway Troops under Captain F.L. Thompson, formerly of Bolton"
states the Bolton Enterprise of July 1949.

Seaman, **Percy Bennett**, Royal Navy
son of Samuel Bennett, Mono Road

Robert Timothy Bennett, 775953, 126th Battalion, Mar 7 1916
born in London, England, husband of Eve Bennett, Mono Road

Charles Bergen, 75th Battalion
Caledon Twp.

Private, **William Henry E. Berney**, 3230764, 1st Central Ontario Regiment, Sept 17 1917
son of George Berney & Agnes Still, Caledon East

Private, **Alvin C. Bible**, 775441, 21st Battalion, Jan 8 1916-May 24 1919
son of William Bible & Sarah Heek, Palgrave

Lance Corporal, **Harry Cecil Bishop**, 3722, Royal Canadian Dragoons, Aug 26 1914
son of Frederick Bishop & Elizabeth Harris, Kent, England
lived in Albion Twp.- brother to Bert Bishop, Albion Twp., killed in France Mar 30 1918
grave I.D.13., Namps-Au-Val British Cemetery, Somme, France

Nursing Sister, **Margaret Louise Black**, CAMC, Apr 10 1917-1919
daughter of John Black & Margaret Ann McCallum, Vaughan Twp.
Nashville area

Ernest Bloom
Caledon East

James Harold Bolton, 285659, 220th York Rangers, Nov 6 1916
son of Abraham Bolton & Lydia Margaret Sykes, Albion Twp.

John Charles Bolton, 3111260, 2nd Central Ontario Regiment, Aug 5 1918
son of Herbert Henry Bolton & Isabella Georgina Guardhouse, Bolton

Bandsman, **James Elliott Bolton**, 172398, 83rd Battalion, Dec 14 1915
son of James H. Bolton & Catherine Elliott, Bolton

Private, **Lambert Ernest Stanley Bolton**, 155001, 1st Pioneer Battalion, Canadian Pioneers
son of Rev. Charles Edward Bolton & Martha Bull, Wiarton, formerly of Bolton
killed June 13 1916, grave – Panel 32, Ypres (Menin Gate), Ieper, West-Vlaanderen, Belgium

Lambert R. Bolton, 679030
son of Herbert Henry Bolton & Isabella Georgina Guardhouse, Bolton

Wesley Abraham Bolton, 769515, 157th Battalion, May 26 1916
son of Abraham Bolton & Lydia Margaret Sykes, Albion Twp.

Robert Bonter

Sergeant, **Clarence Leslie Bowes**, 775454, 126th Battalion, Jan 15 1916-July 1919
son of Alfred Bowes & Catherine Maw, Castlederg

Private, **Leonard Bowes**, 3108900, 2nd Central Ontario Regiment, May 6 1918
son of Isaac Bowes & Rachel Robinson, Castlederg

Private, **Ray Bowes**, 3035744, 1st Central Ontario Regiment, Apr 29 1918
son of Isaac Bowes & Rachel Robinson, Castlederg

Lieutenant, **Alex Clarence Bowles**, MC, 76th Battalion, Aug 11 1915
son of Isaac G. & Elizabeth Bowles, Sand Hill
Military Cross

Private, **Albert Boyce**, 3037673, 1st Central Ontario Regiment, May 13 1918
son of Robert J. Boyce & Flora Downey, Albion Twp.

Dewitt Thomas Boyce, 3108901, 2nd Central Ontario Regiment, May 6 1918
son of Robert J. Boyce & Flora Downey, Albion Twp.

Private, **Everett Leonard Boyce**, 2688628, Canadian Army Service Corps, Aug 14 1918
son of William C. Boyce & Lucy Ann Norris, Albion Twp.

Private, **John Oscar Boyce**, 3108902, 2nd Central Ontario Regiment, May 6 1918
son of William Boyce & Annie Wolfe, Albion Twp.

Gunner, **William Wilfred Boyce**, 338286, 167th Battalion, July 5 1917
son of William C. Boyce & Lucy Ann Norris, Albion Twp.

Lance Corporal, **George Spencer Bradbury**, 201547, 1st Central Ontario Regiment, Nov 15 1915
born in Liverpool, England, employed by William Line, Caledon East
son of Margaret Bradbury, Toronto

Captain, **Emery Bradley**, 83222, 15th Battery, Dec 18 1914
employed in Albion area, son of John Bradley, Hornby

Warrant Officer, **Leslie Bradley**, 11109, 4th Battalion, Sept 22 1914
employed in Albion area, son of John Bradley, Hornby

Private, **John William Bradshaw**, 2251035, #7 Forestry Draft, June 1 1917
born in London, England - friend of Harry Bellchamber, Bolton
employed by Walshaw's Woollen Mills, Glasgow Road, Bolton

Sapper, **John C. Brain**, 769252, 4th Battalion, June 16 1919
son of Edwin Brain & Mary Chisholm, Caledon East

George Breckenridge
lived in the Tullamore area

Private, **Herbert V. Brown**, Royal Tank Regiment
born in County Antrim, Ireland - came to Bolton in 1940's - employed at Rutherfords and Albert Feheley farms, Albion Twp.- after retirement he made his home at the Queen's Hotel, Queen Street North, Bolton

Captain, **James S. Brown**, 36th Battalion, Mono Road

Reginald Lorne Brown, 775449, 126th Battalion, Jan 17 1916
son of William Brown & Mary Ann McKinley, Mono Road

Company Sergeant Major, **Richard Henry Burbridge**, 452363, July 7 1915
born at Sunbury, England, lived in Mono Road area
next of kin - Edward Burbridge, West Malling, Kent, England

Captain, **David Luther Burgess**, MBE, MC, 180th Battalion, Aug 15 1916
son of David Burgess & Charlotte Wurster, Kleinburg, Vaughan Twp.
husband of Christie Dowling, MacDowall, Saskatchewan,
Member of the Order of the British Empire, Military Cross

Henry Burgess, Mono Mills, killed

Wilbert Leonard Burkitt, 769783, 124th Battalion, Jan 6 1916
son of Samuel Burkitt, Kleinburg

Private, **Joseph Patrick Burns**, 142339, Sept 24 1915-Oct 23 1923
son of James Burns & Margaret McElhinney, Palgrave
died from war wounds at Christie Street Hospital, Toronto
interred at Laurel Hill Cemetery, Bolton

Charles Lawrence Burton, 3037310 1st Central Ontario Regiment, Nov 5 1918
son of Robert Burton & Margaret Ann Lawrence, Vaughan Twp.

Frank Burton, 199298, 94th Battalion, Apr 12 1916
son of Robert Burton & Margaret Ann Lawrence, Vaughan Twp.
husband of Edith Burton, Keewatin Ontario

Harry Burton, 775991, 126th Battalion, Mar 18 1916
employed by Francis Jackson, Hammertown area of King Twp.
born in Ripley, Derbyshire, England, son of Mary Ann Wild, Hauthwaite, Notts, England

Driver, **William Burton**, 511498, Canadian Army Service Corps, Jan 3 1916
son of Robert Burton & Margaret Ann Lawrence, Vaughan Twp.

Clifford Bush, employed in Mono Road area

Thomas Bush, 1024188, 234th Battalion, July 12 1916
employed by Jabez Wakely, Albion Twp., born in Norfolk County, England
husband of Martha Bush, Norfolk County, England

Private, **Charles Wilfred Byrne**, 513976, Canadian Army Service Corps, Feb 19 1917
son of James P. Byrne & Alice Pickerell, Albion Twp.

Driver, **Whitney M. Byrne**, 500178, Royal Canadian Engineers, Aug 20 1915
son of James P. Byrne & Alice Pickerell, Albion Twp.

Captain, **Charles Stewart Wallace Calhoun**, 9303, Sept 22 1914
son of Joseph Calhoun & Letitia Allely, Bolton

Major, **Frederick John Campbell Calhoun**, Sept 23 1914, (eye, ear & throat specialist)
son of Joseph Calhoun & Letitia Allely, Bolton

Harold Campbell, 404292, 14th Battalion, May 22 1915
of Nobleton, next of kin- Mrs. J. Tankard, Toronto

Robert James Camplin, 3109778, 2nd Central Ontario Regiment, May 11 1918
of Bolton after WW II, son of James Richard Camplin & Martha Elizabeth Bell, Euphrasia Twp.

George Beverly Carberry, 3037323, 1st Central Ontario Regiment, May 11 1918
son of Edward Carberry & Mary Thomas, Tullamore area

John Carberry
son of William Carberry & Jane Hemphill, Tullamore area

Frederick Cardy, Merchant Navy
of Caledon East area, killed at sea

Thomas Carlyle

Private, **Christopher Isaac Chamberlain**, 3037330 1st Central Ontario Regiment, Nov 5 1918-July 11 1919
son of William Chamberlain & Alice Robb, King Twp.

Private, **William James Chamberlain**, 427188, Canadian Infantry, Central Ontario Regiment, May 10 1915
son of William Chamberlain & Alice Robb, King Twp.
killed at Vimy Ridge, June 17 1917, grave E.12, Petit-Vimy British Cemetery, Pas de Calais, France

Private, **Frank Howard Chapman**, 172125 Queen's Own Rifles, 83rd Battalion, Sept 7 1915
son of Thomas Chapman & Annie Lascelles, Kleinburg area

Private, **George Frederick Chapman**, 2000768, Canadian Army Veterinary Corps, Dec 4 1916
son of Thomas Chapman & Annie Lascelles, Kleinburg area

William Chapman, 663755, 164th Battalion, June 27 1916
born in Portsmouth England, lived in Orangeville area
brother of Frank Joseph Chapman, Carp, Ontario

Winston Chapman

Signaller, **Edwin Lorne Childs**, 775455, 126th Battalion, Nov 12 1915-Mar 1919
son of Thomas Childs & Elizabeth Robinson, Bolton

Thomas Clark, Artillery, Caledon Twp.

Harold Clarke, 234th Battalion, Nov 1916
employed by Thomas McDougall, Albion Twp., Macville

Lemuel Clark, 663693, 164th Battalion, Apr 23 1916
born in St. Thomas - employed in Caledon East area
brother of Jack Clark, St. Thomas

Private, **William Cleaver**, 2251086, #7 Forestry Draft, June 7 1917
born in England, employed at Walshaw's Woollen Mills, Bolton
brother of Elsie Cleaver, Cochrane, Alberta

Lieutenant, **George Herbert Clement** (medical doctor), RCAMC
son of George William Clement & Amy Olivia Wood, Bolton

Private, **Reginald Dan Clifton**, 916290, 198th Battalion, Canadian Machine Gun Corps, Mar 13 1916
son of William & Jane Margaret Clifton, Bolton
husband of Minerva B.Clifton, West Kildonan, Manitoba
killed in France, Oct 1 1918, grave I.B. 20., Sancourt British Cemetery, Nord, France

Company Sergeant Major, **Charles Clow**, 405505, Canadian Infantry, Eastern Ontario Regiment, Apr 5 1915
son of John Nathan & Alice Clow, Lakenheath, Suffolk, England
lived in Bolton area
killed Sept 29 1918, grave 11.A.7., Bourlon Wood Cemetery, Pas de Calais, France

Jack Clow, 820051, Jan 7 1916
son of John Nathan & Alice Clow, Lakenheath, Suffolk, England
lived in Bolton area

Private, **Clifford Edward Coffey**, 3035760, 1st Depot Battalion, Apr 29 1918
son of Kieran Coffey & Annie Hanna, Albion Twp.

Lance Corporal, **George Richard Coker**, 643677, 157th Battalion, Mar 20 1916
born in London, England, raised by Mr. & Mrs. William Sharpe, Tecumseh Twp.

Albert Victor Cole, 3037325, Oct 18 1918
lived in Schomberg area, brother of Mabel Cole, Bethany Ontario

Private, **Edward Collins**, Albion Twp.

Private, **Charles Trevellyn Constant**, A327, 26th Regiment, Jan 21 1915
employed in Mono Mills area, son of William I. & Harriet Constant
Wardsville, Ontario formerly of Northfleet, Gravesend, Kent England
killed Mar 3 1916, St. Quentin Cabaret Military Cemetery, Heuvelland, West-Vlaanderen, Belgium, grave I.A.I.

Albert Cooke, Palgrave

Lance Corporal, **Herbert Arthur Cooper**, 192472, 42nd Battalion, Canadian Infantry, Quebec Regiment, Aug 13 1915
son of William & Minnie Cooper, Toronto, husband of Gertrude M. Black, Toronto
brother-in-law of William H. Black, Bolton, killed Apr 9 1917, Vimy Memorial, Pas de Calais, France

Private, **Robert Cooper**, 149552, 24th Battery, 8th Army Brigade, Canadian Field Artllery
son of John Cooper & Marie Jobson, Mono Road
British War Medal 1914-1920, Victory Medal 1914-1918
Private Cooper was a gunner and fought in France and Belgium in battles at Ypres, Mons, at Vimy Ridge,
April 9 1917 and at Passchendaele from November 7 to November 10 1917

Private, **Hubert S. Corless**, 775460, 116th Battalion, Canadian Infantry, Dec 4 1915
son of Edward Corless & Margaret Snell, Albion Twp.
killed at Passchendaele, Belgium Oct 30 1917, grave X11.A.6., Passchendaele New British Cemetery, Zonnebeke,
West-Vlaanderen, Belgium

Private, **John H. Corless**, 341273, 70th Battery, May 14 1917
son of John Corless & Annie Banks, Albion Twp.

Private, **Wesley Corless**, 3230159 2nd Depot Battalion, Jan 5 1918
son of Edward Corless & Margaret Snell, Albion Twp

Sergeant, **Sydney Charles Cornforth**, 477197, Royal Canadian Regiment, Aug 22 1915
son of Joseph & Clara Cornforth, Stockton-on-Tees, England
lived in Caledon East area, killed Apr 11 1917, grave I.H.5., Barlin Communal Cemetery Extension, Pas de Calais, France

Private, **Harry Charles Courtney**, 3039703, 1st Depot Battalion, June 7 1918-Oct 14 1919
son of Jonathon Courtney & Emily Ann Palmer, Schomberg
British War Medal

Private, **William Victor Coward**, 769464, Canadian Machine Gun Corps, Jan 1 1916
son of James Victor Coward & Emily Burkitt, Vaughan Twp., Nashville area
killed Aug 28 1918, grave VI.D.7., Wancourt British Cemetery, Pas de Calais, France

Private, **Charles William Crewe (Crewse)**, 775461, 126th Battalion, Dec 7, 1915
employed by Robert J. Boyce, Palgrave area, born in Guernsey, Channel Islands
son of Charles William & Emma Crewe, Guernsey, Channel Islands
killed Apr 9 1917, Vimy Memorial, Pas de Calais, France

Sapper, **Richard Criddle**, 2500302, Railway Construction, Depot #2, Apr 17 1918
born in Bristol, England - employed in Bolton area
husband of Eliza Criddle, Ravenna - near Collingwood

Private, **Leo James Cronin**, 3230868, 22nd Battalion, 1st Central Ontario Regiment, Jan 10 1918
son of Richard Cronin & Ann Pender, Albion Twp.

Petty Officer, **William Henry Cross**, RCNVR
born in France, son of John Cross & Frances Deacon, husband of Clara Kidd
father of Madeline Cross, Albion Twp., resided in a small house on west side of highway 50 about midway
between Bolton Heights Road and Columbia Way.

B. Crossley, Mono Road

Cadet, **George Chester Crozie**r, 153518, Royal Air Force
son of Hugh George Crozier & Jessie Drennan, Mono Mills, died as a result of an aeroplane accident at the age
of 19, July 2 1918, buried at Forest Law Cemetery, Orangeville, Plot 25, Grave 10, Forest Section

Sapper, **Sidney Cuff**, 643385, 157th Battalion, Feb 12 1916
born in Folkstone, Kent, England, from the Bernardo Home
lived in the Tottenham area, son of Mrs. Winchester Green, Trainor, Saskatchewan

Private, **John Culham**, 510030, July 23 1915
son of John Culham & Christina Watson, Vaughan Twp.

Harry Cunningham
of Bolton area after WW II

Private, **Frederick Ernest Daines**, 140055, 14th Battalion, July 23 1915
son of George Ernest Daines & Sarah A. Jacques, London England
husband of Edith Anne Allan, Bolton

Alfred Ernest Davies, 775050, 126th Battalion, Jan 11 1916
born in Liverpool, England, employed in Mono Road area
brother of Gertrude Hullwick, Liverpool, England

Vernet M. Davis, 3311686, 2nd Central Ontario Regiment, June 28 1918
son of Henry Davis & Eliza Armstrong, Caledon East

Lance Corporal, **William J. Dawson**, 669107, 166th Battalion, July 18 1916
born in Glasgow Scotland, lived in Vaughan Twp.
brother of Frances Dawson, Dublin, Ireland

Private, **Basil Richard Deacon**, 3235104, 1st Central Ontario Regiment, May 20 1918-Apr 3 1919
son of Richard Joseph Deacon & Ellen O'Callaghan, Lloydtown

Chaplain, **Daisy Dean**, No. 4 Canadian General Hospital Unit, stationed in Greece
daughter of Alexander Dean & Susanna McCort, Sand Hill

Melvin Defoe, 3108926, 2nd Central Ontario Regiment, May 6 1918
born in Sutton, Ontario, employed as a farm laborer in Bolton area
brother of Wesley Defoe, Tottenham

2nd Lieutenant, **Joseph Gordon Dennis**, DFC, 2766, Canadian Army Service Corps, Feb 4 1915, 24737,
Royal Flying Corps, Aug 1917-May 22 1919, Albion Twp.
son of Joseph Dennis & Caroline Treloar, Cornwall, England
Distinguished Flying Cross

Private, **Walter Arthur Mortimer Desmond**, 57617, 36th Peel Regiment, 2161085, Railway Construction &
Forestry Depot, Nov 12 1914-July 25 1917
lived in Mono Road area, brother of Blanche Desmond, Toronto

David Lillie Devins, 3036433 1st Central Ontario Regiment, May 6 1918
son of David Devins & Mary Caroline Hutchison, Vaughan Twp.

Douglas Devins, 207375, 97th Battalion, Dec 29 1915
son of William Devins & Mary Jane Chester, Albion Twp.

Erskine Devins, 18637, 9th Battalion, Princess Patricia Light Infantry, Sept 23 1914
son of William Devins & Mary Jane Chester, Albion Twp.

Garnett Royden Devins, 3232924, 1st Central Ontario Regiment, Mar 14 1918
son of David Devins & Mary Caroline Hutchison, Vaughan Twp.

Private, **Ruban Frank Dobson**, 250086
son of Frank R. Dobson & Elizabeth Thompson, King Twp.

Private, **Arthur Douglas**, 775475, 126th Battalion, Jan 12 1916
son of Minnie Douglas, Matheson, Ontario, employed in Mono Road area

Private, **S. Edgar Douglas**, 405697, Canadian Mounted Rifles, Jan 26 1915
son of Samuel Douglas & Helen Havelock, King Twp.
reported missing - never located, June 2 1916

Private, **Walter Douglas**, 776009, 126th Battalion, Mar 21 1916
son of Minnie Douglas, Matheson, Ontario, employed in Mono Road area

Private, **Charles Dowling**, 109315, Canadian Army Service Corps, Nov 28 1914
son of Bryan Dowling & Sarah Ann Trimble, Bolton

Private, **Victor Downey**, Albion Twp., June 3 1915

Driver, **Walter Gandier Early**, 348088, 3rd Battery, June 1 1915
son of James Early & Anna Belle Hunter, Chinguacousy Twp.

Private, **C. Edwards**

Charles Louis Egan, 225365, Canadian Mounted Rifles, Dec 16 1916
son of Johnston Egan & Margaret Peebles, Vaughan Twp.

Private, **Edward Ewart Elliott**, 2379506, 8th Battalion Canadian Infantry, Manitoba Regiment, Nov 19 1917
son of George Elliott & Eliza Ewart, Albion Twp.
killed Aug 9 1918, grave A.36., Le Quesnel Communal Cemetery Extension, Somme, France

Private, **Elwyn Hayes Elliott**, 3311458, 2nd Depot Battalion, June 4 1918
Cadet, **Elwyn Hayes Elliott**, 173894, Royal Army Flying Corps, July 22 1918-Dec 24 1918
son of Thomas D. Elliott & Helen Evans, Bolton

Corporal, **William Leonard Elliott**, 775478, 126th Battalion, Nov 22 1915
son of Samuel Elliott & Sarah Ann Wilson, Albion Twp.

Bandsman, **Leslie Hilliard Elliott**, 172397, 83rd Battalion, Dec 14 1915
son of Robert Elliott & Jane Hilliard, Albion Twp.

Gunner, **Percy Lorne Elliott**, 338600, Depot Artillery Brigade, May 23 1918
son of Mary Ann Elliott, Bolton

William Trevor Elliott, 3311459
son of Jarvis William Elliott & Mary Catharine McLeod, Albion Twp.

Wilbert Walter Wellar Elmer, 285186, 220th York Rangers, Apr 27 1916
son of Edward Elmer & Rebecca Wellar, King Twp.

Alfred Ennis, 603222, 34th Battalion, Sept 10 1915
of Bolton, son of Thomas Ennis & Rachel Martin, Sussex, England

John Espey, 473215, , Aug 19 1915
son of Henry Espey & Louise Jones, Vaughan Twp.

Russell Espey, 778782, 127th York Rangers, Jan 31 1916
son of Henry Espey & Louise Jones, Vaughan Twp.

Sergeant, **George Arthur Evans**, 104218, 68th Battalion, 1st Canadian Mounted Rifles, July 18 1915-
Jan 23 1919
son of Richard Evans & Jane Craven, Caledon East
British War Medal, Victory Medal

Sapper, **Robert Evans**, 779025 127th York Rangers, Mar 11 1916
lived in Bolton area, son of Mary Evans, Pine Grove-Woodbridge area

George Alfred Eves, 775908, 126th Battalion, Feb 28 1916
lived in Palgrave area, son of Diane Eves, Beeton

Eli Wilson Ewart, 3034412, 1st Central Ontario Regiment, Mar 26 1918
son of William Henry Ewart & Jane Wilson, Albion Twp.

Charles Gordon Ezeard, 285140, 220th York Rangers, Apr 27 1916
brother of Mrs. Charles Holden, Nobleton

Private, **Daniel Donald Fines**, 3230869, 1st Central Ontario Regiment, Jan 10 1918
son of William Fines & Janet McGeachy, Toronto Gore Twp.

Sergeant, **Robert Fines**, 252062, 12th Battalion, Jan 15 1916
son of William Fines & Janet McGeachy, Toronto Gore Twp.

Private, **Island Bellwood Fish**, 441467, 28th Battalion, Canadian Infantry, Saskatchewan Regiment, Oct 2 1915
of Mono Mills, son of Edwin & Sarah Fish, Guelph
died at age 26, Sept 15 1916, Vimy Memorial, Pas de Calais, France

Corporal, **William Charles Fisher**, 838068, Overseas Pioneer Battalion, Nov 29 1915
born in Reading, England, employed in Albion area
brother of Amelia Fisher, Bradford Ontario

Private, **Wilfrid Laurier Fitzpatrick**, 3037345, 1st Central Ontario Regiment, Nov 1 1918
son of Michael Fitzpatrick & Catherine Wallace, Toronto Gore Twp.
The War Service Medal 1914-1918, The Great War for Civilization Medal 1914-1919

Driver, **Cecil Roy Fleming**, 542366, 69th Battery, Dec 11 1916
son of Thomas Fleming & Mary Matilda Nattress, Vaughan Twp.

Private, **John Norman Fleming**, 475847, Princess Patricia's Light Infantry
son of Thomas Fleming & Mary Matilda Nattress, Vaughan Twp., July 17 1915
killed June 7 1916, grave V111.B.91., Boulogne Eastern Cemetery, Pas de Calais, France

Private, **Roy A. Fleming**, 1917
son of Andrew Fleming & Christina McLeod, Toronto Gore Twp.

Private, **Ernest Arthur Foster**, 3037343, 1st Central Ontario Regiment, May 11 1918
son of Richard Oxtoby Foster & Mary Ann Smalley, Nashville area

Gunner, **Aubrey Otis Gage**, 02704, June 12 1915
son of Richard Otis Gage & Louise Hurst, Toronto – later Albion Twp.

Reginald William Gage, 916733, 198th Battalion, Apr 24 1916
son of Richard Otis Gage & Louise Hurst, Toronto – later Albion Twp.

Chris Galbraith
Nobleton

George Francis Gallagher, 1024019, 234th Battalion, Apr 25 1916
of Albion Twp., son of William Gallagher, Toronto

Sergeant, **Ernest Wilfred Garrett**, 404082, Apr 5 1915
of Albion Twp., from the Dr. Bernardo Home, Toronto

Eugene Mathew Garvey, 3037348, 1st Central Ontario Regiment, May 4 1918
son of Mary Garvey, Mono Mills

George Gates, 75th Battalion
Caledon Twp.

Carl George Gillies, 103, Cyclists, Dec 4 1914
son of Thomas Gillies & Lydia Ann Pulford, Bolton

William Allan Gillies, 766380, 3rd Battalion, Nov 29 1915
son of Thomas Gillies & Lydia Ann Pulford, Bolton

Private, **Albert Godbehere**, MM, 775488, 126th Battalion, Jan 4 1916
son of Emma Dungworth, Greenhill, Sheffield, England
employed by Anson McCabe, Albion Twp., Military Medal

Gunner, **William J.Golden**, 3233367, 1st Central Ontario Regiment, Mar 25 1918
son of James Golden & Sarah Jane Gordon, Bolton

Private, **William Alexander Duncan Gordon**, 775487, 126th Battalion, Dec 20 1915
son of Donald Gordon & Eva Ann Marshall, Bolton
Bill Gordon later operated a grocery store and bakery at 23 Queen Street North in Bolton

Lawrence Gould, 466440, Princess Pats, July 10 1915
son of Jacob Gould & Caroline N. White, Bolton
husband of Anna Pearl Gould, Innisfail, Alberta

Lynnwood Gould, 3230784, 1st Central Ontario Regiment, Jan 10
son of Jacob Gould & Caroline N. White, Bolton

Captain, **John Graham**, MiD, Medical Doctor, CAMC, 1915-1919
of Mono Road, son of John Graham & Katherine Oliver, Belwood
Mention-In-Despatches from Field Marshal Earl Haig, for "gallant and distinguished service in the field"
War Service Medal 1914-1918, Victory Medal 1918
Dr. Graham operated a medical practice on Olde Base Line at Airport Road, Mono Road prior to his enlistment.
In 1919 he became a popular and well known medical doctor in Bolton living and practicing at what is now
municipally known as 34 Temperance Street. (House numbering in the village was not introduced until 1971-
1972). He was active in many progressive community undertakings and took an interest in anything designed
for the betterment of Bolton.

William Wilbert Gray, 3311302, 2nd Central Ontario Regiment, June 4 1918
son of Peter Gray & Algerena Laidlaw, Mono Road

George Arthur Green, 907847, 195th Battalion, Saskatchewan Regiment, Apr 19 1916
of Bolton, son of Edward Green & Annabella Ingleden, Kleinburg

Private, **William Arthur Greenwood**, 3233204, , Mar 1918
son of Richard Greenwood & Alice Mouch, Port Colborne
after World War I, W.A. Greenwood became manager of the Imperial Bank in Bolton

Sergeant, **Frederick William Gribble**, 2124919, Skilled Railway Troops, Jan 26 1917, enlisted at Montreal
son of William James Gribble & Arabella Emily Hooper, Kent England
after Wm. Jas. Gribble's death, Arabella married Robert Atwell of Caledon East

Private, **John Joseph Grogan**, 153186, 43rd Battalion, Canadian Infantry, Manitoba Regiment, June 24 1915
son of Joseph Peter Grogan, Albion Twp.
died of wounds, Nov 15 1917
grave XX11. GG. 5., Lijssenthoek Military Cemetery, Poperinge, West-Vlaanderen, Belgium

Tilford Douglas Gunn, 3230381, 1st Central Ontario Regiment, Jan 5 1918
son of William M. Gunn & Jennett Witherspoon, Kleinburg

Private, **James Mathew Guy**, 1009521, 21st Battalion
son of William Guy & Hanna McKenna, Caledon East

Captain, **William Thomas Hackett**, Canadian Army Dental Corps, 169th Battalion, Oct 4 1916
of Bolton & Hockley, son of Thomas Hackett & Margaret Anderson, Bolton
husband of Evelyn J. Hackett, Winnipeg, Manitoba
killed Feb 25 1919, grave XLV.C.7., Etaples Military Cemetery, Pas de Calais, France

Private, **John Stanley Haggerty**, 3058723 75th Depot Battery, May 16 1918
son of Daniel Haggerty & Mary Eliza Smith, Albion Twp., Centreville area, employed by William Crawford, Albion Twp.

Fred Haines, Royal Canadian Dragoons
employed by R. Dooks, Albion Twp. – enlisted at Tottenham

Albert Hainsworth, 2006370, Canadian Engineers, June 28 1917
employed in Castlederg area, born in Leeds, Yorkshire, England
husband of Alice Maud Hainsworth, Leeds, Yorkshire, England

Private, **Joseph Samuel Halbert**, 663165, 164th Battalion, Dec 9 1915
of Mono Mills, son of Robert John & Eliza Ann Halbert, Markdale
killed Oct 9 1918, Haynecourt British Cemetery, Nord, France grave III.A.21.

Sergeant, **Samuel Stanley Clifford Hall**, 3211495 1st Depot Battalion, enlisted at Calgary, Alberta, May 20 1918
of Orangeville & Albion Twp. areas
son of Robert Hall & Mary Jane Moore, Guelph

Trooper, **John Mercer Hamilton**, 643679, 157th Battalion, Mar 9 1916
of Bolton after WWII, son of William Hamilton, Tottenham

Corporal, **Joseph Hanley**, 427871, 69th Battalion, Aug 3 1915
lived in Albion Twp., born in Sudbury – next of kin – Mrs. A. Bolton, Tottenham

Nursing Sister, **Edna Catharine Hanna**, Red Cross Society
daughter of Thomas Henry Hanna & Elizabeth McInnis, Mono Road

Private, **John Arthur S. Hanna**, 3108953, 102nd Battalion, May 6 1918-Apr 3 1919
son of Thomas Henry Hanna & Elizabeth McInnis, Mono Road

Private, **Edward Nelson Harper**, 3037361, 1st Central Ontario Regiment, May 11 1918
lived in Nashville area, born in Devizes, Wiltshire England
son of Elizabeth Harper, Patney near Devizes, Wiltshire England

Private, **James Alfred Harper**, 3037367, 1st Central Ontario Regiment, May 11 1918
son of Alfred Harper & Jane Mitchell, Albion Twp.

Private, **Wilfred Joseph Harrigan**, 3206903, 1st Depot Battalion, Alberta Regiment, Feb 22 1918
son of Daniel Joseph Harrigan & Teresa McCabe, Mono Road
wounded at Cambrai, necessitating the amputation of his left leg

Lance Corporal, **Charles Haskell**, 7044, 1st Battalion, Canadian Infantry, Western Ontario Regiment
employed by Peter Mitchell, Albion Twp.
son of Charles W. Haskell, Guelph, killed June 15 1915
Vimy Memorial, Pas de Calais, France

Sergeant, **Herbert Hawkins**, 775490, 126th Battalion, Jan 12 1916
of Bolton, son of Elizabeth Hawkins, Birmingham, Warwickshire England

James Alfred Henderson, 3107506, 2nd Central Ontario Regiment, Feb 18 1918
son of Andrew S. Henderson & Margaret Amelia Lougheed, Albion Twp.

Private, **Robert Alexander Henderson**, 3035732, 1st Central Ontario Regiment, Apr 29 1918
son of Andrew S. Henderson & Margaret Amelia Lougheed, Albion Twp.

William Henry Hensman, 775811, 126th Battalion, Jan 31 1916
lived at Mono Road, son of Thomas Hensman, Leicestershire, England

Sergeant, **Bruce Hesp**, 1036348, 238th Forestry Battalion, July 25 1916-Apr 23 1919
of Tullamore area & Toronto – born at Stockton on Forest, Yorkshire England
son of William Hesp & Elizabeth Wicks, Bournemouth England
husband of Sarah Theodora Singleton, father of Norman William Hesp, Toronto

Private, **William Roy Hesp**, 3108952, 116th Battalion, May 6 1918-Apr 8 1919
son of Henry Hesp & Susannah Williamson, Albion Twp.
The War Service Medal 1914-1918
Service at the Front Medal, The Great War for Civilization Medal 1914-1919
Before he left for overseas service, Susannah Hesp penned these words to her son in a pocket sized Bible given
to him – "read this little book, hallow its teachings. It will help you in your difficulties. May the Lord help you
to do what is right and bring you safely home. But, if we never meet in this world again, may we all meet in
Heaven. – from Mother to Roy."

William Henry Hewitt, 3110429, 2nd Central Ontario Regiment, June 6 1918
son of Richard Hewitt & Elizabeth Guilliant, Kleinburg area

Sergeant, **Henry William Hickey**, 11202, 4th Battalion, 1st Central Ontario Regiment, Sept 22 1914
lived in Caledon East area, born in London, England
son of Walter Hickey, Honeywood, Ontario
Sergeant Hickey was recommended to receive the Victoria Cross on May 24 1915 but did not live to receive the
honour, killed May 30 1915, Vimy Memorial, Pas de Calais, France

Albert Hill, 3111119, 2nd Central Ontario Regiment, July 24 1918
son of George Hill & Jane Cutting, Nobleton

Private, **Henry Lewis Hilliard**, 3037356, 1st Central Ontario Regiment, May 11 1918
son of Samuel Hilliard & Margaret Hunter, Kleinburg

Russell Tyndall Hilliard, 3037362, 1st Central Ontario Regiment, May 11 1918
son of Samuel Hilliard & Margaret Hunter, Kleinburg

Fred Hinds, Palgrave

Corporal, **Albert E. Hoar**, 41218, Sept 25 1914
lived in Albion Twp., born in South Wales; next of kin - G.T. Hoar, Montreal Quebec

Private, **Frank Hodgson**, 536066, 4th Canadian Division, Aug 12 1916-1918
lived at Mono Road, born in Kendal England
son of R.W. Hodgson, Kendal England

Frederick John Holder, Caledon East

Private, **David Hood**, 20th Battalion, 1915-1917
friend of George & Edith Beauchamp, Glasgow Road, Bolton

Corporal, **George Thomas Howard**, 164628, 75th Battalion, Canadian Infantry, Central Ontario Regiment,
Nov 10 1915
son of George & Joanie Howard, King Twp.,
killed Apr 9 1917, grave 1.B.15., Canadian Cemetery No. 2, Neuville-St.Vaast, Pas de Calais, France

Corporal, **George Alexander William Hubbard**, 42051, 7th Battery, Sept 24 1914
of Bolton after WW II, born in Canning Town, Essex England
next of kin - William Hubbard, South Woodford, Essex England

Sapper, **George James Hugill**, 778274, 127th York Rangers, Jan 5 1916
grandson of John Hugill, Woodbridge

Gunner, **Leonard Percival Humphreys**, 340963, 75th Battalion, July 6 1916
son of William Humphreys & Susan Ireland, Kleinburg

Norman Hunter, 907398, Mar 18 1916
son of William Hunter, Bolton

John Wilfred Hutchinson, 258652, 1st Depot Battalion, Saskatchewan Regiment, Feb 5 1918
son of William John Hutchinson & Elizabeth Drummond, Caledon East

Sergeant, **William Norman Hutchinson**, DCM, MM, 11241, 4th Battalion, Sept 22 1914-Apr 24 1919
son of William John Hutchinson & Elizabeth Drummond, Caledon East
Distinguished Conduct Medal
Military Medal, The 1914-1915 British Star, The British War Medal, The Victory Medal 1914-1918

Private, **Frederick Ireland**, 3231020, 2nd Depot Battalion, 1st Central Ontario Regiment,
Jan 18 1918-Feb 20 1919
son of Alfred Ireland & Frances Clubine, Albion Twp.
"Frederick Ireland served in England and France and suffered a gun shot
wound to the left leg in the calf area" according to his nephew Bruce Ireland.

Corporal, **Robert Henry Ireland**, 285223, 220th Battalion, Apr 1916-Apr 1919
son of Alfred Ireland and Frances Clubine, Albion Twp.
"Robert Henry Ireland saw service in England and France. By horse and wagon, he transported supplies to the
front lines in France under heavy fire. His buddy was killed nearby. He was affected some by German gas, lived
on bully beef in cans and was half starved sometimes. He got $1.10 per day" according to his son Bruce
Ireland.

Private, **Ernest John Jackson**, 775507, 3rd Battalion, Canadian Infantry,
Central Ontario Regiment, Nov 7 1916
of Bolton, son of Emily Sadler, Horsham England
killed July 10 1917
grave 11.E.10., La Targette British Cemetery, Neuville-St Vaast, Pas de Calais, France

Frederick Sidney Jackson, 11250, 4th Battalion, 36th Regiment, Sept 22 1914
born in London England - son of Alice Jackson, London England
employed at Walshaw's Woollen Mills, Glasgow Road, Bolton

Private, **Samuel Joseph Jackson**, 700068, 101st Battalion, Dec 6 1915
son of Rachael Ann Jackson, Mono Mills
killed Apr 9 1917, Vimy Memorial, Pas de Calais, France

Corporal, **Ross Kenneth Jaffary**, 775509, 126th Battalion, Jan 22 1915
son of William Alfred Jaffary & Amy E. Newlove, Albion Twp.

Private, **William John James**, 775971, 126th Battalion, Mar 9 1916
son of William James & Fannie Emma Beamish, Bolton

Loftus Percy George Jewitt, 2000770
son of William Jewitt & Harriet Sheardown, King Twp.

Gunner, **George Williamson Johnston**, MM, 2022070, 102nd Battalion
employed by Charles H. Rutherford, Albion Twp., Castlederg
Military Medal

Robert Johnston
son of John Johnston, Vaughan Twp.

William Johnston
son of John Johnston, Vaughan Twp.

Carl Jones
Vaughan Twp., killed

John (Jack) Edgar Jones, 126th Battalion
son of James Jones & Ellen Lyness, Palgrave

William Jones, Mono Road, killed

Private, **George Wesley Clifford Judge**, 2498498, York & Simcoe Foresters, Sept 12 1917
son of George Judge & Jennie Carberry, Mono Road

Sergeant, **Samuel James Judge**, 136219, 74th Battalion, Aug 30 1915
son of James Judge & Martha Goodeve, Mono Road

Lieutenant, **Selwyn Evans Judge**, 406334, 36th Peel Battalion, Royal Army Flying Corps, Apr 14 1915
son of William L. Judge & Maria Evans, Caledon East

Andrew Ivan Kaake, 3037372, 1st Central Ontario Regiment, May 11 1918
son of Thomas Kaake & Elizabeth Goodfellow, King Twp.

Private, **Dalton Kearns**, 3108965, May 6 1918-June 8 1919
son of Charles Kearns & Jane Ann Corbett, Caledon East
The War Service Medal 1914-1918
The Great War for Civilization Medal 1914-1919

Garvin Kearns

Private, **George Kearns**, 234th Battalion
Mono Road

H. Keelan, Mono Road

Albert Kelly

Trueman Kelly, Mono Road

Captain, (Chaplain), **William Terrance Kelly**, 3371, 2nd Division, 1915-1918
son of Bernard Kelly & Catherine Minnock, Albion Twp.
served under General Logie

Private, **Harold Kemp**, 14th Battalion

Private, **Albert Alexander Kennedy**, 775514, 126th Battalion, Nov 20 1915
son of Hugh & Hannah Kennedy , Bolton

Lester Kerr

Private, **Edward James Killeen**, 1051423, Nov 17 1916
son of James Ambrose Killleen & Mary Rossney, Caledon East

Private, **Farrell Ambrose Killeen**, 3030909, 1st Central Ontario Regiment, Nov 5 1917
son of James Ambrose Killeen & Mary Rossney, Caledon East

Private, **Henry George King**, 3108966, 1st Depot Battalion, Oct 29 1918
of Vaughan & Albion Twps., born in Windsor, Birkshire England
son of Edward King & Ada Slade

Bennie Laceby
son of Thomas Laceby & Margaret Walker, Bolton

Arthur Langley
employed by Robert Crisp, Albion Twp.

Private, **William Frank George Langmead**, 142242, 76th Battalion, Sept 14 1915
born in England, next of kin – Mrs. Albert Fleming, Sand Hill

Corporal, **John W.H. Laughlin**, 407058, 36th Battalion, June 10 1915
of Mono Road, born in Youngstown, brother of George Laughlin, Mono Mills

Sydney Lawrence, 257th Battalion, Apr 3 1919
Bolton

Arthur James Leadbetter, 643687, 157th Battalion, May 1 1916-Feb 9 1918
of Albion Twp. near Tottenham, son of James Leadbetter & Anne Jane Mann of Otterville
husband of Minnie Leadbetter of Aylmer

Everett Salton Learoyd, 504411, Divisional Signallers Company, Mar 20 1916
son of Rev. William Henry Learoyd & Rhoda Mary Holman, Kleinburg

Harold Gordon Learoyd, 503171, Divisional Signallers Company, Feb 18 1916
son of Rev. William Henry Learoyd & Rhoda Mary Holman, Kleinburg

Private, **Byron Redvers Leavens**, 1024440, 234th Battalion, Nov 13 1916-Mar 25 1919
son of Frank N. Leavens & Alberta Catherine Snider, Bolton
Byron Leavens was Bolton's Postmaster from July 19 1927 to the time of his death January 2 1945.

Fred Lefeuvre
employed by Stewart H. Cameron, Albion Twp.

Private, **Richard Lefeuvre**, 775767, 126th Battalion, Feb 14 1916
employed by Stewart H. Cameron, Albion Twp.
born at Guernsey, Channel Islands, son of Richard Lefeuvre, Montana U.S.A.

Lieutenant, **Basil Roy Lepper**, 304275, Canadian Field Artillery
son of Dr. James William Lepper & Maria Elizabeth Carter, Bolton,
killed in France, Sept 27 1918, grave 1.B.1., Sains-Les-Marquion British Cemetery, Pas de Calais, France

Lieutenant, **Euston Lepper**,
son of Dr. James William Lepper & Maria Elizabeth Carter, Bolton

Lieutenant, **James Lepper**
son of Dr. James William Lepper & Maria Elizabeth Carter, Bolton

Private, **Charles Lillie**,
of Mono Mills, killed

John Lince, 727434
Bolton, gassed, Sept 19 1917

Lieutenant, **Roy Eli Lindsay**, 1081481, Engineers, July 6 1916
son of William Lindsay & Catharine Gibson, Albion Twp.

Private, **Davison Alexander Lindsey**, 277187, 1st Depot Battalion, June 6 1918
son of James Lindsey & Elizabeth Davison, Albion Twp., Macville area

Private, **Oliver Graham Lindsey**, 502206, Engineers, Dec 15 1915
son of James Lindsey & Elizabeth Davison, Albion Twp., Macville area

Private, **Eugene Liscombe**, 775515, 126th Battalion, Nov 3 1915-Apr 3 1919
Bolton - friend of Frank N. Leavens, Bolton

Sergeant, **William Chester Little**, 472819, 46th Battalion, Dec 1915
son of John Little, Tullamore
killed in France Mar 26 1917, grave VI.G.9., Villers Station Cemetery, Villers-Au-Bois, Pas de Calais, France

1st Lieutenant, **Leroy Stanley Livingston**
son of Robert Henry Livingston & Emma Maude Perkins, Toronto Gore Twp.

Private, **Robert William Livingston**, 3037373, Military Police
son of Robert Henry Livingston & Emma Maude Perkins, Toronto Gore Twp.

Lieutenant, **Ewart Gladstone Lloyd**, 300081
son of Alfred Levi Lloyd & Elizabeth Ann Shrigley, Lloydtown

F. Locke

Private, **Arthur Given Long**, 407039, 18th Battalion, Canadian Infantry, Western Ontario Regiment
son of Rev. James Arthur Long & Mary Ann Given, Toronto
lived in Albion area, killed Mar 29 1916
grave 11.N.6., Ridge Wood Military Cemetery, Heuvelland, West-Vlaanderen, Belgium

Robert Lougheed, Mono Road

Major, **Alexander Addison MacKenzie**, Governor-General's Body Guards & Fourth Canadian Rifles, 1914
son of Donald MacKenzie & Lydia Ann Addison, Vaughan Twp.

Sergeant, **Donald Ross MacKenzie**, 778132, 2nd Battalion, Canadian Railway Troops
son of Donald MacKenzie & Lydia Ann Addison, Vaughan Twp.
killed Mar 30 1918
grave A.10., Fouilloy Communal Cemetery, Somme, France

Private, **Thomas Macklin**, 776048

Lieutenant, **John Fletcher MacLean**, 1090284, 15th Battalion, 1916-1919
of Bolton later, son of H. McLean, Minnedosa, Manitoba

Private, **Reginald Frank Maples**, 663780, 116th Battalion
of Mono Mills, killed Aug 15 1918
Bouchoir New British Cemetery, Somme, France grave 11.B.56.

Clinton Martin

Howard Martin, Caledon East

Private, **John Melville Martin**, 3035763,
Mono Road

Private, **Edward Mason**,
born in England, employed by Walshaw's Woollen Mills, Glasgow Road, Bolton
presumably killed at Vimy Ridge between April 7 and April 10 1917. The May 11 1917 issue of the *Bolton Enterprise* states Mrs. Edward Mason and little girl were living at the home of Mr. & Mrs. Milford C. Moffatt (Hannah Jane Matson) in Albion Township at this time.

Private, **Lawrence Mathews**, 775828, 18th Battalion
son of Thomas Mathews & Rachel VanWyck, Mono Road
killed in France, Apr 12 1917

Robert Mathews
son of Thomas Mathews & Rachel VanWyck, Mono Road

Private, **Isaac Oliver Matson**, 3233899, 1st Central Ontario Regiment, Sept 29 1917
son of Isaac Matson & Jane Wilson, Albion Twp.

Private, **Oscar Maw**, 3311340 2nd Central Ontario Regiment, Nov 1 1917
son of Fred Maw & Margaret Speers, Albion Twp.

Private, **Thomas Maw**, 3035336 1st Central Ontario Regiment, Nov 26 1917
son of Fred Maw & Margaret Speers, Albion Twp.

Leo Maxwell
son of R.J. Maxwell, Bolton

Private, **Earle Vincent Mellow**, 434893, 50th Battalion, Medicine Hat, Alberta
son of George Mellow & Christina MacTaggart, Albion Twp.

Charles Merril, Caledon Twp.

Lieutenant Colonel, **Armour A. Miller**, 19th Battalion, Canadian Infantry, Central Ontario Regiment, June 14 1916
killed June 21 1918 grave 1.M.24., Gezaincourt Communal Cemetery Extension, Somme, France

Herbert Miller, Vaughan Twp., killed

George Mills, 52nd Battalion
born in England, employed by Richard Hutchinson of Sand Hill
killed 1918

Private, **Thomas Mills**, 10672, 4th Battalion, Canadian Infantry, Central Ontario Regiment
raised by Mr. & Mrs. Thomas Cooke, Albion Twp.
killed Apr 12 1916, grave 1.H.5., Chester Farm Cemetery, Ieper, West-Vlaanderen, Belgium

Frederick Minton

William Minton

George Mintram
employed by Milton Downey, Albion Twp., Castlederg

Sergeant, **George F. Mitchell**, Dental Corps
son of John F. Mitchell, Sand Hill

H.A. Mitchell
son of John F. Mitchell, Sand Hill

Melville Mitchell

Sergeant, **Shephner W. Moore**, 91st Battalion
son of William Robert Moore & Jennie Blain, Albion Twp.

Edward Morgan
a "home" boy from Vaughan Twp., employed at Walshaw's Woolen Mills,
Glasgow Road, Bolton, killed

John Morgan
Vaughan Twp., killed

Private, **Thomas Morrissey**, 775537, 126th Battalion, Jan 12 1916
son of Rose McCarty, Adjala Twp.

Reeve Wilson Morrison
son of Thomas J. Morrison & Carry Rankin, Bolton

Private, **Elmer A. Moss**, 775535 87th Battalion, Canadian Infantry, Quebec Regiment, Jan 8 1916
son of Abraham Moss & Catherine Bible, Albion Twp., killed Aug 15 1917, Vimy Memorial, Pas de Calais, France
British War Medal, Victory Medal

John Henry Mullen,
son of James Joseph Mullen & Elizabeth Hanlon, Albion Twp.

Private, **Patrick Andrew Mullen**, 3031721, 1st Central Ontario Regiment, Jan 3 1918
son of James Joseph Mullen & Elizabeth Hanlon, Albion Twp.

Private, **George Watson Munro**, 775534, 18th Battalion, Canadian Infantry,
Western Ontario Regiment, Jan 1 1916
son of Peter Munro & Annie Watson, Albion Twp.
killed in France, Aug 22 1917
grave 1.M.15., Aix-Noulette Communal Cemetery Extension, Pas de Calais, France

Gilbert Munro
son of Gilbert Munro & Sarah Hollingshead, King Twp.

Private, **Gordon McDonald Munro**, 3108980 1st Depot Battalion, May 6 1918-Jan 16 1919
son of Peter Munro & Annie Watson, Albion Twp.

Private, **James Watson Munro**, 2125190, Engineers
son of Peter Munro & Annie Watson, Albion Twp.

Private, **William Watson Munro**, 775525, 21st Battalion, Canadian Infantry,
Eastern Ontario Regiment, Nov 20 1915
son of Peter Munro & Annie Watson, Albion Twp.
killed at Vimy Ridge, May 22 1917
grave 11.L.2., Wimereux Communal Cemetery, Pas de Calais, France

Private, **David Edgar McAllister**, 447134, 49th Battalion, Canadian Infantry, (Alberta Regiment) 1915-1918
son of Thomas McAllister & Jane Mitchell, King Twp.

Private, **Robert Stanley McAllister**, 447281, 49th Battalion, Canadian Infantry, (Alberta Regiment), 1915
son of Thomas McAllister & Jane Mitchell, King Twp.
killed at Battle of Ypres, June 3 1916
grave Panel 24-28-30, Ypres (Menin Gate) Memorial, Ieper, West-Vlaanderen, Belgium

William J. McBain, 1024395, 234th Battalion, Oct 25 1916
born in Dufftown, Scotland, husband of Caroline Godson, Lloydtown

Corporal, **Walter Campbell McBride**, 681827, 58th Battalion, Canadian Infantry, Central Ontario Regiment,
May 10 1916
son of William John McBride & Isabella Rowley, Palgrave
killed at Bois duSart, France, Aug 26 1918
grave V11.J.21., Vis-En-Artois British Cemetery, Haucourt, Pas de Calais, France

Corporal, **William George McBride**, 551406 Fort Garry Horse - Canadian Mounted Rifles, Dec 22 1914-Dec
14 1918
son of William John McBride & Isabella Rowley, Palgrave
wounded in France and lost left arm
William McBride was the acting Postmaster in Palgrave from 1947 to 1951

Albert John McCaffrey, 340357, 69th Battery, transferred to Dental Corps, Apr 6 1915-1918
son of Patrick J. McCaffrey & Alice McKenna, Caledon East

Corporal, **Wilbert Lawrence McCaffrey**, 775989, 116th Battalion, Mar 15 1916
son of Patrick J. McCaffrey & Alice McKenna, Caledon East
killed at Cambrai, France, Sept 29 1918
grave B.20, St. Olle British Cemetery, Raillencourt, Nord, France,

Private, **John Archibald McCallum**, 651581, 18th Battalion, Canadian Infantry, Western Ontario Regiment, Jan 31 1916
son of Neil McCallum & Jane Jeffrey, Vaughan Twp.
killed Aug 26 1918, grave V.B.4., Wancourt British Cemetery, Pas de Calais, France

John Duncan Earl McCallum, 512533, 3rd Division, Mar 21 1916
son of Duncan McCallum & Sarah Cherry, King Twp.

Thomas Alex Eric McCartney, 2683846, , Apr 26 1918
son of Henry McCartney & Margaret Ann Dunn, Caledon East

Captain, **Daniel Milton McCaughrin**, 71263, Canadian Engineers, Nov 10 1916
son of Daniel McCaughrin, husband of Eva McCaughrin, Mono Road

Captain, **Roy Cecil McCort**, No. 6 Battery, May 4 1916
son of Alexander McCort & Harriett Burgess, Albion Twp.

Private, **Jesse Byron McCubbin**, 475959, Princess Pats, July 28 1915
son of Alexander John McCubbin & Kate Williams, Bolton

Lieutenant, **Perry McCubbin**, 1006045, 228th Battalion, Northern Fusiliers, Mar 20 1916
son of Alexander John McCubbin & Kate Williams, Bolton
husband of Elizabeth McCubbin, North Bay

Stewart McCutcheon, 3233077, 70th Battery, Mar 18 1918
son of William T. McCutcheon & Sarah J. Stewart, King Twp.

Flight Lieutenant, **Walter S. McCutcheon**, Royal Canadian Bicycle Brigade and
Royal Army Flying Corps, 1915
son of John A. McCutcheon & Minnie R. Snider, King Twp.
The following information has been supplied by Donald Campbell, a nephew of Flight Lieutenant Walter S. McCutcheon "Uncle Walter joined initially, the Royal Canadian Bicycle Brigade in, I believe 1915. He suffered serious injury at one point and, on recovery, was no longer able to sit on a bicycle saddle, whereupon he joined the brand new Royal Army Flying Corps, as the R.A.F. was first known. In 1919, the R.A.F., as we know it, was created and Uncle Walter trained in England for some years as a flyer. My understanding is that he came home in 1926. Because of his transfer from the "Cyclists" to the Flying Corps, his records are in England."

Major, **William Franklin McCutcheon**, 513095, No. 2 Canadian Army Service Corps, Oct 15 1916
son of William Robert McCutcheon & Nancy Hunter, King Twp.

Lance Corporal, **James Joseph McDevitt**, 775532, 18th Battalion, Canadian Infantry, 1914
son of William McDevitt & Susannah McDonald, Caledon Twp.
severely gassed at Vimy Ridge
War Service Badge - Class "A", 1919
The Great War for Civilization Medal 1914-1919

Bertram McDonald, 775907, 126th Battalion, Feb 28 1916
son of John & Martha Ann McDonald, Albion Twp.

Private, **Elwon David McDonald**, 775884, 18th Battalion, Canadian Infantry, Western Ontario Regiment
of Caledon East, son of John A. McDonald & Nellie Watson, Brampton
died at age 22, Apr 13 1917
Vimy Memorial, Pas de Calaise, France

John McDonald
Vaughan Twp., killed

Roy McDonald

Edward McDonough
son of James & Hannah McDonough, Vaughan Twp.

Frank McDonough
son of James & Hannah McDonough, Vaughan Twp.

Private, **John Joseph McDonough**, 775652, 126th Battalion
son of James & Hannah McDonough, Vaughan Twp.- husband of Margaret Egan, Toronto

William McDonough
son of James & Hannah McDonough, Vaughan Twp.

William McElwheney
Vaughan Twp.

John McFadgen
son of James & Elizabeth McFadgen, Vaughan Twp.

Lance Corporal, **William Beaton McGillivray**, 513219, Princess Patricia's Light Infantry, Eastern Ontario Regiment
son of William McGillivray, Vaughan Twp., Nashville area
killed Sept 28 1918, grave A.23. Mill Switch British Cemetery, Tilloy-Les-Cambrai, Nord, France

Donald Alexander Swanson McKay, 11309, 4th Battalion, Sept 22 1914
of Mono Road, son of Sinclair McKay, Thurso, Caithness Scotland

Seaman, **Neil McKay**, 2128A, Royal Naval Reserve, HMS "Newmarket"
husband of Hughina McRay of Achow, Sweney, Lybster, Wick, Scotland
employed by Stewart A. Cameron, Albion Twp., killed July 17 1917
Portsmouth, Naval Memorial, Hampshire, United Kingdom, Panel 27

Private, **William McKay**
worked for various farmers in the Bolton area

Flight Lieutenant, **Charles John Weylie McKeown**, 490793, 204th Battalion, 1916, Royal Flying Corps, 1917-1919
son of John James McKeown & Sarah Gray, Sand Hill
Flight Lieutenant McKeown was a prisoner of war in Germany for 10 months

Captain, **David Fuller McKinley**
son of William McKinley & Maria Fuller, King Twp.

Private, **John James Stanley McKinley**, 3108978, 2nd Central Ontario Regiment, May 6 1918
son of William John McKinley & Elizabeth Burk, Caledon East

Private, **James Henry Campbell McMahon**, 475536, 126th Battalion
son of Henry McMahon & Mary Maude Cubbins, Palgrave

Corporal, **Thomas D. McMahon**, MM, 136094, 1st Canadian Mounted Rifles, Saskatchewan Regiment, July 26 1915
born in Dublin Ireland, son of Florence Shipton, London, England
employed by John James Coulter, King Twp.
killed Oct 26 1917, grave - Panel 18-26-28, Ypres, (Menin Gate) Memorial, Ieper, West-Vlaanderen, Belgium
Military Medal

Thomas McMaster
Nobleton

Private, **Earl N. McMinn**, 775539, 87th Battalion, Canadian Infantry, Quebec Regiment, Jan 24 1916
son of William A. McMinn & Martha J. Taylor, Palgrave
killed May 20 1917, grave 7.C.21., Canadian Cemetery No. 2, Neuville-St. Vaast, Pas de Calais, France

Private, **William McNair**, 928654, 47th Battalion, Canadian Infantry, Western Ontario Regiment
husband of Emma Place, father of Stuart, Alf, Emily & Herb, Bolton
killed Sept 3 1918, grave 111.E.15., Ligny-St. Flochel British Cemetery, Averdoingt, Pas de Calais, France
British War Medal 1914-1920, Victory Medal 1914-1918

Sergeant, **John Cole Nattress**, 904189
son of Joseph Nattress & Ann Jane Cole, Bolton

William Neil

Robert Nelson
Castlederg

Lieutenant, **John Wesley Newlove**, MC, (medical doctor) United States Army
son of James H. Newlove & Jane Watson, Albion Twp., Macville
Military Cross

Private, **James Newman**, 234th Battalion

Corporal, **Charles Chester Nichol**, 11272, 4th Battalion
son of William R. Nichol & Sarah E. Porterfield, Sand Hill, Sept 22 1914

Private, **James Wardlow Norris**, 3109001, 102nd Battalion, stretcher bearer, 1917-1919
son of James H. Norris & Isabella Martin, Albion Twp.

Private, **Charles D. Norton**, 3035998
son of Alsey Norton & Margaret Ellen Devins, Bolton

Richard Overbury
of Bolton area after WW II

Joseph O'Leary

Private, **Arthur Palmer**
son of Joseph Palmer & Alice Porter, Albion Twp.

Ralph Palmer
son of Joseph Palmer & Alice Porter, Albion Twp.

Wilmer Palmer
son of Joseph Palmer & Alice Porter, Albion Twp.

Russell Parker, Nobleton

John Alexander Parr, 3311355
son of Samuel Alexander Parr & Sarah Jane Kelly, Toronto Gore Twp.

Charles Cecil Patterson, 721455, May 1918, returned to Canada, Aug 22 1919
son of Archibald Patterson & Alice Dickson, Vaughan Twp., Nashville area

John Ernest Patterson, 3037224
son of John Patterson & Margaret Crawford, Albion Twp.

Flight Lieutenant, **Wilford A. Patterson**, 2022562, Royal Flying Corps
son of David Patterson & Henrietta Robinson, Albion Twp.

Arthur Payne, Nobleton

Harry Payne
employed by Charles Bolton, Albion Twp.

William Payne
of Nobleton, employed by Thomas Dowzer, Albion Twp.

Fred Pellatt
born in England, employed in Albion Twp. area

Sergeant, **Oliver James Penrice**, 1024248, 234th Battalion
son of James Penrice & Mary Jane Williamson, Albion Twp.

Corporal, **James Michael Perdue**, 11279
son of Michael Perdue & Prudence Sparrow, Caledon East

Private, **John Hilliard Gray Perdue**, 3311378, 8th Battalion, Canadian Infantry, Central Ontario Regiment
son of John H. Perdue & Elizabeth Gray, Caledon East
died at sea enroute to France, Aug 13 1918
grave Panel 2., Halifax Memorial, Nova Scotia

Private, **William Tupper Perdue**, 775550, 126th Battalion, Jan 13 1916
son of Michael Perdue & Prudence Sparrow, Caledon East

John Henry Perry, 3109016, 2nd Central Ontario Regiment, May 6 1918
son of John Perry & Margaret Jane Mail, Albion Twp., Mono Road

Sapper, **Arthur Leroy Phillip**s, 778505, 127th York Rangers, Jan 26 1916
son of Jesse Phillips & Margaret Egan, Vaughan Twp.

William Phillips
son of George Phillips & Sarah Carson, Albion Twp., Palgrave

Chaplain, **Joseph Michael Pickett**, served for three years
son of John Pickett & Mary Ann McLelland, Albion Twp.

Albert W. Pilson, 768001, 50th Battalion, July 24 1915
son of Erastus Roger Pilson & Elleoner Ellen Mullins, Bolton

Corporal, **Cuthbert Samuel Pitchford**, 141834, 54th Battalion, Canadian Infantry, Central Ontario Regiment
son of Samuel & Elizabeth Ann Pitchford, Caledon East
enlisted at age 15, 1915
killed in France, Sept 2 1918
grave 11.D.25., Dury Mill British Cemetery, Pas de Calais, France

Sapper, **Joseph Prest**, 285631

Corporal, **John James Proctor**, 643655, 4th Battalion, Feb 12 1916
of Mono Mills area, son of George & Ann Proctor, Hockley
killed Nov 16 1918
Etaples Military Cemetery, Pas de Calais, France - grave L.D.16

Private, **William S. Proctor**, 3107979 2nd Depot Battalion, Oct 23 1917-Apr 24 1919
son of Joseph O. Proctor & Isabella Wiley, Caledon East

Major, (Chaplain), **Ernest Edgar Pugsley**
Palgrave

Private, **Culver Benson Purvis**, 540094, 3rd Division, Cyclists Corps
son of Charles B. Purvis & Florence Collver, Bolton

Lieutenant, **Maxwell Cline Purvis**, Air Force
son of Charles B. Purvis & Florence Collver, Bolton
according to the June 12, 1974 edition of the *Bolton Enterprise*, "Maxwell Cline Purvis, Q.C., a Toronto barrister, died last week. He will be remembered by older residents when his father conducted a general store business here during World War 1. Deceased established a notable record as a flyer during World War 1, piloting a Handley Bomber the longest distance into Germany. He was severely wounded while on a mission."

James Raeside, 404180
son of William Raeside Sr., Kleinburg

John Raeside
son of William Raeside Sr., Kleinburg

Corporal, **Robert Morris Raeside**, 404181, Canadian Machine Gun Corps
son of William Raeside Sr., Kleinburg, killed Apr 13 1917
grave 1.C.19., Bois-Carre British Cemetery, Thelus, Pas de Calais, France

William Raeside
son of William Raeside Sr., Kleinburg

John Lester Raine, 3109018, 2nd Ontario Regiment, 1917
son of John Raine & Eliza Bowles, near Tullamore

Leonard Rawn
son of John Rawn & Jane Henry, Caledon East

Captain, **Charles E. Read**, MC, 15th Battalion, 48th Highlander, 1915-1919, Military Cross
son of William Read & Isabel McGlinch, Toronto
According to his son Richard, "Captain Read was the last officer of the 48th Highlanders to be wounded during World War I, which occurred in November 1918." Charles Read and Mrs. Read with their family moved to Bolton about 1942.

Private, **Joe Reynar**, 3311544
Bolton

John Ernest Rhoebottom (Robotham), Mono Road

Sergeant, **William Randall Richardson**, 600, Canadian Army Dental Corps, Feb 8 1917-Oct 20 1917
son of Dr. William Richardson & Ada Christina Hickling, Barrie
after World War II, Sergeant Richardson established a dental practice in Bolton

Jere Riddell, Mono Road,

Sergeant, **W. Harry Rimmer**, 170th Battalion
son of John & Henrietta Rimmer, Bolton

Alvin Robb, 3037413
son of James Robb & Elizabeth Ballard, Vaughan Twp., Nashville area

Leonard Robb, 778369, 127th Battalion, 1916
son of Robert Robb & Sarah Smith, King Twp.

George Robinson, Mono Road

Nursing Sister, **Hattie Robinson**
daughter of George A. Robinson, Caledon Twp. near Inglewood

Captain, **Howard Parker Robinson**, (medical doctor), CAMC, Apr 5 1917
son of Dr. Thomas Harvey Robinson & Annie C. Hill, Kleinburg

Nursing Sister, **Laura Robinson**, 1915, 1919
daughter of George Arthur Robinson & Mary Edna Kaake, King Twp.

Private, **George James Rolley**, 670130, 166th Battalion, July 5 1916
son of John Rolley & Jane Moffatt, Albion Twp.
husband of Mary Coulter, Beeton

Private, **Percy John Roulston**, 652148
employed by R. W. Burrell & Son, Caledon East

Ashton Rowley
son of John Rowley & Sarah Elizabeth Taylor, Albion Twp.

Holland Bracken Rowley, 775168
son of John Rowley & Sarah Elizabeth Taylor, Albion Twp.

James Richard Rowley
son of Richard Rowley & Charlotte Walton, Albion Twp.

Norman James Stanley Rowley
son of Francis John Rowley & Ellen Elizabeth Lyons, Albion Twp.

Private, **Thomas J. Rowley**
son of Benjamin Rowley & Rebecca Jackson, Albion Twp.

Driver, **Cecil James Ruse**, 273696
Palgrave

Private, **Albert W. Ruston**, 2621 Canadian Army Service Corps, Divisional Ammunition Corps, 1914
son of Richard F. Ruston & Margaret Beasley
Lemburg, Saskatchewan - formerly Albion Twp., contracted pneumonia in Toronto and died Sept 12 1915,
interred at Laurel Hill Cemetery, Bolton

Lieutenant, **Frank Stewart Rutherford**, Royal Canadian Engineers, 1914
son of Henry Rutherford & Mary Ann Cassidy, Albion Twp.
Dr. Rutherford, BA. Sc, LL.D was appointed Deputy Minister of Education for the Province of Ontario serving
from January 17 1946 to July 8 1951 under the governments of Premiers George Drew, Thomas L. Kennedy and
Leslie Frost.

Private, **Lloyd George Rutherford**, 3109020
son of Albert S. Rutherford & Hannah R. Tindale, Albion Twp.

Private, **Tindale Rutherford**
son of Albert S. Rutherford & Hannah R. Tindale, Albion Twp.

Captain, **Stanley David Rutledge**, 34559, 2nd General Hospital Corps, 1914
son of John Rutledge & Maria Hesp, Bolton

Tony Sacre
of Bolton area after WW II

Bill Salwarsky
born in Russia, employed in Nobleton area

Hartley H. Sanderson, 3234232, 1st Central Ontario Regiment, Apr 30 1918
son of Augusta Sanderson & Ellen Beatty, Caledon East

William John Sanford, 3236557, Canadian Garrison Regiment, Nov 11 1917
born in Shelburne, employed in Palgrave area, husband of Edith, Shelburne

Private, **Stephen James Sanford**, 1024353, 234th Battalion, Sept 30 1916-Mar 1919
born in Chatham, Kent, England, employed by Bert Bishop, Albion Twp.
next of kin - mother, Georgina Sanford, Chatham, Kent, England

Seaman, **Fred Saturday**, Navy
husband of Grace Rivett, King Twp., employed by Cold Creek Trout Club

Private, **Cecil George Savage**, 725052, 109th Bttalion, Dec 22 1915
brother of Arthur Savage, Meaford - employed in Palgrave area

Fred Henry B. Saxon, 408118, 37th Battalion, June 10 1915
born at Streetsville - next of kin - Mrs. Carrie Saxon, Streetsville
lived in Bolton area in later years

Private, **Eley Scott Scarlett**, 201264, 3rd Battalion, Oct 8 1915
of Mono Mills, born in England, son of James & Celia Scarlett
of "The Hermitage", Linden Grove, Taunton, Somerset, England
killed Dec 11 1916, Villers Station Cemetery, Villers-Au-Bois, Pas de Calais, France grave 111.C.19.

Private, **Arthur Scott**, 725226 109th Battalion, Canadian Infantry, Central Ontario Regiment, Feb 8 1916
was a Dr. Barnardo Home boy from England who from the age of 10, was raised by Mr. & Mrs. Charles H. Rutherford (Florence Black), Albion Twp.
killed Aug 15 1917, grave I.J.9., Aix-Noulette Communal Cemetery Extension, Pas de Calais, France

Corporal, **Frederick Scowen**, 775178, 126th Battalion, Dec 20 1915
employed in Mono Road area, next of kin - Annie Scowen, London, England

William Albert Seal, 55116, Nov 10 1914
born in Portstade by Sea, Sussex England, son of Benjamin Seal, Sussex England
husband of Minnie Seal, Toronto, employed in Caledon East area

Sergeant, **Gilbert Henry Searle**, 767087, 123rd Battalion, Dec 27 1915
born in England, employed in Castlederg area, Albion Twp.
son of Henry J. & Ellen Annette Searle, Brampton

Private, **Leonard John Searle**, 135307, 1st Battalion, Canadian Infantry, Western Ontario Regiment,
July 28 1915, born in England, employed in Castlederg area, Albion Twp.
son of Henry J. & Ellen Annette Searle, Brampton, killed July 2 1916, grave 52.33725., Nunhead (AllSaints) Cemetery, London, United Kingdom

Private, **John Joseph Sharp**, MM, 643407, 116th Battalion, Feb 12 1916
son of William & Rachael Sharp of Tecumseh and Vaughan Townships
Military Medal, killed Aug 14 1918
grave A.9. Boves West Communal Cemetery Extension, Somme, France

Sergeant, **Sidney Shaw**, 5756, Princess Patricia Light Infantry, Sept 23 1914
was a Scout Master in Bolton, born in India
son of E. Shaw, Portsmouth England, died in Toronto after World War I

Private, **Hugh James Sheardown**, 3109025, 2nd Central Ontario Regiment, Oct 27, 1917-1918
son of James Sheardown & Sarah Ann Campbell, King Twp.

Private, **Lawrence Sheardown**, 3235189, 1st Central Ontario Regiment, May 21 1918
son of Charles Sheardown & Louisa Vanderburgh, King Twp.

Private, **William Tyndill Sheardown**, 1010293, 229th Battalion, Apr 5 1917, enlisted at Moose Jaw, Sakatchewan, son of George Sheardown & Mary Maud Lundy, Bolton
husband of Ethel Adeline Stinson, La Fleche, Saskatchewan

Albert Shepherd, Mono Road

George Shepherd, Mono Road

Peter T. Shepherd, Mono Road

Harold Walter William Shinn, 763289, 122nd Battalion, Feb 12 1916
born in England, employed by Alfred Tindale, Albion Twp.
son of Emily Pearson, Kingsway, London England

Private, **Robert Slade**, 775189, 126th Battalion, Dec 27 1915
employed in Mono Road area
son of Edith Slade, Bridgewater, Somerset England

George Smart
employed in Albion Twp., enlisted at Gravenhurst

Archie Smith, 838183 147th Grey Battalion, Dec 4 1915
born in North Bay, employed in Nobleton area
brother of Mrs. Leonard Ross, Cookstown

Fred Smith

Private, **James Campbell Smith**, 3037414, 1st Central Ontario Regiment, May 11 1918-1919
son of James C. Smith & Florence MacMurchy, Vaughan Twp., Nashville area

Sergeant, **Joseph Smith**, 722193, 108th Battalion, Mar 2 1916
son of John Smith, Albion Twp., husband of Margaret Smith, Stonewall, Manitoba

Private, **Thomas Edward Smith**, 775957, 38th Battalion, Canadian Infantry, Eastern Ontario Regiment
brother of Harry Smith, Nashville, employed by Richard Mashinter, Albion Twp
killed in France June 28 1917, grave 11.A.6., La Chaudiere Military Cemetery, Vimy, Pas de Calais, France

Private, **William Ernest Smith**, 775571, 126th Battalion, Jan 12 1916
from the Dr. Bernardo Home, England - lived in Mono Road area

Albert Smithers, 778124, 127thYork Rangers, Dec 21 1915
son of Thomas Alexander Smithers & Mary Agar, Vaughan Twp.

William Smithers, 778452 127th York Rangers, Jan 6 1916
son of Thomas Alexander Smithers & Mary Agar, Vaughan Twp.

Private, **Patrick Sarsfield Arthur Smyth**, 887724, 46th Battalion, Jan 24 1916, Canadian Infantry,
Saskatchewan Regiment
son of Thomas & Mary Ann Smyth, Vaughan Twp.
Nashville area - husband of Mary Smyth, Humbolt, Saskatchewan
killed Apr 12 1917, Vimy Memorial, Pas de Calais, France

Colonel, **Arthur Evans Snell**, CAMC, Aug 24 1914, May 21 1920, Croix de Guerre, CMG DSO, MiD
son of Samuel J. Snell & Elizabeth Evans, Bolton
husband of Henrietta F. Fleischunaun, London
Croix de Guerre, Companion of the Order of St. Michael and St. George, Distinguished Service Order
Mention-in-Despatches - 4 times
Colonel Snell was appointed Deputy Assistant Director Medical Services of the Canadian Army Medical Corps on
September 13 1915, Assistant Director Medical Services on May 17 1916 and Deputy Director Medical Services
on July 17 1918 .

Sergeant, **Charles E. Snell**, MM, 300604, 34th Battalion, Aug 18 1915
son of William Snell & Florence Dean, Albion Twp., Macville
Military Medal

Private, **Albert Earl Snider**, 3037416, 'C' Company, #78 Infantry, May 11 1918-Mar 24 1919
son of Harvey Snider & Elizabeth Starratt, King Twp.

Private, **Roy Manley Sparrow**, 252494 28th Battalion, Canadian Infantry,
Saskatchewan Regiment, Mar 15 1916
son of Samuel Sparrow & Annie Shaw, Sand Hill
killed in France May 8 1917
Vimy Memorial, Pas de Calais, France

Elgin Speers, 3311384, 2nd Central Ontario Regiment, June 3 1918
son of Alexander D. Speers & Margaret Benson, Caledon East

Victor Spencer
Caledon Twp., killed

Lance Corporal, **Charles Spendiff**, 928466, Jan 14 1916
son of Percy Spendiff, Fonthill, employed in Mono Mills area

Erle Charles Spinks, 3109026, 2nd Central Ontario Regiment, May 6 1918
son of Charles Spinks, Caledon East

Private, **William Squires**, 228084, 201st Battalion, Feb 24 1916
son of Mary Ellen Squires, Bolton

Private, **Gordon Thomas Stanfield**, 775570, 126th Battalion, Jan 8 1916
son of Emily Stanfield, Palgrave

Lance Corporal, **Phillip Stephenson**, 681435, Canadian Machine Gun Corps, Mar 13 1916
son of Jane Stephenson, Yorkshire, England
employed by Ebenezer Armstrong, Albion Twp., killed Nov 3 1917
grave XX1.HH.17., Ligssenthoek Military Cemetery, Poperinge, West-Vlaanderen, Belgium

Lyle Stewart
son of Robert Stewart & Minnie Davis, King Twp.

Roy Stewart

Russell Stewart
son of James Stewart & Martha Armstrong, Caledon East

Private, **James Edward Stinson**, 853604, 117th Battalion, Mar 23 1916
born in Palgrave, husband of Elizabeth Stinson, Allandale

Private, **William Thomas Stinson**, 2191, 126th Battalion, Sept 26 1914
employed in Palgrave area, son of Hiram Stinson, Orangeville

Alfred Ernest St. John, 467182, Sept 6 1915
son of Thomas Roe St. John & Mary Roulston, Palgrave

Private, **James Alexander St. John**, 1025, 8th Canadian Infantry Battalion, 1914
son of Thomas Roe St. John & Mary Roulston, Palgrave

George Arthur Stokes, 3231706, 1st Central Ontario Regiment, Jan 28 1918
son of George Sr. & Maude Stokes , Bolton

Private, **Albert Strong**
son of Stephen Strong & Sarah Jane Norris, Albion Twp.

Private, **Earle Joseph Strong**, 463716, 7th Battalion, Canadian Infantry,
British Columbia Regiment, Aug 7 1915
son of Joseph T. Strong & Margaret Broley, Albion Twp.
killed Nov 10 1917
grave Panel 18-28-30, Ypres (Menin Gate) Memorial, Ieper, West-Vlaanderen, Belgium

Private, **Frederick Robert Oliver Strong**, 3311386, 2nd Central Ontario Regiment, June 3 1918-Dec 1918
son of Stephen Strong & Sarah Jane Norris, Albion Twp.

Private, **Albert Stronge**, 775564, 116th Battalion, Canadian Infantry, Dec 23 1915
son of Annie Stronge, Toronto, employed by William Shore, Palgrave
killed at Vimy Ridge, May 21 1917
grave C.13., Petit-Vimy British Cemetery, Pas de Calais, France

Fred Stubbs, 142169, 76th Battalion, July 27 1915
son of James Stubbs & Esther Harrison, Bolton

Private, **Wilfred Joseph Stych**, 775573, Canadian Infantry, Jan 17 1916-Aug 27 1918
son of Joseph Stych & Mary Emma Lyons, Ballycroy, Eastern Ontario Regiment

Private, **George Essington Styles (Stiles)**, 3035755, 1st Central Ontario Regiment
employed in Albion Twp. area, son of William Stiles, Toronto, Oct 12 1918

Private, **George Swindle**, 775577, 126th Battalion, Jan 24 1916
born in Bangor, Ireland – lived at Ballycroy, next of kin, William Swindle, Ireland

Lieutenant, **William Colborne Sanders Switzer**
son of John C. Switzer & Martha Sparrow, Bolton

Earl Sykes
Bolton, killed

Private, **Edwin Arthur Tatum**, 775580, 126th Battalion, Jan 10 1916
son of Edwin Tatum & Jesse Heitman, Palgrave

Sergeant, **Frederick A. Taylor**
son of Jeremiah Taylor & Jane Stewart, Palgrave

Private, **Harry Taylor**, 126th Battalion
employed by James H. Newlove, Albion Twp., Macville

William Thatcher, of Bolton after WW II

Sergeant, **Charles Ernest Thomas**, 45340, T.D. Engineers, Jan 15 1915-Feb 5 1919
son of William Thomas & Hannah Wilson, Vaughan Twp.
Canadian Engineers Medal 1914-1915
The Great War for Civilization Medal 1914-1919
British War Medal 1914-1918

George Thomas
lived in the Tullamore area

Private, **Robert Franklin Thomas**, 3235638, 19th Battalion, June 4 1918-Oct 1 1919
son of Robert H. Thomas & Sarah McWade, Albion Twp.,

Captain, **F.L. Thompson**, Winnipeg Forestry Battalion
Bolton

Private, **George William Thompson**, 775579, 126th Battalion, Nov 7 1915
son of Alice Thompson, Palgrave

Private, **William Thompson**, 126th Battalion, Nov 11 1917
employed at Mr. Clarke's, Castlederg, killed

Private, **Alfred Tomsett**, Mono Road

Private, **Albert Nelson Train**, 234226, 52nd Battalion
son of John Train & Ann Gummerson, Vaughan Twp.

Cadet, **George Morley Train**, 540252
son of John Train & Ann Gummerson, Vaughan Twp.

Albert Trainor, 151966
son of Michael J. & Ellen Trainor, Kleinburg

Lance Corporal, **John William Tribble**, 541678, 4th Canadian Signal Corps, Canadian Engineers, Dec 1915
son of Adam Tribble & Mary Louise Kingsbury, Albion Twp.
killed at the Battle of Ypres Oct 23 1917
grave V1.E.4., Nine Elms British Cemetery, Poperinge, West-Vlaanderen, Belgium

Private, **James Turner**, Canadian Engineers
of Bolton area after WW II

James Russell Turner, 643410, 75th Battalion
son of George Turner & Margaret Quigley, Palgrave, killed Nov 14 1917
grave Panel 18-24-26-30, Ypres (Menin Gate) Memorial Ieper, West Vlaanderen, Belgium

John Spurgeon Veals, 3060186 1st Depot Battalion, May 25 1918
son of Charles Gillard Veals & Catharine Herbert, Cavan Twp.
According to the Caledon East United Church History and the Salem United Church History, Rev. Veals was born in Omemee and entered the Ministry in 1920. He served at several Churches before taking charge of the Mono Road Circuit which was comprised of Macville, Sand Hill and Salem United Churches. He ministered there from 1941 to 1951. In 1960 he retired and moved to Caledon East where he remained until his death.

Charles Veer, Caledon Twp.

William Walder

Private, **Albert R.Walker**, 775592, 116th Battalion, Jan 10 1916
son of John Walker & Agnes Marshall, Palgrave
killed Aug 8 1918, grave Sp. Mem. Hourges Orchard Cemetery, Domart-Sur-La-Luce, Somme, France

Captain, **Robertson Roy Walker**, Dentist, CADC
son of Rev. George Walker & Louisa M. Robertson, Bolton

Captain, **Stanley Arthur Walker**, Medical Doctor, RAMC, 6th Cheshire Battalion
son of Rev. George Walker & Louisa M. Robertson, Bolton
killed Oct 14 1916, grave V111.A.9. Lonsdale Cemetery, Authuile, Somme, France

Wesley W. Walker, 775593
son of John Walker & Agnes Marshall, Palgrave

Sergeant, **Adam Wallace**, DCM, MM and Bar, 405455, 35th Battalion & 26th New Brunswick Battalion
Aug 23 1915-May 17 1919
son of Robert J. Wallace & Mary Jane McGee, Bolton,
Distinguished Conduct Medal; Military Medal and Bar; The Great War for Civilization Medal 1914-1919;
The War Service Medal 1914-1918

Captain, **Herbert Ellerslie Wallace**, Medical Doctor, CAMC, Apr 19 1916
son of Dr. James M. Wallace & Jane Agnes Craig, Edwardsburg Twp.
husband of Annie E. Bonnar (daughter of Dr. David Bonner & Catherine McCauley)
father of Margaret Annie Wallace, Bolton. Captain Wallace was a Bolton physician prior to the war and located
on King Street. He moved to the former Bowes residence on Nancy Street in October 1908.

Captain, **Nathaniel Clarke Wallace**, 81st Battalion, Oct 9 1915
son of Hon. N. Clarke Wallace & Belinda Gilmour, Vaughan Twp.
husband of Louise Burritt Lockhart

Thomas Wallace
of Mono Road, son of William Wallace & Annie Ingoldsby - hotelkeepers at Lockton

James Walsh

William James Walton, 721696, Jan 7 1916, enlisted at Stonewall Manitoba
son of Abraham Walton & Ellen Blain, Albion Twp.

Norman Butler Walton, 441907, "A" Company, Mar 1 1916, enlisted at Winnipeg Manitoba
son of Isaac Walton & Mary Armstrong, Vaughan Twp.

John W. Ward
Vaughan Twp., killed

Lance Corporal, **Sydney Mason Ward**, 775583, 126th Battalion, Nov 12 1915
of Bolton, born in Ashford, Kent England – son of Elsie E. Ward, Peterborough

P.J. Warden

Thomas Joseph Warden, 775209, 126th Battalion, Jan 14 1916
born in Warwick, England – husband of Ada Warden, Mono Road

Private, **Stanley C. Warrell**, 193400, 13th Battalion, Canadian Infantry, Quebec Regiment
Vaughan Twp.
killed Sept 23 1916, Bouzincourt Ridge Cemetery, Albert, Somme, France - grave 111.D.12.

Earl Warwick

Arthur Watkins, Caledon Twp.

Lieutenant, **Charles Harold Watson**, Canadian Field Artillery
son of George C. Watson & Margaret Ann Bell, Albion Twp., 4th Brigade
killed at Amiens, France Aug 11 1918
grave 111.D.18., Rosieres Communal Cemetery Extension, Somme, France

Thomas Wilford Watson
son of Thomas Blakely Watson & Mary Ann Robinson, Albion Twp.

Wilfred Alexander Ross Watson, 3109701,
son of James Watson & Esther Ann Harper, Albion Twp.

Charles Watts, Caledon East

Richard Watts, Caledon East

William Watts, Caledon East

Nelson Wauchope, 3037447
son of Samuel Wauchope & Maria Ellen McDonald, Albion Twp.

James Webster
Mono Road, killed

Sergeant, **Edward J. Weeks**, 112996, 36th Battalion
born in England, employed in Albion Twp. area of Macville

Thomas Allison Weir, 340349, 69th Overseas Battery, Nov 14 1917
son of Thomas Weir & Martha Blair, Caledon East

Wilbert Wellar
son of Nelson Wellar & Janet MacGillivray, King Twp.

Joseph Wesley Welwood, 888226, 188th Battalion, Feb 19 1916-Nov 15 1916
son of John Welwood, Caledon Twp., near Orangeville

Norman Welwood, 745246, 116th Battalion, Jan 7 1916
son of John Welwood, Caledon Twp., near Orangeville

Captain, **Thomas Richard Welwood**, (physician), No. 10 Tr. Depot, Sept 15 1916
son of John Welwood, Caledon Twp., near Orangeville
husband of Martha Cicely, Neudorf, Saskatchewan

Private, **William James Welwood**, 663223, 164th Battalion, Canadian Machine Gun Corps
son of John Welwood, Caledon Twp., near Orangeville
killed Oct 30 1917
grave XX1V.F.23., Tyne Cot Cemetery, Zonnebeke, West-Vlaanderen, Belgium

Harry White, Mono Road

Private, **George Whitehead**
born in England, employed by Jarvis Elliott, Mono Road, enlisted at age 16
received wounds necessitating the amputation of a leg

Lieutenant, **Henry Alvin Whitmore**, DSO
Vaughan Twp., Distinguished Service Order

Roy Whitmore, Vaughan Twp.

Charlie Wicks, Mono Road

Norval Williams
son of Harry Williams, Churchill area of Albion Twp.

Thomas H. Williamson
son of Frank Williamson & Delia Hall, Albion Twp.

Albert Henry Wilson, 3039399, 1st Central Ontario Regiment, May 25 1918
son of Thomas Wilson & Martha Wilson, Sand Hill

Charles Hunter Wilson, Royal Flying Corps
son of John Condie Wilson & Amelia Jane Haas, St. George, Ontario
After World War II Charles Hunter Wilson became a popular medical doctor in Bolton. His practice and residence was located at the former Dr. John Graham home at 34 Temperance Street.

Private, **Frank R. Wilson**, 135243, Canadian Infantry, Manitoba Regiment
son of William George Wilson & Eliza Ann Dean, Albion Twp.
killed at Flanders, France, Aug 21 1916
grave Mem. D.7., Railway Dugouts Burial Ground, Ieper, West-Vlaanderen, Belgium

John Parr Wilson
son of John Wilson & Martha Parr, Albion Twp.

Reuban Calvin Wilson, 535486
son of John Wilson & Martha Parr, Albion Twp., Medical Doctor

Private, **Richard Wilson**, 234th Battalion
son of Thomas P. Wilson & Eliza Hamilton, Albion Twp.

Robert Mervin Wilson, 2498385, Forestry Corps, Oct 31 1917
son of William James Wilson & Mary Ann Nelson, Albion Twp.

Victor Wilson, Caledon Twp.

Private, **Wesley Wilson**, Bolton

Henry Wimpenny
son of George Wimpenny & Margaret Carey, Albion Twp.

Thomas Wise, Nobleton

Trooper, **Elmer Witherspoon**, 225364
son of David Witherspoon & Mary Blough, Kleinburg

Wilbert David Witherspoon, 114396
son of David Witherspoon & Mary Blough, Kleinburg

George Mills Wolfe, 106636
son of Richard Wolfe & Martha Jane Mills, Albion Twp.

Private, **James Alfred Wolfe**, 229403, 61st Battalion, June 5 1915-Apr 12 1919, enlisted at Winnipeg
son of Captain James A. Wolfe & Ann Verner, Albion Twp.

Sergeant, **John O. Wolfe**, MM, 865865
son of Richard Wolfe & Martha Jane Mills, Albion Twp.
Military Medal

Lieutenant, **Lloyd Wolfe**, 624689
son of Richard Wolfe & Martha Jane Mills, Albion Twp.

Herbert Wesley Wood, 3038473
son of Alfred Wood & Angeline Copithorn, King Twp.

Howard Wood, 3037439

Corporal, **Robert Edgar Wood**, 775585, 126th Battalion, Jan 11 1915, Mar 1919
son of John C. Wood & Prudence Hannah Fox, Bolton

Private, **William Henry Wood**, 775584, 116th Battalion, Canadian Infantry, Jan 11 1915
son of John C. Wood & Prudence Hannah Fox, Bolton
died of wounds in France, July 23 1917
grave H.15., Bruay Communal Cemetery Extension, Pas de Calais, France

Sergeant, **Harry Wheeler Woods**, MM, 57040, 20th Canadian Battalion, Nov 11 1914
lived in Mono Road area, born at Hartlepoole, Durham England
next of kin - James Woods, Sparkbrook, Birmingham England, Military Medal

Alfred M. Wright
employed by Herb Downey, Albion Twp.

Private, **Walter A. Wylie**, 910934, 196th University Battalion, enlisted at Yorkton, returned to Canada, Jan 27 1919, son of William Wylie & Sarah Archer, Theodore, Saskatchewan, husband of Lillian Blanche Robinson, father of Glenna, Allan and Donald

Donald Wylie has supplied the following information about his dad's war service which is copied from the February 11 1919 edition of the Yorkton Press. "It is a far cry from Theodore to the battlefields of Europe but the boys of the prairie town lost no time in responding to the call for men. Among the many enlisting from that point were three boys of nearly the same age. They had been inseparables at school while sitting at the feet of that prince of educators, the late Peter Yemen, and as a trio they enlisted in the 196th University Battalion.

Of the three Private Thomas L. Tracy and Private R. W. Mercer served in the Canadian Motor Machine Gun Corps and at Passchendaele, Tracy was killed and Mercer wounded. Mercer was again wounded in the great drive made by the Germans on 21st March last but he is again in the field and acting as despatch rider in the army of occupation in Germany.

Private Walter A. Wylie was wounded by shrapnel in the battle of Amiens and the section in which he had been was wiped out by gas a few days afterwards. He returned to his home on January 27.

Privates Wylie and Tracy are well known in Yorkton, Private Wylie attending Collegiate and both taking their Normal course here. Immediately prior to enlistment Private Mercer was teller in the Union Bank at Wawota."

Moving from Saskatchewan to Bolton in 1932, Dr. W.A. Wylie became a prominent citizen and popular family physician in the village. His practice and residence was at 69 King Street West, now the location of the Allan L. Naiman law firm, and then at the corner of Ann and Sterne Streets in 1941, on the lot presently occupied by the Town of Caledon Fire and Ambulance Building.

Sergeant Major, **William Edward Yarranton**, also served in the Boer War
son of William Yarranton and Sarah Baldwin, Worchester England
He lived at Mono Road in the house now owned by Alex and Edith Hutchinson on Airport Road.

George Young, Mono Mills

⟪⟪ PART II ⟫⟫
CANADA IN WORLD WAR II
1939-1945

Barely twenty years had passed before The Great War of 1914-1918 acquired a new name: *World War I.* For despite the great dreams of peace and international cooperation that followed the "war to end all wars", a second conflagration, a conflict even wider than its predecessor, soon flared around the globe. By the time it ended in 1945, World War II had embroiled almost all the countries on the planet, some by choice, some in response to invasion or attack, still others solely by virtue of their location. Canada became deeply involved right from the beginning and, just as in the first war, played a far greater role than anyone thought possible, given the country's population, wealth, and traditional attitude toward military strength.

Again, a Recipe for War

Ironically, most of the countries drawn into World War I in 1914, found themselves involved again in 1939 even though they had taken special steps to prevent such a thing. On January 10, 1920, a League of Nations (with Canada as an independent, contributing member) was formally established to preserve peace by settling disputes through negotiation and compromise. It was a lofty ideal but in reality, too much to hope for. Even while the agreement was being signed, there was civil war in Russia; French troops were fighting in Syria; communist troops from Hungary were attacking Bulgaria; British troops were fighting in Afghanistan; there was war between Russia and Finland; Poland invaded the Ukraine, and Japan was making incursions in Manchuria. Meanwhile, barely noticed on the world stage, a strange character named Benito Mussolini had established himself as leader of the Fascist Party of Italy. In Germany, an equally strange - and equally obscure - character by the name of Adolf Hitler had taken over a tiny group of activists and renamed it the National Socialist German Workers Party.

Germany Slides into Fascism

Although the League of Nations did indeed resolve some disagreements successfully, it failed a most crucial test when it did not intervene with Germany and Italy in the mid-1930s. Although the first and most dramatic defiance came from Italy - it invaded Abyssinia (Ethiopia) in 1935 - it was Germany, under Adolf Hitler, and the Nazi Party that made it clear that the League of Nations was ineffective.

In retrospect, the rise of Nazism and militarism in Germany may well have been inevitable because of the terms of the Treaty of Versailles that ended World War I. Under this treaty, Germany was forbidden to re-arm in a manner that would enable her to wage war. This was a reasonable enough concept given the country's policies in the years before and after 1914. But the treaty also dictated an extensive set of harsh and impoverishing provisions, including the loss of territories and loss of industry and patents (like the patent for aspirin). These latter impositions were especially important because they reduced Germany's capacity to make the huge reparation payments that the treaty also demanded. All these terms, along with civil unrest, monstrous inflation, and unemployment had created a huge pool of resentment in Germany, one that Hitler and his party found opportune in the 1920s and 30s.

Nobody Said "Stop!"

In 1935, in direct violation of the Treaty of Versailles, Germany introduced compulsory military service and then, in 1936, defied both the treaty and the League of Nations by re-militarizing the Rhineland. In the same year, the League sat on its hands while Italy invaded Ethiopia. Within the next two years Germany reclaimed the territory it had lost and took in even more. Across the world in Asia, Japan had taken control of Manchuria, had invaded China, and was threatening the entire Asian subcontinent. War, a worldwide war, it seemed, was imminent.

Unlike the period before World War I, the years leading up to the second great conflict were not marked by huge, universal military buildups. Just before 1914, all the important countries of Europe had large forces and had no hesitation about using them. Prior to 1939, only Germany and Italy (and Japan, in Asia) were engaged in building military strength in a big way. Yet even these countries did not have particularly overwhelming strength. Italy never got itself close to the level that Mussolini imagined, and not until well into 1940-41 did German war production really start to roll. (For the invasion of Poland in September 1939, the German army relied principally on horse-drawn transport.) Still, the German armed forces were far more ready than Britain and France, the only countries likely to oppose them. Russia was even less ready, especially since Stalin had executed many of his generals in the 1930s, and the U.S., unprepared and full of out-dated equipment, was officially 'isolationist'.

Appeasement Doesn't Work; War Begins

By 1939, it was apparent to almost everyone that if Hitler remained in command in Germany - and to a lesser extent, if Mussolini continued to run Italy's affairs - then sooner or later, they would have to be opposed militarily. Yet for reasons that continue to be debated, the soon-to-be Allies conducted a policy of appeasement. Led by Britain, the Allies stood by while Hitler and Mussolini formed the Rome-Berlin Axis in 1936. They stood by while Germany annexed Austria in 1938, and then they agreed to sacrifice Czechoslovakia for what they thought was peace. Italy, having successfully defeated the spear-carrying Abyssinian army with its tanks - the invasion was actually agreed to in advance by the foreign ministers of Britain and France - now invaded Albania and began to threaten Greece.

Despite all this frightening activity, and despite the fact that both Axis powers had added virulent anti-Semitism to their governing policies, the Allies still found a positive element in the mix. Hitler and the Nazi Party, along with Mussolini and the Fascist Party, were unalterably opposed to communism, and if there was one principle on which both the Allies and the Axis were on-side, that was it. Thus the Allies took comfort in the belief that their appeasement policy was containing international communism. That cloud of illusion, however, was blown away in 1939 when Germany signed a non-aggression pact with the USSR (among the terms of which was carving up Poland). Thus when Germany marched into Poland on September 1, 1939, the Allies knew the jig was up. Two days later, Britain and France declared war.

Canada Gets Into the Fray

Across Canada, in those first days of September, radios in every home were tuned to the latest news, awaiting word from the House of Commons in Ottawa. What would Canada do? For just as Canadians have a reputation of hoping for compromise until the last possible moment, they also have a reputation for getting into the fray when they are needed. Everyone knew the country would be involved. Nevertheless, in 1939, Canadians didn't want a war. Like every one of the Allies, this country had been generally supportive of the policy of appeasing Hitler. Prime Minister William Lyon Mackenzie King had even publicly thanked British PM, Neville Chamberlain, for sacrificing Czechoslovakia in 1938. Canada's collective memory of The Great War was still strong; there were still unpaid debts from the conflict; and Canadian unity was still hurting from the conscription crisis.

In addition, during the late 1930s, the country was indulging in its peculiar national habit: the belief that most of the problems were "over there", and until it was necessary to do something, it would do nothing. However, once Britain declared war, the 'something' took precedence over the 'nothing' and Canada was soon into it. Significantly, Canada did not declare war until September 10, an expression of its independence from Britain and of its power to make a declaration on its own. Although the British government had already said, "It is hoped that Canada would exert her full national effort as in the last war" when Prime Minister Mackenzie King inquired about Britain's expectations, King was merely being courteous. Canada felt she was her own boss now.

The date of September 10 had a special significance for this country for in the Atlantic only the day before, the ocean liner S.S. Athenia, with many Canadians aboard - including some from this area - was sunk by German U-boats. The date also marked the second time in the twentieth century that Canada would enter a military conflict with almost nothing to offer by way of equipment or forces, and by the end of the affair become a major player. On September 16, 1939, for example, just six days after the declaration of war, the first convoy to leave Halifax for England was under way, protected by a Royal Canadian Navy escort: just two destroyers and one flying boat; it was all the country could muster! Yet by the end of the war, Canada had the world's fourth largest navy.

War Around the World

While Canada was gearing itself up to participate in the conflict, a string of military events changed the world so rapidly and so profoundly that this country's role as a supplier of armed forces and of war material, as a protector of the air and the oceans, and as a great food bank, grew daily in importance. Poland fell to Germany in a few weeks. (Its defence was made even more impossible when the USSR invaded from the east.) Then in the spring of 1940, Germany took Norway, Denmark, Belgium, Holland and Luxembourg, and on May 24, invaded France.

Before 1939, the French, in what was clearly one of the most inept pieces of strategy in both world wars, had planned to hold off Germany with a line of forts, called the Maginot Line. The Germans simply went around the forts and France fell in a month. The British Expeditionary Force, sent to France in 1939, was hurriedly evacuated.

Then, with France defeated and Britain on its knees, Italy declared war on both countries. There followed the legendary air war, the 'Battle of Britain', in the fall of 1940 in which the Royal Air Force (with many Canadian pilots involved) held off the mighty Luftwaffe. Meanwhile in Asia, Japan invaded Indo-China (Vietnam) and in North Africa, Italy attacked Somaliland and Egypt, British protectorates, and from Albania launched an attack on Greece. That attack failed badly so Germany took over in 1941 and quickly succeeded. Germany also took Yugoslavia that year after the Yugoslavian leadership, on the brink of joining the Axis powers, was overthrown by a pro-Allies coup. The German war effort also spread to North Africa in order to bail out the Italian army there, and in 1941, in a major shift of strategy, Germany turned on its erstwhile partner, the USSR, and launched a great drive to the east.

On the oceans, the German navy, particularly the U-boat section, was sinking thousands and thousands of tons of Allied shipping, especially in the Atlantic, and even within sight of the Canadian coast in the Gulf of St. Lawrence. (On the surface, the German and British navies had helped spread the fighting; for example, a naval battle on the River Plate between Argentina and Uruguay had brought the war to South America in December 1939.) In December 1941, because it wanted a free hand in the Pacific Ocean for its conquest of southern Asia - and perhaps Australia - Japan made a pre-emptive strike on Pearl Harbour.

In the air, the Battle of Britain had demonstrated the importance of aerial warfare, a fact that became underlined when the U.S. joined the war, after Pearl Harbour. That attack and its aftermath (the Battle of Midway in the Pacific, for example) proved the value of aircraft

German U-boat (U-190) surrendered off the coast of Newfoundland in 1945.

German U-boat (U-889) shown after her surrender to RCN ships off Shelburne, Nova Scotia, May 1945.

carriers and of mass bombing techniques. Over the remainder of the war, it was the bombing of war production facilities, perhaps more than anything else, that ultimately defeated the Axis powers, especially Germany.

By early 1942, every country in the world was either directly involved in the war or, if neutral, remained so only with maximum effort. But it was from this point on, with Allied air forces bombing Germany relentlessly, Allied navies developing ever better convoy styles and submarine detection techniques, and the sheer weight of personnel and material the Allies could produce, that the defeat of Germany and Japan in 1945 became inevitable. (Italy surrendered in 1943.) Yet to accomplish this took a massive effort from the Allies. It involved everything from a teenage girl making bomb triggers in Malton, Ontario, to the 130,000 Allied troops that landed on the beaches of Normandy in June 1944, to the Canadian Cree and American Navajo people who taught Allied troops native languages that would stymie Japanese codebreakers. In Canada, there was not a citizen anywhere who was left untouched by this war.

By December 1939, the 1st Canadian Division was in England, training at Aldershot near Salisbury Plain. Many other regiments followed, including the Lorne Scots from Peel and Dufferin, which left for Europe in January 1940. The 2nd Canadian Infantry Division reached England in mid-1940. (In this book you can read the letters written by our local men from England during this training period.) However it was not until 1943 that Canadian land forces really saw action, and then, a lot of it.

Canadian Forces in the Air

In the air it was a different story. So many young men crossed the Atlantic to join Britain's Royal Air Force that by the fall of 1939 there were more Canadians flying with the RAF than with the Royal Canadian Air Force. Soon "all-Canadian" fighter squadrons were formed and facilities were set up to train Canadian airmen. By August of 1940, the No. 1 Fighter Squadron of the RCAF was engaged in battle over Germany. About 80 Canadian airmen flew in the famous Battle of Britain, some in the all-Canadian RAF 242 Squadron. In the following years, the Royal Canadian Air Force had a major part in the night bombing raids over Germany. It was costly, too. During a daylight mission to Hamburg, Germany, for example, on March 31, 1945, when the war in Europe had only about five weeks to go, eight Canadian Lancaster bombers were shot down by Messerschmitt jet fighters. By the end of the war in 1945, the RCAF had 48 squadrons on duty, patrolling the Atlantic out of bases in Canada, and serving overseas out of bases in Britain, Africa, Italy, northwest Europe, southeast Asia and the northern Pacific. In total, a quarter of a million men and women served in Canada's air force during the war. Of this number 17,101 never came home.

...On Land

In 1943, the 1st Canadian Armoured Brigade accompanied the British in their advance to Florence after the fall of Rome on June 4, 1943 and right after that, the first Canadian infantrymen landed in Sicily. The Italian campaign was a tough slog for the Canadian troops. By the time they were withdrawn in early 1945 and sent to Holland and France, almost 100,000 had fought there, and 5,764 lost their lives. (First-hand accounts of the fighting in

Italy, with all the dangers and difficulties encountered, are set out in the letters from local servicemen.) The army made an even larger contribution in northwest Europe, participating in the difficult advance toward Germany after D-Day. They played a key role in the liberation of Holland where, to this day, the grateful people of that country keep the memory of Canadian soldiers vigorously alive. Some 237,000 of our country's men and women served in the campaigns of northwestern Europe, and of that number 11,336 were left behind.

A little known exception to the under-use of Canadian land forces in the early years of the war is the futile defence of Hong Kong in 1941. Although the British had already decided to write off this crown colony and its 20,000-man garrison in the event of war with Japan, the Canadian government somehow agreed to send a contingent there just a few months before the attack on Pearl Harbour. On November 16 of that year, 1,975 unready, poorly equipped and under-trained troops arrived. Japan attacked on December 18 and the British governor surrendered on Christmas Day. 575 Canadians died in Hong Kong, many of them in prison camps.

...and On the Oceans...

The Royal Canadian Navy was barely large enough to be called a navy in 1939, but by 1943, it had pretty much taken over responsibility for the northwest Atlantic. It was a significant accomplishment; in fact, naval historians today still cite the example of how Canada in almost no time at all built a fleet large enough to alter the outcome of the war. By 1945, 100,000 men and 6,500 women had served in almost 500 fighting vessels of various types (with over 2,000 fatal casualties). Much of the work of the RCN was in convoy patrols, protecting the vast shiploads of Allied supplies from the U-boats of the German navy. But for the RCN it was not just convoy work in the Atlantic. Over a hundred vessels and 10,000 sailors took part in D-Day. By the end of the war, the navy had even sent the *HMCS Uganda* to the Pacific to help the US Marines in their assault on the island of Okinawa.

Landmark Encounters

Historians argue over the most important event in the Pacific theatre: Midway, Guam, Okinawa, Pearl Harbour of course, and the bombing of Hiroshima and Nagasaki are major contenders. In North Africa, key battles are Tobruk and the tank wars in the desert. In the Atlantic, it is any one of hundreds and hundreds of convoys that did or did not make it to England or Russia out of Halifax, St. John's and New York. In Europe, the clear nod is given to the D-Day invasion at Normandy on June 6, 1944. There were 14,000 Canadians in this attack. They took Juno Beach, and by the end of the day, two Canadian regiments had fought their way about ten miles inland, farther than any force from the British or American armies on either side of them. Before dawn, RCAF bombers had dropped 860 tons of bombs over Normandy, and fighter squadrons provided cover over the beaches, in what was a clear, beginning-of-the-end for the German forces.

However, of all the landmark battles, struggles that have national significance - like Vimy Ridge in the First World War - no name stands out more sharply for Canadians than Dieppe. Like Vimy Ridge, this clash on the 19th of August, 1942 cost the lives of a very large percentage of the attackers - about 5,000 Canadians charged the beach; more than 900 were killed with almost 2,000 taken prisoner - but unlike the Vimy Ridge battle, Dieppe was a monumental failure. Usually called a "raid" now, rather than a battle, this "reconnaissance in force" as the military referred to it, was a product of inadequate training, overly complex strategy and insufficient support. It did not achieve a single one of its objectives, although some military historians argue that it provided useful information for the D-Day attack some two years later.

Everybody Pitched In

Canadian women served with great honour in both world wars, and in the Second World War applied their talents, skills and dedication in all three branches of the services. Their duties spanned many areas of responsibility, and men serving in the army, air force and navy relied on women's expertise on countless occasions to help achieve success. They were not only a vital part of the actual military effort. Thousands of women during World War II - even more than in the first war - besides maintaining the home front, raising children, and keeping families together, rolled up their sleeves to work in defense plants and offices and farms. Although they willingly took over these jobs during the war years to fill the gap, many returned to their former roles when the war was over. However, the experience of working outside of the home led many women to continue along this path, thus stimulating yet another effort on the part of women to seek equal status in the world.

On the home front, women, men, even children when necessary and possible, contributed to a vital part of the Canadian war effort: namely, industrial production and food production. Almost every home had a 'Victory Garden' in an attempt to be self-sufficient so that as much food as possible could be exported overseas. Agriculture, especially in Ontario and the western provinces, boomed during World War II taking up the energy of everyone on the home front. Everyone, that is, except those who were working in the factories. Canada built ships, bombers, fighter planes, tanks, jeeps, trucks, almost a million land vehicles altogether, in the course of the war. Many from this area made the daily trek to Malton to work in the factories there.

And Then It Was Over

When Germany's inevitable surrender finally occurred, and Victory in Europe (V-E Day) was proclaimed on May 7, 1945, boisterous celebrations were held throughout Canadian communities, including Bolton and many of our local villages. Japan hung on until the 2nd of September (V-J Day) and a world, by now totally exhausted, celebrated yet again. After six years of total commitment it was time for the Canadian boys - and girls - to come home again. It was time to take up the lives they had left behind, get back to the business of earning income and being part of a family and a community that had other things to do than think about war. It was not an easy task for a person engaged in heavy combat for a period of time to revert to a former lifestyle. Adjustments and patience were required in all areas. However, with the passage of time, the difficult memories subsided and throughout Canada, our local communities included, a generally more relaxed atmosphere soon began to prevail.

The men and women of World War II, whose stories are found on the pages that follow, had done it for Canada yet again. They had put their hopes and dreams on hold, reluctantly left their families, forced themselves to turn their backs on people they loved, to go off and fight a war, in the clear knowledge that some of them might not come back - as indeed many did not. It's not something that comes naturally to most people and certainly not, it would seem, to Canadians. Yet when the sacrifice is necessary, as it obviously was in 1939, this is a country that proves it can do more than its share. Just as it had in World War I, Canada made its presence felt in a profoundly important way in the second great conflict of the twentieth century. And it was possible because of the sacrifices by men and women in communities like Bolton, Caledon East, Palgrave, Nobleton, Nashville, Kleinberg and others in the Caledon area. These men and women had worked the farms and factories, had run the offices, clerked in stores and taught in schools: ordinary men and women who became extraordinary because they knew it was necessary. On the pages that follow, are some of their stories.

Ken Weber

⫷⫷ Chapter Eight ⫸⫸
– 1939 –
World War II Begins

It has been said that the Second World War was a continuation of the First World War with similarities in their cause and result. The peace, which existed between them, spanned a period of twenty years and eleven months. Rumours of another conflict began to surface in 1938 and the year 1939 saw increased speculation that war was inevitable. It became a reality in September of 1939, and by December 31 of that year the first Canadian troops arrived in England.

S.S. Athenia Torpedoed by German Sub

The September 8, 1939 edition of the *Bolton Enterprise* states:

The terrible atrocities of war were brought home with full force in the news late Sunday night that S.S. Athenia of the Donaldson Line has been torpedoed one day out from Belfast by a German submarine. The fact that three Bolton citizens were aboard intensified the horror. The incident was the first major stroke of the war and is one which has fired Britons and Canadians to great determination.

The passenger list of the Athenia when it was torpedoed included the names of Firth A. Jaffary and Mr. and Mrs. George Hamilton of Bolton. The liner had left Glasgow at noon Friday, Liverpool at 4 p.m. Saturday and Belfast on Saturday night for Montreal, its passengers happy in the thought that they were racing for home, safe from the war. Then in the dark hours of the morning had come the blast of the torpedo as it struck the ship's hull, the screams of the victims and the dazed moments until the crew manned their life boat stations and the passengers took to the boats.

The sinking brought home to Britons, for the first time, despite three air raid alarms during the first 24 hours of Briton's war with Germany, the fact that they were in a grim and terrible struggle. From the flaring newspaper headlines and the radio they learned that Germany had struck its first blow, only a few hundred miles away.

Nothing, short of the bombing of London or another British city, could have been calculated so to arouse British bitterness, anger and determination more than the torpedoing of a British passenger liner jammed with men, women and children.

The millions of people in London, southeast England and the midlands had arisen after a night's sleep broken by air alarms - for which they blamed Hitler personally - to hear the news which roused memories among the middle aged of the campaign of the German U-boats in the World War.

The British liner, Athenia, was left to sink when rescue ships started for Scottish and Irish ports with at least 1,000 survivors of its 1,347 passengers and crew. Hundreds of Canadians and Americans were among the passengers and crew of the Montreal bound Cunard-White Star (Donaldson) liner.

The Athenia's master, Captain James Cook wirelessed "Passengers and crew, except those killed by explosion, took to boats and were picked up by various ships". This news came hours after the first word from the ship that it had been torpedoed and was sinking rapidly.

News arrived in Bolton Wednesday morning from Firth Jaffary in a cable to his uncle,

Wyatt A. Jaffary, saying, "Back in Ireland again". Later, word came through that Mr. and Mrs. George Hamilton were safe aboard the American S.S. City of Flint and landed safely at Halifax. Word of their safety was received with great joy here.

Recruitment Begins

Later it was reported in the Bolton Enterprise -

1941 recruitment poster.
COURTESY PUBLIC ARCHIVES OF CANADA

Camp Borden has been closed to all civilians. A smartly clad guard of the R.C.A.S.C. will stop you and politely inform you that no admittance is allowed as war has been declared. Buildings already in process of erection are being speeded up by the recent knowledge that Canada is at war. Fourteen new tanks will bring the total at Camp Borden up to 16 light tanks and 12 Carden Lloyd armoured carriers. Their crew consists of a commander, gunner and driver. They are 12 feet long, 5 feet wide and 8 feet high. Weighing about 6 tons, they have bullet proof armour and have a 125 horsepower motor and drive on a caterpillar track.

In the same shipment were eight aeroplanes consigned to the Commanding Officer, R.C.A.F. Station at Camp Borden. They were securely enclosed in sealed boxcars, tonnage of each indicated at 75. There was one machine in two boxcars, it was stated.

◇

The voluntary registration of Canadian women was arranged for the week of September 25th to 30th inclusive. Bureaus were opened at Dr. A.F. Reynar's office in Palgrave, Hanton's Hotel in Caledon East, Mono Road Public Library, Sand Hill Orange Hall, Bolton Town Hall and at W.H. Taylor's store at Castlemore.

Bolton Enterprise - September 29, 1939
Several from this town and district have been disappointed when they attempted to enlist with an overseas unit. They report that no more men are required at the moment. The government will not allow skilled workmen to enlist and in this connection it has been pointed out by a Minister, "You can train a man to be a good soldier much quicker that you can train him to be efficient on the farm".

◇

Among the first soldiers to enlist in this district were Arnold Thompson, son of Mr. and Mrs. Alf Thompson of Bolton and Walter McKee of Sand Hill. Arnold Thompson began his training in Toronto and Walter McKee was stationed with an anti-aircraft unit at Kingston.

Bolton Enterprise - November 3, 1939
Four Bolton young men were among the new recruits who took the Oath of Allegiance to King George VI at Brampton Armouries. They have signed up with the Lorne Scots, Peel, Halton and Dufferin Regiment in the non-permanent forces. They are Alf McNair, Cal Daines, Walter Schild and John Whitbread.

Other Bolton men who have been members of the Lorne Scots for some years are Joseph Studholme, Roy Studholme, Russell Bell, Charles Calladine, Fred Roden, Joseph Nicholson, Ernest Hart, William Norton and Ernest Robertson as well as Jack Robertson of Mono Road.

Recruits are flocking to join the Canadian forces at the rate of 500 a day as Canada attempts to bring its numbers up to full wartime strength.

Bolton Enterprise - April 26, 1940
Officers-in-training, numbering 42, while on a cross country trek, camped over night on the banks of the Cold Creek, near the Fresh Air Camp on Mrs. Fuller's farm. They had marched from Toronto on Monday, wearing full battle dress, steel helmets, and carrying rifles and bayonets, to bagpipe music. By swinging along at 120 paces to the minute, which is a brisk walk, the young officers got a real taste of what is expected of "buck" privates. They proceeded north Tuesday over the rough route of the 12th line and will return to Toronto the latter part of the week.

Training camp in Shilo, Manitoba. Note names on tanks.

COURTESY JEAN PROCTOR

Bolton Enterprise - May 10, 1940
Colonel Arthur E. Snell, C.M.G., D.S.O., M.B., O.St.J., Chief Commissioner of Canada's St. John Ambulance Brigade, whose headquarters are in Ottawa, is inspecting first aid and air raid precaution corps from coast to coast. Colonel Snell recently inspected the largest unit in Canada at Vancouver where he took the salute as 400 men, women and children in the uniform of St. John Ambulance Association marched past. A native of Bolton, Colonel Snell, is a son of S.J. Snell, early druggist and postmaster. He is a nephew of Mrs. T.D. Elliott of this place.

This is the same Colonel Snell who performed so bravely in the First World War and was decorated for his efforts in that conflict.

Bolton Enterprise - May 24, 1940
Wilfred Byrne, son of Mrs. James Byrne and a native of this place, recently left Toronto for an eastern point with a large troop movement. Private Byrne served in the last Great War and is one of the first veterans of this district who has been accepted for overseas service again. He is a member of the 48th Highlanders Reserve Unit.

Bolton Enterprise - May 31, 1940
Laude Wilson has joined the Canadian Active Service Forces and is now at Camp Borden.

◇

Troops have been moving to Camp Borden this week. At least seven trains passed through this point on the CPR over the weekend, loaded with soldiers for their summer quarters. More followed during the week. The troop movement to Camp Borden recalls the great traffic of soldiers on the CPR through Bolton to the same destination during World War 1. At that time there were a great many troop trains which waited here when Bolton was a junction point. The station and yards were alive with soldiers.

Bolton Enterprise - October 18, 1940
In the recently organized Forestry Corps of the C.A.S.F. a native of this district is a company commander. Major C. Roy McCort, son of the late Alex McCort and Mrs. McCort is officer commanding No. 9 Company, which was recruited in Montreal. The personnel were carefully chosen from among the lumberjack and woodsmen in order to bring this important

branch of our military machine to the highest standard. Major McCort, a civil engineer, has been general manager for several years of one of Quebec's largest pulp and paper industries, and is a veteran of the last war. He is a graduate of Toronto University.

Two Views of Canada's First Week of War

The Evening Telegram - September 1939

In the first week of their country's participation in the war, Canadians had two very different pictures presented to them.

One was of Thornton Mustard, principal of the Toronto Normal School, giving up his place in a lifeboat to a woman and waving good-bye to his wife from the deck of the Athenia. It was an example of heroic self-sacrifice.

Another picture is not so inspiring. With an abundance of food there has been a scramble by hoarders to secure a supply far beyond their normal needs, with the effect that a temporary and local shortage in some commodities has been created. The hoarders have not cared that others might not get even their normal supply, or that fruit might rot on the market for want of sugar to preserve it. Prices have been raised without let or hindrance. Too many have let unintelligent selfishness rule.

Hoarders and price-raisers are enemies of the state and are dealt with as such in some countries. Here they have so far been permitted to operate .... As yet the price of no necessity of life has been pegged and no hoarder or price-raiser has been brought to book.

Mr. Mustard's calm action was the essence of bravery. He gave up a chance of safety for the alternative of probable death.

The hysterical action of hoarders is contemptible. They have carelessly deprived others of necessities in fear of a shortage which was nonexistent until created by themselves or in anticipation of enhanced prices which they themselves have helped to create.

Mayor Day of Toronto stated - "If hoarding continues, drastic action will have to be taken in order that everyone will get a fair share of the commodities available".

⫷⫷⫷ Chapter Nine ⫸⫸⫸
– 1940-1941 –
News from Overseas

Wherever the local men and women were stationed, The Bolton Enterprise made sure that they received copies of their weekly newspaper. They encouraged them to write letters, which would be subsequently printed in The Enterprise. A number of local servicemen were prolific writers and their letters, with detailed descriptions of various experiences, provide an interesting glimpse into their lives overseas and in Canada. Without such letters a wealth of important information would have been lost to present generations.

◇

Halifax, Nova Scotia
March 8, 1940
Quite regularly every Tuesday for some weeks past I have been receiving your paper. It comes like a letter from home and gives me much joy; also the occasional sorrow, to read its interesting columns. Your sports commentator especially is to be congratulated for his excellent description of the hockey games and his enthusiastic support of the victorious Bolton teams.

I cannot tell you how much I appreciated your thoughtful kindness toward men in the service, so please accept my sincere thanks for sending me the good old Bolton Enterprise.

Yours very truly,
Gunner Walter C. McKee

p.s. - My six months service has been pleasant indeed. I am associated with a splendid lot of fellows doing a very interesting and difficult piece of artillery. Army routine and discipline is certainly no hardship. We have plenty of warm comfortable clothing for bed and body.

We eat the best of food - fresh, clean and wholesome, plain and plentiful. Our every desire is to share in putting a stop to the world menace of peace.

W.C.M.

Addresses on the move; Toronto Daily Star.

Letters from England

Bolton Enterprise - January 26, 1940

Aldershot Camp, North Tourney Barracks, England
December 28, 1939
Dear Editor:
Just a line to enclose my sincere appreciation of the kindness of the people of Bolton, who so thoughtfully sent that telegram, or as it is called here, cablegram. Believe me

this was a very pleasant surprise. They handed me the telegram just as I was leaving parade this afternoon. I've got all the names figured out and got a count of 33. From this distance there was nothing I could have asked for more than that heartfelt tribute from home.

Believe me you can realize there is a war on over here. These blackouts are very hard to get used to. It gets dark at 4.30 p.m. here, which is 11.30 a.m. in Bolton. We haven't had any word of our leaving England - likely before March or April.

We had a big snowfall yesterday, the first we have had, but it's not cold like Canadian winters. It's damper and cooler than our country, but still not winter. Most of the boys are suffering from colds.

I have only had one day in London. They keep us confined to barracks to keep us under control. We are about 38 miles from London. I get five days leave on January 2. I am going to visit Harry Young and then perhaps have a couple of days in old London.

Well guess that is all for now, but please convey my deepest appreciation to all who sent the cablegram, and believe me I'll carry that as long as it holds together. I often think of the people back home and wish I was parading the streets of Bolton again, but I'm not sorry I joined the army either. Thanks again in advance.

Yours very truly,
Alf McNair
B Co., - B76401
Toronto Scottish

◇

Toronto, Ontario
January 21, 1940
Dear Editor:

Received your paper O.K. for which accept thanks. Am leaving Toronto for an eastern training camp and would like to be able to call on you but time will not allow. Kindly remember me to the people of Bolton and community. Would be pleased to hear how everything is at home, and thanking you again, I am,

Yours sincerely,
H.E. Wallace
B94215 R.C.O.C.
No. 2 A.F.W.

Bolton Enterprise - March 15, 1940

Word from soldiers who are training with the C.E.F. at Aldershot Camp in England is to the effect that they are meeting many old Bolton friends in different units. Here are some of the boys who have been visiting one another: Delbert Robertson, son of Mr. & Mrs. William Robertson, Irwin Boyce, of Toronto, son of the late Mr. & Mrs. W.C. Boyce of Bolton, Lloyd Herman, son of Rev. Frank and Mrs. Herman of Markham and formerly of Bolton, Harry Nelson, son of Mr. & Mrs. Louis Nelson, Alf McNair, son of Mrs. E. McNair and Arnold Thompson, son of Mr. & Mrs. Alf Thompson.

Bolton Enterprise - April 5, 1940

Aldershot, Salamaca B,
March 10, 1940

I was handed a Bolton Enterprise this afternoon by Private Alf McNair. I was never so glad to see a paper as this one. As I have not received a letter from home yet, it was full of news to me. After I read it I passed it on to Sergeant Harry Nelson and he passed it on to more of the boys from Bolton. There are a lot of Bolton boys here - that is, men from in or near Bolton.

The weather has been very nice - like our first of May weather at home. The army is getting settled down to hard training and blackouts. Can you think of Toronto without a light and all the traffic and NOT a light? The only light is when the searchlights go on and then you want to see them out, for a very good reason. Can you guess why?

I do not know when we move but I think it will be soon.

Private Arnold Thompson, B94281
No. 2 Army Field Workshop
R.C.O.C.

◇

Aldershot, Hants, England
April 22, 1940

Well sir, I have just finished reading the April 5th issue of the Bolton Enterprise and must say that it certainly bucks a fellow up considerably to read first hand news of home.

Since arriving here I have run into quite a few chaps in various regiments from Bolton and vicinity with whom I exchange various items of interest gleaned from the pages of the Bolton Enterprise.

During my first few weeks here I found the nightly blackouts rather awkward and depressing, but must say that I now find them quite exciting and extremely interesting.

Would be pleased if you would pass on my compliments and best wishes to my good friend, J.P. Sullivan, as I notice he is again the proud father of a baby girl.

Thanking you once again on behalf of the boys and myself for your kindness in forwarding the Enterprise, I am,

Yours sincerely
Private H.E. Wallace
Reg. No. B94215, R.C.O.C.
No. 2, A.F.W., Base P.O.
C.A.S.F. Canada

Bolton Enterprise - May 17, 1940
Walter Young received a letter from his father. W.H. Young, who lives in Poole Dorset, England, that he saw in the news moving pictures, Private Alf McNair on a motorcycle escorting their Majesties, the King and Queen, at Aldershot Camp in England. Mr. Young says that he is working practically night and day, seven days a week, in the wartime rush in the Old Country.

Aldershot, May 4th

Just a line to thank you for the Enterprise. While I have been away from Bolton for fifteen years, I am still greatly interested in happenings of the district, and I find much news of interest to me. I was sorry to read of the death of Albert Pilson.

It is a small world after all as when I landed here about the first person I saw was Sergeant Harry Nelson and Private Arnold Thompson. I then met Irwin Boyce and Alf McNair and we had regular old boys' reunion. I have not met Lloyd Herman yet. He is the son of Rev. Frank Herman, formerly of Bolton. Alf McNair left last week for another camp somewhere in England. I guess we will all be going before long, as things look bad. Tell Bill Gordon I met his brother-in-law the other night and was quite surprised. Well I guess I will close for now, as I have to put the light out. They go out in our camp at 9.30 p.m. and we get up at 5.30 a.m. They really are giving us quite a lot of hard training, but I think the bunch from good old Bolton will give Hitler quite a battle when we meet, which I sure hope will be soon. Later on we are getting a picture taken of our guard so I will send you one. I will also get the Bolton lads together for a picture for the Enterprise. I will say good night.

I remain,
Your friend,
Driver Delbert Robertson

P.S. We are no longer called Private in our unit. We are called "Driver".

◇

Dear Editor:

If you think the readers of the Enterprise enjoy my letters you may publish this one. My last letter dealt with a trip to London, and this one deals with a recent trip to Nottingham. As we thought we were experienced travellers we started out full of confidence, which I am sorry to say, we soon lost. We first went to Waterloo and then by underground railway to St. Pancreas' Station, which is clear across the mighty metropolis of London. We then took the train to Nottingham. As we were trying to get away and travel by daylight in order to miss the blackout we neglected to have the R.T.O. sign our pass. We arrived in Nottingham just at dark, but they would not let us out at the station. We started to work on the pass question and after an hour of interviewing various officers of the Imperial Army we were released.

It was dark and as it was a black out situation we went to the police station in order to find where Mr. Davidson lives. I had known his son in Canada. After taking practically the wrong route in every direction we met another man in still another police station and he took us right to the home of the Davidsons. We sat up very late while they asked many questions about Canada.

Well it seems to be quite the thing to have tea in bed in England and the Davidson household was no exception. After breakfast our host took us out on a sightseeing tour showing us places of historic interest. He first took us to the Nottingham Castle which is located on the peak of a great hill, perched high on a rock. It can be seen from a great distance. It was destroyed by Oliver Cromwell and was rebuilt fifty years later. In peacetime it is used as a museum. At present it is occupied by one of the oldest regiments in England, The Scot Greys, as a barracks. Right under the castle is a pub (beverage room) that has been in service continually since 1169. Here they make beer and wine in solid rock vats. In fact the whole place is cut out of solid rock. We spent several hours in the caves behind the pub and under the castle.

Next we went to Standard Hill where "Bonnie Prince Charlie" raised his standard to reclaim the throne of England. Under this are still more caves that would take days to penetrate. In fact they say that some of them have not been entered for 200 years. As buildings are being torn down here they are finding more caves. We were taken to the point where Oliver Cromwell set his guns to destroy the castle.

Home to the Davidsons' we went and sat down to an English dinner, which was a dandy. The English really expect you to eat, and eat we certainly did.

Next day Mr. Davidson took us to a pub which was said to have been Dick Turpin's place of hiding. He is said to have ridden his horse, Dark Bess, through a window when the police were after him. The window, however, was small, and how he got his horse through it, is still a mystery to me. We walked through Donkey Streets where you can shake hands with someone in upstairs windows. On to Sherwood Forest we went, the home of the famous Robin Hood. Today it remains still a forest, but, of course, it is a park and one of the prettiest I have ever been in. Our leave was shortly up and we had still time to visit the Border Army Church where the colors of the famous border regiments over a long period of years have been deposited. As we examined the colors we were greatly impressed with the long service seen by these regiments in all parts of the world. Upon leaving again to return to our barracks we realized more than ever the great contribution made by these gallant English regiments in order to maintain freedom. We were proud we were soldiers of the British Empire.

Arnold Thompson

Bolton Enterprise - December 6, 1940

November 3, 1940
Dear Editor:
At the instigation of a friend of mine in Toronto you were good enough to forward me recently copies of the Bolton Enterprise, including the 1938 "50th Anniversary" issue, upon which - although perhaps somewhat belated - I must first of all offer you my congratulations. As twenty-four years have elapsed since I last saw a copy of the Enterprise you can easily imagine the interest and excitement I had as I eagerly scanned its pages and of the many happy recollections they brought back to me, and I am indeed very grateful to you for sending them on to me.

I was more than pleased to read that the Enterprise was still in your very capable hands and also that you are apparently enjoying good health to enable you to do so. Your association with Bolton and its interests has extended over a very long period and you have rendered excellent public service which more than merits the praise and appreciation of the townsfolk.

Perhaps you say to yourself: "Yes this is very nice, but just who are you?". Probably those who knew me a quarter of a century ago will have some difficulty in recalling me. I only resided in Bolton over a period of five years and was but a youth devoid of any outstanding accomplishments there is obviously no particular reason why they should. However, to the inquisitive I would say that I arrived in Bolton early in 1911 and resided in its suburb (Glasgow), where I was employed for the greater part of that time at the Woolen Mill until the time of my enlistment. I was twelve months at Camp Borden and other centres when I left for overseas with the 170th Toronto Battalion and was ultimately discharged in England after a lengthy stay in hospital, Christmas, 1919, where I have remained ever since.

I had many happy associations with Bolton and it has often given me much pleasure to recall them, in fact I really think my heart is still there. You will, perhaps, remember me more clearly as one of the pioneers in the scout movement in 1911, for in conjunction with Adam Wallace (a very worthy colleague) we were entrusted at your behest, and with your assistance, to inaugurate a troop of boy scouts. As a result a very fine troop of local boys subsequently developed, and many happy times we spent together in our scouting activities. Some of the boys at the time whom I can vividly recall, perhaps better than they can me, are: Adam Wallace whom incidentally I was very pleased to read had distinguished himself with the M.M. and bar and D.C.M. in addition to his rank. I also attained the rank of Sergeant, but lacking the marked characteristics and abilities of Adam, retired minus any decorations, your son Byron (in whose company) I had the pleasure of several hikes over the English countryside, Monty Gould, Hector Bonner, George Stokes, Whitney and Wilfred Byrne (unfortunately we had not the persuasive abilities to get

Whitney to become scout minded); Charles Hesp, Alma Macdonald, Vernon Robertson and Lorne Childs (with whom I also spent many pleasant times rambling the lanes in the south of England prior to his proceeding to France).

Much water has flowed under the bridge since then and I suppose Bolton has changed so much that I would hardly recognize the town as I knew it. Nevertheless it is good to read of its progress and I sincerely hope it will continue to do so; nothing would give me greater pleasure than to revisit the old town and wander through its by-ways and talk over reminiscences such as are at present in my mind with some if not all of my former colleagues.

But, as you are well aware, war is again upon us and Canada is once again playing a very important part and Bolton is also doing her share. These are perilous days for us in the old country, with air raids playing such havoc, but we have the will to win and are neither dismayed nor dispirited; Germany will never win the war by destroying our towns and cities and the morale of the people is still unshaken. There is still plenty to be seen and we are not short of foodstuffs. Our sincere hope is that the time is not far distant when we will bring the enemy to his knees so that things can resume their normal course with Peace once again restored and the fear of war forever removed.

It has been a great pleasure to write you these lines, yet perhaps a liberty; if so, I hope you will excuse me as I felt that I simply must put into writing a few of my thoughts after perusing the interesting papers you so kindly sent me.

With all good wishes for the future, hoping that you and your family are spared to enjoy many more years and wishing Bolton and its townspeople every success.

Believe me,
Yours sincerely,
Harry Rimmer,
Liverpool, 13, England

I remember my dad, Roy Hesp, mentioning Harry Rimmer a highly regarded man who was employed, along with many others in the vicinity, by J. (Joshua) Walshaw & Son Limited on Glasgow Road in Bolton. This firm, located across the road from the farm then owned by my grandparents, Henry and Susannah Hesp, successfully operated a woollen mill with the chief line of production being high grade bed blankets. Later, the management devolved upon Joshua's son Edward, under whose direction contracts were obtained from the Defence Department to produce large quantities of blankets for the military. Harry Rimmer enlisted in the army and my dad and he met again in England.

Bolton Enterprise - January 3, 1941

November 24, 1940

Dear Editor:

I thought you might be interested in hearing about London after all the air raids. So here goes to try and tell you of last Sunday when we made a trip to greater London. We went to the underground. All lines were running normally with the exception of Waterloo, so we took it.

Everything was O.K. except travelling was slow. It was so slow we decided to get out and walk. We found things much the same. In fact we had to walk all afternoon before we saw a bombed house. As we wanted to see the worst of it we changed our course and saw some of the damaged parts. One hotel, five storeys high, had been hit and split down the centre. A man's coat was hanging on a wall with a looking glass beside it not even broken. We saw a number of houses with blackened shingles where a fire had broken out. As far as we could find out all public services were going on as usual. We did not see any children running around without any place to go. In fact many looked better cared for than many children in Toronto. As evening came people came out of their homes with blankets and made their way to the shelters. They have games for the children and picture shows for the grown-ups. In fact some of the shelters are like hotels only you do not have to pay. If Hitler thinks he can break the hearts of the English he will have to increase things a lot. I wish to say a word concerning the A.F.S., the organization who put out the fires. They are doing splendid work. In a building I was visiting, a bomb dropped and a fire resulted. In fifteen minutes the fire was out with no light and little noise. If there is anyone who reads this and has friends in or around London, from whom they have not heard since the bombing started, I will look them up and have them write, if the address is forwarded to me.

Yours sincerely,
Arnold Thompson

Bolton Enterprise - October 3, 1941
Gunner Walter McKee wrote the following letter from England to his father, Mr. James McKee of Sand Hill.

Dear Dad:

It is a great joy indeed to honor your 81st birthday by writing these few lines. It is quite a while since last I wrote you but you may always be assured that no news is good news. I have tired of office work and have been released by the Major and for the past five weeks I have been on the guns. I have passed on the rifle, the machine gun and the Bofors anti-aircraft and anti-tank guns. It is very interesting indeed and, of course, just what I like very much. Tomorrow I will make a start at the electrical equipment used with the anti-aircraft gun. It is called a predictor and by looking through it at the plane the gun is electrically pointed so that the shell fired will hit the plane (that is if everyone does his work correctly.) We had a little rifle shooting today and I was fortunate enough to have a better score than the instructor. Just now part of our battery is stationed with another battery at Manston aerodrome. That is the nearest aerodrome to France or Germany. We are guarding the place with anti-aircraft guns but in the four days that I have been here only one German plane came near us and he was 3 1/2 miles up. He came down out of the clouds and dropped four bombs that did no damage and then beat it back over the channel again. One gun scored a shot in its wing but did not hit badly enough to bring it down. We were sorry it didn't come close enough for us to have a shot at it, but we may have our turn later.

We are living in tents that are so camouflaged that you couldn't tell them from haystacks. The weather is fairly good so it is a healthy change. I shall be glad to go into the barracks when the cold weather comes. The County of Kent is much like the southern part of our County of Peel. There is a great deal of gardening and fruit growing. This year wheat and barley are grown more extensively and there is a bumper crop and in good shape too since there have been no bad storms. It looks like very old times in Ontario to see some of the farmers cradling and binding by hand. They do the little fields, roadways and patches with the cradle. The farmer just here is using a Chalmers tractor on a Deering 7-ft. cut binder. No sheaf carrier but boys go about the field and put the sheaves in rows and men follow later and stook them up in long stooks. The wagons they use are short and dumpy and carry about one-half we are used to in Ontario. Of course, often only one horse is used. The ground is always cultivated just as soon as the grain is shocked so that a big load would be too heavy to draw. You should see the hay stacks here. They are a bit of a mechanics' job. The top of the stack is thatched so nicely that you wouldn't think there's one straw out of place. Our nearest villages are Minister and Ramsgate-by-the-sea. We are 24 miles from France. Dover is just along the coast a short way. On clear days we can see the coast of Belgium and France. We see the bombers leave here and see the flares of the bombs as they burst on the coastal towns and seaports. We can see the German searchlights and the flash of their anti-aircraft shell in the sky. While we lose some planes the squadrons of this aerodrome have been fairly fortunate having lost but a few planes. It is quite a sight to see the squadrons taking off to join with the others in an attack on Germany. Often we can hear the planes but cannot see them as they are far above the clouds as much as seven miles from the ground.

Since we are only seventeen miles from Canterbury I will go there and see the world famous cathedral and the Archbishop, who is the head of the Church of England. I saw the outside of the cathedral as we came through Dartford. It is an immense building and a wonderful piece of architecture. So far I haven't taken a hand at harvesting yet over here. Some of the infantry and engineering units have been released on leave to help out in the harvest. I often think many of us would be better giving a hand with it instead of standing by watching others. But, of course they still talk of an invasion and are not taking any chances being caught unready. Sept. 1 is supposed to be the big day but I think Hitler may see fit to postpone the date since he has really more than he can handle with Russia.

In early July I had my furlough to Scotland where I again saw Annie Ireland and daughter, Pauline. Bombardier Robertson and I had a very enjoyable time together. We did some fishing in the Leven River but caught none. We used only flies. I am enclosing some snaps which explain themselves. The quad-Lewis machine gun is used on planes that are low flying or diving at our position. They are good for only a short range of about 600 yards. I would have gone to Ireland but couldn't as only those with relatives are permitted to go there. If I have another leave I must visit the County of Ayr, Scotland, and see where the McKee's originated.

Remember me to my old friends at Sand Hill. Many I would like to write and hear from, but I don't like writing letters as you very well know. I will bring this letter to a close with the most sincere wish that you remain healthy and happy to enjoy the return of many more birthdays. There will be a great many changes in the community before I get back - many have taken place already.

Your son,
Gunner Walter Carson McKee
4th Lt. A.A. Battery, R.C.A.,
C.A.A., Can Lt. A.A. Regt.,
R.C.A., Base Post Office, England

"Keep in touch with the folks at home"

ON ACTIVE SERVICE
WITH THE
CANADIAN FORCES

THE SALVATION ARMY

England Friday 13. 194~

Letter to Harold Baxter of Caledon East from Bill Evans.
COURTESY SHIRLEY CANNON

A Visit With the Queen

Bolton Enterprise - October 31, 1941

Henry Rutherford, son of Mr. & Mrs. J.H. Rutherford, Albion, writes his sister, Miss Martha Rutherford in part as follows:

I went about thirty miles on Wednesday helping to move some coal, not a bad job, as we didn't work very hard, and had a nice trip there and back. This is really a very nice country. The places all look very neat and well kept up. All the farmers, who make stacks, seem to thatch a roof on them. A great many houses have thatched roofs, or tile, or slate with very few wooden ones. It is sure quite different to Canada.

On Thursday most of us were told at noon that we could fall out for guard at five o'clock. They always pick the neatest soldier as a stick man and give him a pass for one or two days. They said there would be three stick men and as a treat they were sending them to London on Friday to a party. Smitty, Adams and I got the call. So on Friday we got ready and got into a truck and went to London. They were opening up a new Victoria League Club for soldiers. There were about 35 nursing sisters, 100 airmen, 10 sailors and about 75 from the army, from all parts of the Empire, but none from this island. There were about 30 of us in a room and we were asked not to smoke as we might have a distinguished visitor. No one seemed to know who but at 3.05 she came. It was the Queen and I suppose this will always be a big day in my life. She was in no hurry to look around and get out. She spoke to nearly everyone, asking questions, spending maybe about twenty minutes in there and then going out into the garden and stayed there a good while speaking to the rest of the people. My, she is a wonderful person. Guess I should be able to soldier better now. I couldn't start to describe what she wore. I guess all her outfit was a mauve color and she didn't want anyone to remember she was the Queen at all. We all took a ride on the subway when the party was over. It is surely a fast way to get about the city. Saw a little sign of bombing but not very much. Still think I like Scotland much better.

Christmas in England

Bolton Enterprise - January 31, 1941

Somewhere in England
Dec. 27, 1940.
Dear Editor:
Perhaps your readers will be interested to know how some Canadian troops spent Christmas in old England. I had been invited to a house party some days before Christmas and right up until the week before there was doubt whether leave would be granted. Just about the time hope had died I was told I was to have three days leave.

My pass came through early Christmas Eve and I was off. I had to make my way through greater London and as I walked through the deserted streets I heard singing coming from the underground shelters, "Hark! the Herald Angels Sing", and I stopped at intervals to listen to old carols being sung under such strange circumstances. As I gazed around at the desolate ruins with their blacked rafters, broken walls, piles of brick and cement, windows with no glass, my spirit was lifted by the seriousness of the singers. It impressed me as one who had seen a friend near death fall into a peaceful sleep, knowing full well he will recover, just as I know London will rise again, mightier, finer and more beautiful than ever. I hurried on.

I was the last of the guests to arrive at the home of my friends. Their welcome possessed that warmness that always puts one at ease. Tea was immediately served. The houseguests represented well the British Commonwealth of Nations. In addition to myself there were two English Tommy soldiers, a New Zealander, a South African, an Australian and a Hindu of the "Selkirk" regiment. As the hour was late and we were tired from our trips we were shown to our rooms.

Tea was served in bed at eight the next morning, but breakfast did not follow until ten. Our host was most apologetic for the meal. But we had eggs, bacon, jam, toast and butter, and tea and coffee. After breakfast we were escorted on a short hike across the beautiful moor of the estate, where we saw hares, foxes and other wild game. We were back in time to hear the King's speech. Conversation got on the time of day it was back home in each of our countries and it sure was puzzling.

I was interested in my Hindu friend and I asked if I could see his girker, a big knife he carried in his belt. Nearly as soon as I had asked I knew I had done something wrong. But he gravely withdrew it from its sheath and handed it to me. Of finest steel, it was eighteen inches long with a slight curve. The handle was nicely carved. I asked several questions about it, which he answered with seriousness. To my astonishment when I handed it back to him, he resolutely rolled up his sleeve and drew the sharp blade across his arm, making a nasty gash. It seems that all members of his regiment had made the vow never to draw their girker without spilling blood.

Dinner was served. If England is starving that table sure did not look like it. Before we ate, toasts were offered to the King and to absent friends. As this toast was drunk more than one tear glistened down the cheeks. Our thoughts went back to other Christmases and our friends in the homeland. The glasses were thrown into the fireplace and broke to bits. No one would again drink from those glasses. Our host felt the dinner was not rich enough for us, but after army food it was delightful to say the very least. Following dinner we sat around the open hearth and told of our homeland. And so to bed. We were up early the next morning and rushed back to duty after our 1940 Christmas.

Sincerely,
Arnold Thompson

P.S. As I was addressing this letter "Jerry" dropped two bombs blowing our door and breaking all windows. Nobody hurt and all goes well.

Evacuating Women and Children after Bombing

Bolton Enterprise - June 27, 1941

May 27, 1941.
Dear Editor:
I thought it possible that the folks at home might like to know something of the treatment given the unfortunate people of England who have suffered the bombing of the German planes and have lost their homes as the result.

Sometime ago I was sent to a city that had had a hard night of enemy bombing from the air. We arrived about nine o'clock. The buildings were still smoking and dust still hung heavy in the air. Rescue parties were still working frantically removing the wounded and dead from the debris. Breakfast was already being served to the evacuees. It consisted of hot soup, beans, toast and jam. Hot tea had already been served since daylight.

We were detailed to get women and children ready to leave for billets. First clothes must be found for those who had lost everything. Two blankets were supplied to each. The difficult job was to gather each family together. This is a very big task. The names of the older children and mothers are taken down. The young children, who did not know their names, were separated. Our next move was to their homes, or the site where once the house stood. We salvaged any clothes and blankets that could be found. It was a trying time with frantic mothers asking for their children. One would tell you her youngster was three and had curly hair while another was four and had black hair. After the families had been gathered together the Red Cross distributed blankets and clothing and exercised a general supervision over the whole job. It is wonderful to see how thankful the mothers are for any little kindness. Despite the anxiety the brave mothers wait their turn to see if their children can be found, or if need be, to identify the bodies.

One little woman I saw was sitting with a baby in her arms and a little girl seven years of age by her side. I asked her what she was short of and she simply said, sadly, her boy. I investigated and found the lifeless body of the little fellow crushed beneath a wall. I was deeply touched. Later I found that she had only recently received word that her husband had not returned from a flight over enemy country.

Dinner was served at one o'clock and this was a very good meal for all. Most of the afternoon was taken up getting the evacuees ready to go to their new homes. Some fortunate ones had friends in the country, while for the majority billets had to be located. This is a large order. Tea was served at four o'clock. We were then loaded on trains and sent to different towns. The rain, which was helping the AFS, was not making our job any easier. Inside the train all blinds were drawn. The children and the mothers were very tired with nerves at the breaking point. Not a word of complaint could be heard and each tried to help the other as much as possible.

Some of the small children would let a blind slip up and even this little light would show up to a German plane observer above. When this happened we all ran for a tunnel and remained there until the all clear sounded. When the train started moving it was bad. When the train stopped we could hear the bombs dropping in the distance. After being stopped on account of the bombings we passed on our way to the next station where hot tea and milk were served and we all felt better as the result. At this point we were to be relieved here but our relief had to go to another place. We just carried on. About midnight our part of the train was cut off as we had reached the billets arranged for us.

Most of us know what a job it is to move small children at night. With no lights and in a small town it was a real task. The Red Cross workers made it easier and were at the station to meet us. In two hours everyone was in bed. As soldiers our job was through but the Red Cross workers had days of hard work ahead. Practically everything these people possessed was lost. They must be clothed and fed. Agencies that are doing this work for the unfortunate families which have been bombed from their homes are doing work of the highest order. You people in Bolton should help them all you can.

Arnold Thompson, B94281

A Soldier's Poem

Bolton Enterprise - November 21, 1941

Private Vern Robertson, a Bolton boy on active service overseas. has asked us to publish the following poem:

A Reminder
Please remind the people who know us
Ere we left our country to roam
That there's nothing that fortune can bring us
As good as a letter from home

We watch every day for the mailman
We hope there's a letter to-day
If he passes along without pausing
We despondently wander away

So try and send us a letter
A word from across the foam
For there's nothing a soldier so prays for
So much as a letter from home.

A Spitfire fighter plane.

Bags German and Falls in Cool Waters of the Channel

Bolton Enterprise - August 29, 1941

It meant a parachute jump into the English channel, a bit of a swim and a ride in the rescue launch, but Pilot Officer Norman R. Dick, a 20-year-old fighter pilot, got back to the mess in time for tea. Pilot Officer Dick, is a son of Dr. R. A. Dick of Canora, Sask., a native of Bolton, and is a nephew of T. A. Dick of this place. He belongs to the newest Canadian fighter squadron. It went out Tuesday for its first big operation. Its job was to escort bombers in daylight raids over France.

The squadron had a big day - it shot down four Messerschmitt fighters. Norman Dick got one of them in a fierce three-minute fight, but came out of the aerial brawl, with a damaged limping plane. The youngster had to bail out, and after a long descent, the cold waters of the channel were there to greet him. Rescue launches were there to save and he was pulled aboard, one of four airmen rescued from the channel during the day. During the fight Norman R. Dick shot down two Messerschmitts and saved the lives of at least two companions when his cannon fire literally blasted the Nazis out of the air.

Dick, a graduate of the Royal Military College, will be twenty-one this week, is already a veteran of dozen sweeps over France, but he confessed, "This is the first time anything has happened to me and they shot everything but me." Asked to list the damage to his plane, he replied, "Engine hit. Control column put out of commission. Right wing tip torn off right to the aileron. Three cannon shells through the wing. Covering of one machine gun completely ripped off. Left wing riddled. Reflector sight splintered and radio, I think also hit. Elevators damaged. All I had was a good rudder control and left aileron control."

≪ Chapter Ten ≫
– 1942-1943 –
Living in War Time

Spin-offs from the war affected almost everyone in one way or another. Gasoline rationing was necessary which created a challenge for motorists and careful planning was required in order to meet a person's needs. Food rationing imposed another hardship. Borrowing food stamps took place from time to time, but not often, because it was rare when a person possessed any to spare. Adjusting to the situation required perseverance and people plodded on through the ordeal.

Local businesses were converted and became part of the war industry. With a shortage of men, women did not hesitate to play a meaningful role while working at munition factories in Bolton, Malton and Toronto. A bus, owned and operated by Stan Broad who was at that time the Dodge car and truck dealer located on the south side of King Street East at Humber Lea Road, made daily trips to Victory Aircraft Limited of Malton. This is where some of the mighty Lancaster bombers were built. It was a familiar sight to see the workers boarding the bus each day at the intersection of King and Queen Streets in Bolton. Similar scenes were taking place in Caledon East, Palgrave and so on. Women also had their share of overseas experiences and three women's stories are included in this chapter.

During this time most local stores on Bolton's main street closed on Thursday afternoons. Some store-owners, including Alex Barry and Ervan (Wilkie) Wilkinson, used this time to help farmers with their harvest, which was greatly appreciated by those who received such assistance.

The Cigarette Fund was established and people assembled regularly to prepare parcels for local people serving abroad. Those involved in this undertaking were a happy group enjoying each other's company while they packed cigarettes, chocolate bars and other small items for shipment overseas.

Pilot training exercises provided an opportunity for local airmen to stray into home territory showing off their flying skills to those fortunate enough to witness such daredevil exhibitions.

Rations

Bolton Enterprise - February 13, 1942

Based on the mileage system, gasoline rationing after April 1 will allow the motorist less than a gallon a day, for under the ration plan, motorists in category "A" will only be able to travel 5,400 miles in a year. Ration tickets will be issued every three months, it is also understood, and can only be used during the months designated. Unused tickets will be valueless if carried over from one quarter to the next. The motorist, using his car daily, would be limited to about 13 miles a day, but under the system, the motorist may use up his three month quota as he chooses, either spreading it evenly over the days or "banking" it up for extended trips. Books of ration tickets will be issued good for April 1 to June 30; July 1 to September 30; October 1 to Dec. 31, and Jan. 1 to March 31.

VICTORY BONDING

Wartime messages from Canada's government, 1939-1945.

The Local War Industry

Bolton Enterprise - June 27, 1941

A contract for construction of latest type bomber, involving an outlay of over $25,000,000, was announced by Munitions Minister Howe. National Steel Car Corporation Limited, Malton, Ont., was given the contract to construct Martin B-26 bombers, and the contract cost is exclusive of the cost of engines, propellers and instruments.

"The Martin B-26 is the last word in United States design of a medium bomber, combining high speed and great range," said Mr. Howe. "The planes are to be built in the company's Malton plant and the contract provides that R. J. Magor, president of National Steel Car, will be personally responsible for the management and administration of this plant."

The Martin B-26, known as the "Flying Torpedo," is powered with two engines, driving two four-bladed propellers. The ship weighs some 13 tons and is faster than many pursuit planes now fighting in Europe. "It is reputed to be the most formidable plane of its type designed to date in America, and perhaps in the world," munitions and supply officials said.

The fire power from its defensive gun positions firing in every direction makes the Martin the most heavily defended plane in its class. It has a tail turret for rear defense, and a power operated twin-gun turret for other defense. The fuel supply is carried in self-sealing tanks. Armor is provided to protect the skilled pilots and gunners in combat.

COURTESY PUBLIC ARCHIVES OF CANADA

Bolton Enterprise - May 8, 1942

The announcement was made on Wednesday that Dick's factory in Bolton has been leased to a Toronto manufacturing company and will be used for wartime production. The B.M. Engineering Co. of 80 Market Street, Toronto have taken over the property on a long term lease, according to Major Edwin Meredith, a representative of the company, who was in Bolton early in the week attending to initial details and organization.

Major Meredith said that new machinery would be installed as hurriedly as possible and the plant started on production of what he termed "100 per cent war work, manufacturing tools, dies, stampings, forgings and other precision work". He estimated that fifty men would find employment, working in two shifts. He said an addition to the factory is contemplated to house the necessary wood-working machinery.

The need for skilled machinists is one of the problems. Major Meredith explained that age is no consideration and older men and others experienced in machine work should answer the advertisement appearing on another page of The Bolton Enterprise this week, if they desire employment.

The Dick factory owned by Thomson A. Dick, is of brick construction, well lighted, and modern in many of its details. It replaced a larger one on the same site destroyed by fire thirty years ago. The firm of William Dick and its successor, T.A. Dick, manufactured agricultural implements, which were known with favor from almost coast to coast. The original Dick plant in Bolton stood on King Street opposite the Jaffary residence.

The factory has a splendid water power and dam in connection, a factor, no doubt, which helped to entice The B.M. Co. to locate here.

The question of living accommodation for the extra workers and their families is one which might well receive the attention of the Council and the Board of Trade. It must be considered that a great many large houses in Bolton are occupied by only one or two persons, and the possibility of leasing a flat appears practical and perhaps a solution to what may turn out to be a vexatious problem. At the moment there are no unoccupied houses in Bolton and it may be propitious at this time to commence building a number of modern dwellings.

Bolton Enterprise - May 19, 1944
Warrant Officer Bruce Robertson, R.C.A.F., son of the late Rev. D.A.Robertson, was in Bolton on Monday. Bruce has charge of the bombing test station situated on the fair grounds here for the past few weeks. The trailer, with glass dome, houses equipment which registers the accuracy of bomb aimers on passing planes. The aimers create a flash which is registered and determines just how accurate a real or dud bomb might have been. Bruce's brother, David, is with the forces in Italy, and his sister, Joy, is a missionary in far away Africa.

Three Women's War Experiences

Lois Egan (Heppell), a niece of Helen Egan (Oldfield), has had in her possession this account of her aunt's experiences serving with the Red Cross during World War II and has graciously allowed us to print it here. I think you will find it interesting.

In August of 1939 I chanced to see an article in a Toronto newspaper that the wife of an official from Finland was looking for women recruits to drive ambulances. I wrote to her offering my services and received a courteous reply stating that the newspapers had misinterpreted her meaning, but she had taken the liberty of forwarding my letter to Mrs. Plumptre of the Canadian Red Cross Society. I was contacted and asked to join the Evening Division of the Transport Corps as a volunteer. My hopes were high that I would be sent overseas as an ambulance driver. The Transport Division was quite an active group; drilling at the Armouries every Sunday afternoon; taking courses in motor mechanics, home nursing and First Aid, besides working at our full-time daily jobs. I was in charge of procuring drivers from amongst our own members for driving duties in the evenings and weekends, on receiving request from the Society. We had a duty roster of the number of hours worked to be filled out each month. These rosters showed a total of from 50 to 90 hours per month. Every evening and on weekends a crew of our girls stood at the ready for emergency calls in the building that housed the ambulance. I can only remember two such emergency calls for our crew.

In August of 1943, I finally received notice that I was to be prepared to go overseas at a moment's notice. Five of us from Toronto left the Union Station for Montreal, where we stayed overnight. Five girls from Ottawa and Montreal joined our group and we headed for Saint John, N.B., where Jackie Grimmer joined us. After a delightful few days in Saint John we embarked, with two war correspondents, on the SS Mosdale, a 3,000-ton freighter, for a solitary crossing of eleven days. At Liverpool, we were met by a Red Cross official who warned us to remain on board the Mosdale for the night as they were experiencing nightly raids. I passed this information on to the girls and whether or not they stayed on board, I still don't know.

The next morning we entrained to London, where we were met by Mrs. Lee and drivers to take us to Corps House, 'our home away from home'. After a week's hospitality leave, I was posted to the Canadian Nursing Sisters' Club, Maple Leaf #3, 58 Cromwell Road to the position of General Duties. I had a fair amount of time off

John Hesp in front of Maple Leaf Club in London. COURTESY MARGARET HESP

and was thrilled to be able to tour around London for the nine months I was stationed there.

In April of 1944, after a few weeks training in handi-crafts at Burlington Gardens, I was sent to Scotch Corners in Yorkshire to join Unit No. 16 as Welfare Officer and to be billetted with No. 10 until such time as No. 16 was to be sent overseas. After six delightful weeks of double daylight saving time, Dorothy King, Isabel Willis and I were switched to No. 2 General Hospital in Whitby on the coast, where we were joined by Jean Lamb. Jean had been out to Italy with a unit and had to return when the order came through that all married girls had to return to London. However, on the way she learned that her husband had been killed in action, and eventually she joined our Unit. Jean and I had an interesting month in Whitby exploring and seeing the sights - then moved with No. 2 Unit to Southampton, and then to Ford Manor.

We were aroused at 3 a.m. one morning and given our last mail in England. I had a letter from my sister enclosing a newspaper clipping of my landing in France. This proved to be a good omen and we arrived safely via Hospital Ship at Mike's Beach on D-Day plus 63. The Unit was trucked to about five kilometers outside Bayeau, where we were again billetted with No. 10 Unit. I assisted for a short time on the night shift in the annex of the operating room doing odd jobs, mostly mending plastic gloves for the surgeons and pouring tea, etc. This was at the time the American planes had mistakenly bombed the Allies, when a mix-up of flares occurred.

After a short time, No. 10 moved up to Antwerp and we took over their patients and had a chance to get acquainted with our duties. We stayed in this area until mid-November. It had rained considerably and we were glad we were equipped with high army boots to wade through the gumbo. Our next move was to Ghent, Belgium in open trucks over very dusty roads. Our hospital was set up in a three-storey modern building, with terrazzo floors, on the bank of one of the canals. It was interesting to watch the many barges being hauled along by a rope slung over the shoulder of nearly always, a woman. Our billets were in a collaborator's house about ten minutes walk from the hospital. The hours were regular with weekends off and Jean and I again found the countryside a good place to explore, often hitchhiking in army vehicles. We found the drivers very protective and would often go out of their way to deliver us to our destination.

No. 2 C.G.H. was a twelve hundred-bed hospital. Dorothy King was in charge of our little group and she stayed in the office and recreation room. Isabel had the top floor with Jean on the first floor and I had the second floor, which included the Officers' Ward, which made it that we each had from 300 to 400 patients to see very day. It was a lot of walking on those terrazzo floors, carrying a basket of supplies.

We shortly ran out of Penelope patterns - and as we had a roll of coarse natural fibre resembling burlap - I asked the boys if they would like the crests of their units drawn on this material and they could then work them with threads using the colours of their regiment. This idea caught on and I would often collect about fifteen of them during a day, take them to the Mess, iron them and bring them back the next day. Incidentally, one of the officer patients was an artist and would draw these crests on the material by the dozen, which helped a lot. We also had kits of belts to be tied and needlepoint kits.

A the time of V-E Day, Jean and I were delegated to go to a Processing Unit set up just outside Brussels where some of the Ex POWs were flown in to be documented, refitted with clothes and necessities. We had a booth with Red Cross supplies alongside a similar one run by the British Red Cross. The Ex POWs would come through our tent in groups of twenty. Most of them were too stunned to take much note of our wares. To me it was a very emotional time: No. 2 Hospital closed down in July and Jean was posted back to London while I went on to Brussels as a driver for two weeks, while one of the drivers was on leave.

My next posting was No. 2. C.C.S. in Apeldoorn, Holland to take over from Jean Ellis (Wright). The Colonel of this Unit had been our family doctor years ago in Bolton, Ontario and several of the nurses had been with No. 2 so I felt at home immediately. The patients were anxiously waiting for their yellow tickets to arrive signifying they were on the way home. It was hard to get them interested in any of our crafts, as all they could think of was how to get their names on the roster for Canada. The war now being over, the duties of the doctors and nurses were more relaxed and a group of us enjoyed a number of trips to Amsterdam - for bowling and ice-skating.

In early November No. 2 C.C.S. sent their remaining patients to England and home and the hospital closed down. Ten of us set out for a week's cultural leave in Denmark in two station wagons. When we arrived in Hamburg to stay overnight at the Leave Centre Hotel, six big German boys stood lined up by our car. We scrambled out of there in a hurry, taking only part of our baggage with us. I had left my kit bag and when we came to drive off in the morning, it and all the other small luggage was gone. We were lucky they hadn't touched the station wagons. Our leave in Copenhagen was very interesting - attending lectures in the morning and afternoon - all about Denmark and its five-year plans. The Matron and I were entertained to a typically Danish dinner by a Danish family with only the twenty-year-old girl who could speak English, although the others tried from time to time amidst great hilarity. It was a very interesting week; especially as we were assigned Danish escorts, and we really appreciated the steaks, eels and seafood after army rations.

On my return, I went directly to No. 1 Hospital in Nijmegen. This Unit had come up from Italy with Pheme Walker in charge of the Red Cross personnel. On December 5th, the children of all the workers in the hospital were to be given a Christmas Party and presents which was their traditional custom. We had some felt by the yard and suggested to the patients that if I cut out toy animals, would they stitch and stuff them. One of the boys spoke up and said he was a tailor by trade and if I would give him the material, he would cut out the animals and see that the whole project was done. He did an excellent job and the stuffed animals were keenly appreciated by the children. It was estimated that approximately five hundred children would be attending the party, but nearly one thousand turned up and the facilities and supplies were greatly taxed; also the strength of the nurses who were ladling out the rice pudding and chocolate sauce. It was a day to remember by everyone.

No. 1 C. G. H closed after the Christmas Season and I returned to London to work in Burlington Gardens until the 1st of March and returned home on the Ile de France in a cabin with 20 other gals, which in peacetime was meant for two. Fortunately my sister and brother-in-law welcomed me to their home on a farm while I completed a course in accounting, after which I returned to Toronto to the usual routine. My grateful thanks go to the Canadian Red Cross Society, and to Margaret Duff in particular, who put my name on the roster for work on the continent. It was the most satisfying feeling to know that one did contribute to the war and peace effort and yet enjoyed every minute of it.

Helen Egan Oldfield, although not in the best of health, was 90 years of age in January, 2002.

◇

Doris Evans (Porter) of Bolton, Ontario writes of her 'Life in the CWAC"
I went in the army when I was eighteen years old, a farm girl fresh out of high school. This is the time when - could we have afforded it - I would have been heading off to university. Instead I went into a life which didn't offer any diploma, but succeeded in defining my future in much the same way as four years of university might have done.

I did my basic training at the Macdonald College campus in Ste. Anne de Bellevue, Quebec. This was my first foray into "La Belle Province" and I loved it. No matter what their bad press might suggest French Canadians are warm and friendly and *fun*! Back in Toronto they didn't know what to do with me. Most of the women there were older, had been out in the work force and knew what they wanted to do. I had Grade 13, which was looked upon in those days as the epitome of education for women in particular. They finally sent me off to a training course in basic office procedures geared to the military way of doing things. Letters were carefully typed with each paragraph numbered and always ended "For your information and necessary action please."

So I set out to serve my country and be part of the war effort in a uniform and I was very proud of it. The pay was $1.20 a day! But when you consider that was on top of food, clothing, housing, medical care and supervision, it wasn't too bad. In army parlance this was summed up as "Rations, Quarters, Duty and Discipline". The civilians who worked in many of our offices made about $40. a month and had to provide all of the extras for themselves.

In addition to Toronto I served in an administration school in Kemptville, Ontario and the military headquarters for New Brunswick at Saint John. I must say I fell in love with the Maritimes and hated to leave. To this day they have a completely different outlook on life down there. I was ashamed of the military from Ontario who looked down on things there as unsophisticated and showed it in their attitude. The Maritimers hated the guys who came from "Tranna" - and with good reason. I denied everything and told people I came from a little place in Ontario and got along fine.

Girls weren't allowed to go overseas until they were 21, which happened to me in December 1944. I immediately applied to go on draft to England. By the time I got on a list it was April and on May 8, 1945 V-E Day came. I can't say I was sorry the war was over. We had a military hospital in Saint John and the maimed and mutilated veterans were a familiar sight on the streets. One day I was going on the street car to West Saint John when it had some kind of backfire and let out a tremendous bang. In seconds one young fellow in uniform had dived under the long seat at the side of the car!

I was disappointed not to be going overseas of course and then a miracle happened. Ships were going over to bring home the waiting troops and travelling pretty light. So they sent several contingents of women over to take on some of the jobs of fellows who had been there for years, to free them up to come home. So in June, I set off for a year of duty in England. Some of our girls went to the continent where there was a large Canadian presence in Appeldoorn, Holland.

I wound up at a dream posting called Khaki University of Canada. Khaki University was a phenomenon of forward thinking launched by a government then, as now, not noted for such things. There were a lot of men and women sitting over there waiting to get home whose post-war plans were to go to university. So the president of the University of New Brunswick was brought on board, the location of one of our Canadian base hospitals used for a campus and, in September 1945, Khaki University opened its doors to over 600 students. All had served in England and Europe. In two semesters they could obtain a high school diploma or first year university credits. It was hugely successful. I was posted there on the administrative staff and had the best year of my military career.

I went overseas on the Ile de France and came back on it as well. It was quite a beautiful ship. We travelled in the first class area, but with ten double-decker bunks in each large stateroom! But even though they were still in wartime mode, the meals were wonderful.

I look back on four years service in the Canadian army with pride and with joy. I never fired a shot in anger nor was I ever shot at. So my contribution at best was very peripheral. But it was a worthwhile effort just the same and an experience I am very glad I had.

A photo of Doris Evans (Porter) appears on the front cover of this book. Doris still lives in the Bolton area and is active in many areas in the community.

◇

Laura Stewart (Matsche) writes from California of her experiences in the RCAF. She was Sergeant Laura Stewart of Albion Township. She enlisted in March 1943 and was discharged in November 1946.

After basic and course training, plus a month or two in a precision squad, I had the most enjoyable job of my life. It involved having all "other ranks" posted to #5 SFTS (Service Flying Training School) Centralia reporting their arrivals to me. I signed them in and directed them to the sections to which they were assigned. One day, 60 Australians appeared at my window in the headquarters orderly room. We had not received a signal about their arrival, or received their records. It was imperative that I accurately obtain their names, home addresses and their next of kin in case they were killed before their records arrived. This was a bit of a challenge, when their As and Es sounded like OY to me. When all ranks were posted away from #6 SFTS, I wrote the travel warrants for them, which they exchanged for train tickets and accommodations.

In my spare time, I devoured the Air Force Administrative Orders. When Command tried to find fault with a warrant I had written, I took great joy in always being able to prove my action correct by quoting applicable sections from the AFA Orders. I was only a Corporal, with no hope of becoming a Sergeant as our station establishment for five administration female Sergeants was already filled.

Rumours stated that dental assistants were needed overseas. I applied to remuster to this field. Before being allowed to do so, I had to wait for a male Flight Sergeant (two ranks above me) to be posted in so that I could teach him how to do my job. Six months later I was a Sergeant dental assistant. Hopes of going overseas were dashed when they found out that women were not strong enough to handle the field dental equipment.

The Life of a Bandsman in the RCAF

Bolton Enterprise - March 19, 1943

Dear Editor:

I get the Enterprise every week from home and am always very glad to get it. I wonder if you realize how nice it is for us fellows who are so far from home to get the hometown news? I see by the paper that you are interested in information about local boys who are in the services, so I will try and tell you something about the activities of our band here at "Y" Depot. We came here in November, a twenty-eight-piece band, and were made very welcome, as a band is supposed to add pep to a station. Our job is to try and help boost the morale of the boys with our music. I think we have been successful to a degree as the other day we rated a column in the Halifax Mail, which I enclose. We also broadcasted last Thursday night on the "Wings over Canada", program, at 8.30. We rehearse about five hours a day and play for route marches and inspections every week. We also play at boxing matches and at the Forum when the Air Force hockey team plays. We have a good team, Bobby Baner is one of the players and they won the Enterprise - April 17, 1942 Halifax Senior Hockey League title, on Saturday night, the score being 7-1.

The life of a bandsman in the R.C.A.F. is no cinch, and there is never a dull moment. We have a fine bandmaster, whom we all respect both for his personality and musical ability. He is well known to Mr. Napier, the Bolton Bandmaster. I like the military life and would not hesitate recommending it to any young man. Bolton Band was going strong when I was home on leave and I hope it continues to do so. You always support it in the paper which is a fine gesture of public spirit, and every boy in Bolton should take advantage of the opportunity to learn to play in the band, when you have about the finest teacher you could possibly get. With best regards,

Sincerely Yours,

A.C.1 C.H. Strong, Bandsman. No. 1 Depot R.C.A.F. Halifax

The Jamboree Cigarette Fund

Bolton Enterprise - July 30 1943

The Jamboree Cigarette Fund have received many acknowledgments of receiving cigarettes but few are as interesting as the following airgraph letter from L.A.C. Ted Sandford of the R.A.F. India Command. Ted is the son of Mr. & Mrs. Charles Sandford of Nashville and is a former member of the Imperial Bank staff here. The letter follows:

Your carton of cigarettes, dated February 8, 1943, arrived to-day. Incidentally, it is my first parcel since arriving in India. The mail is just beginning to find me. The cigarettes are in excellent condition and quite fresh. Quite a contrast to those that we buy which are musty due to dampness. I am writing this in my tent. The view as I look out is in marked contrast to any of the familiar sights around beautiful Bolton. As far as the eye can see there is nothing but barren rock and sand. Occasionally there are goat herds or camel caravans. The monsoons are with us now and although we haven't rain, the winds are terrific. Sand storms have ones eyes smarting and clothes saturated. Kindest regards to all members of the Jamboree Committee and here's hoping you have the biggest show ever this year. Thanks again for the cigarettes.

Flying Low Over Bolton

During the war years the people of the Bolton area were favoured from time to time with spectacular aerial manoeuvres by local RCAF airmen piloting, on most occasions, a Harvard aircraft. John Armstrong, a former employee of the Imperial Bank at Bolton, and Albion Township resident Douglas Speirs were known as two of these pilots who were exceptionally skilled and performed daringly. John Armstrong later became a Squadron Leader and Douglas Speirs a Flying Officer. Unfortunately, John Armstrong lost his life during the war as did two other former Bolton Imperial Bank employees, Sergeant Pilot Alan Bone and Flight Lieutenant Stan Cotterill.

Harvard planes similar to the ones used for training purposes.

COURTESY LANCE RUSSWURM, KITCHENER

Sometimes a plane could be seen spiralling earthward and levelling out so low it was frightening to some. The distinct roar of a Harvard aircraft engine was impressive to me but not to others who reported some flights to RCAF authorities. I admired the sound and sight of the aircraft and marvelled at the pilots' abilities.

Bruce Wilson lived on a farm, located at the corner of King Road West and Coleraine Drive, with his parents Claude and Lila Wilson, and brothers, Murray and Ormie. He recalls John Armstrong flying so low between their house and barn on one occasion that the hens in the barnyard scattered in all directions. Armstrong continued on towards Bolton dipping down out of sight and up again over the Village. Bruce also remembers being told about another flyer who landed in a nearby farmer's field in a Tiger Moth to take the hired man for a ride. After returning his passenger he clipped a telephone line with the tail wheel while taking off and trailed the wire back to his base.

Melville Hands also remembers John Armstrong flying low above the Humber River coming from the area of Jim Goodfellow's Mill and Dam (formerly McFall's) past the Howard Furnace Company building on Mill Street, where Melville was employed, and lifting up to clear the bridge on Queen Street and then out over the west of Bolton.

I remember another time when I heard the sound of a low flying Harvard but it was not a pleasant experience. It occurred on a foggy Saturday morning in the spring of the year. The sound indicated the plane was nearby and I ran towards the noise, which seemed to be towards the hill behind our barn in the direction of the Wilson farm. It was obvious the pilot was lost and was flying low trying to get his bearings. I was soon at the top of the steep hill and the sound was coming closer to me. I stopped and strained trying to see the plane because it seemed to be coming directly towards me. I was about to fall to the ground when the aircraft roared slowly by at the very edge of the hill. The two airmen could be seen for a brief moment through the fog and one looked directly at me with a frightened expression on his face. The aircraft was only a few feet from me. The aircraft flew out over the valley towards Glasgow Road and the sound indicated it had turned westward towards the extended hill ridge. They would have to increase their altitude in order to clear the hill. In a few minutes there was no sound and I knew they must have landed and I hoped safely.

I ran across the field towards King Street West, climbed the fence, crossed the road and over Wilson's fence and into a field. In the mist I could see the plane upside down having bogged down in the soft ground and flipped over. By then, Claude Wilson had transported the two uninjured airmen to his farmhouse in his 1936 red GMC 1/2 ton pick-up truck. They phoned officials at Camp Borden to report the accident. Bruce Wilson remembers the only damage to the aeroplane was the plexiglass over the cockpit being broken. He also recalls the wings were removed and the Harvard loaded on to a truck and transported back to Camp Borden. Evidently, the soft ground and the expert piloting had saved the plane from extensive damage and prevented injuries to the airmen.

The Fifth Kick-Off of the sale of War Bonds in the fall of 1943. The Navy men in uniform marched from HMCS York, where they were stationed, to the Toronto City Hall. Viola Fletcher and Bernice Snell, both engaged to Corless brothers, were there as spectators.

COURTESY ARTHUR AND VIOLA CORLESS

⟪⟪ Chapter Eleven ⟫⟫
– 1944 –
Fighting Continues In Italy - D-Day

On June 10, 1940 Italy declared war on Britain and France. Australia, Canada, India, New Zealand and South Africa declared war on Italy the same day. Italy was soon given full treatment as the only equal ally of Germany. However, by July 1943 Mussolini had fallen as leader of the Italian military and Germany took control. In time Germany's strength weakened and on May 2, 1945 the unconditional surrender of the German forces in Italy took effect. A number of servicemen and servicewomen from this area served in Italy, where over one-third of its land is ruggedly mountainous. They fought, and some died, under terrible conditions.

D-Day, or the invasion at Normandy, France, got underway just before dawn on June 6, 1944 with a heavy concentration of Canadian troops making their way ashore. A tank driver with the Royal Canadian Armoured Corps remembers it being a horrifying experience while roaring at full throttle from a barge into the water. The portion of the tank above the tracks was covered in a shroud to prevent water from entering the interior. In complete darkness the tank was propelled directly forward without the driver knowing if or when the tracks would take hold of firm ground. Fortunately, he successfully directed the tank to shore and was one of those courageous Canadians taking part in this invasion. Canadian regiments, with others, made their way inland and by August of 1944 Paris was under full control of the Allies. This invasion marked another step towards complete victory, which would become reality the following year.

The Italian Front

Bolton Enterprise - March 31, 1944

A Bolton soldier had an unusual experience in Italy recently. Corporal Allan Kirby was making a rice pudding in the house in which he was billeted when a shell knocked the chimney off the building. When Allan got back to stirring his favorite pudding again he thought it seemed rather thick. On examination he found it was filled with pieces of brick and mortar. The incident brings to mind a poem which was popular in the last war entitled "The Haggis of Private McPhee". McPhee, however, suffered a worse fate as a shell blew his haggis all to h - - - .

Bolton Enterprise - May 5, 1944

Private Frank Horan, son of Mr. & Mrs. J. Frank Horan, 5th Line Albion, has arrived back home from overseas. He arrived at the Exhibition grounds on Monday night and on Tuesday got back to his home. Private Horan is a battle-hardened veteran of France and Italy, and was wounded at Ortona. It was the first time he had seen his parents, brothers and sisters, since 1939, he having landed in England on New Year's Eve that year.

He had little to say of his experience. With the Canadian force that landed at Brest, as France collapsed, and advanced towards Paris before being recalled by Lieutenant General McNaughton, he described this experience as "a nice train ride in box cars".

"I landed in Sicily with the first attack, and saw the completion of the Sicilian campaign", he said. After that he was in the hospital for a short time with malaria, but went back into action and "the next dose I got was at the Moro River".

Hit by shrapnel in the leg at Ortona, he minimized his wound. His greatest dislike throughout Sicily and Italian fighting was the German trench mortar fire, although "it doesn't kill as many as machine gun and shell fire". It was his fourth time in hospital beds while he convalesced from his wound before returning to Canada.

Bolton Enterprise - May 12, 1944

Dear Committee:

I received word from your secretary stating that no word had reached you from the boys in Italy regarding the many cigarettes sent here by you folks. I think that I can assure you that word will be received from all the boys in the very near future. Bubs and I have just received the first Jamboree cigarettes in Italy and it is quite likely that the same goes for the other boys in this theatre. Our mail situation is very good. There have been one or two flying accidents of late which has interrupted the service a little but not seriously. From all accounts there are quite a number of Bolton boys in Italy. Unfortunately I have never met any of them. Ted Reeves was asking another chap from our regiment to be remembered to me, while I was spending an 8 day leave at the famous 8th Army rest centre. I also missed Nemo Robertson by a couple of days. On another occasion I must have walked past where Bill Chamberlain was living because when our outfit moved out of a front line position into a rest camp I found out after that we had passed right through Bill's regiment. The weather here now is grand. I am sitting out on the side of a hill and wher-ever I look I can see snow-capped mountains. The scenery is something to marvel at so long as a - - - - - - - - isn't in the same picture.

Somewhere in Italy.   COURTESY CAPTAIN DOUGLAS F. HERSEY, (RET'D)

These poor people are taking quite a trimming and they certainly look awful. They will sell their souls for clothes and will steal them again if you are not on the bit. When the Germans were rushing through here a couple of months ago they were cleaned out. I see a bunch of our stout-hearted little "spits" rushing over to harass Jerry. I can also hear the big guns rolling around like thunder. When one first hears big ones it makes you wonder but in most cases you soon get used to them and then you like to hear them so long as they are ours. Jerry has them too. Well I guess that I have prattled enough for now. I have other letters to write so I should at least make a start at them. Again I send you my sincere thanks and I hope that your next Jamboree is bigger and better than ever. -

Sincerely yours,   Allan J. Kirby

D-Day

Bolton Enterprise - June 9, 1944

EISENHOWER'S ORDER

LONDON, June 6 - General Dwight D. Eisenhower issued the following order of the day to his invasion troops today:

Soldiers, sailors, and airmen of the Allied Expeditionary Forces:

You are about to embark on a great crusade. The eyes of the world are upon you and the hopes and prayers of all liberty-loving peoples go with you.

In company with our brave allies and brothers in arms on other fronts you will bring about the destruction of the German war machine, elimination of Nazi tyranny over the oppressed people of Europe and security for us in a free world.

Your task will not be an easy one. Your enemy is well-trained, well-equipped, and battle-hardened. He will fight savagely. But in this year of 1944 much has happened since the Nazi triumphs of 1940 and 1941.

The United Nations have inflicted upon the Germans great defeats in open battle, man to man. Our air offensive has seriously reduced their strength in the air and their capacity to wage war on ground. Our home fronts have given us overwhelming superiority in weapons and munitions of war, and have placed at our disposal great reserves of trained fighting men. The tide has turned and free men of the world are marching to victory.

I have full confidence in your courage, devotion to duty, and skill in battle. We will accept nothing less than full victory. Good luck and let us all beseech the blessing of Almighty God upon this great and noble undertaking.

ALLIED PEOPLE PRAY FOR VICTORY

Canadians, calmly receiving news of the invasion, turned to the altars of their faith to pray for victory and peace. A joint service of solemnity was held in Bolton and a continuance of prayer is urged by the Canadian Prime Minister and Allied leaders.

Advancing on the Beachhead.

Bolton Enterprise - July 21, 1944

Dear Mr. Editor:

Received cigarettes yesterday and certainly glad to get them. We can get along without eat or sleep for a few days but not without smokes, and we smoke more over here in France than ever. I certainly take my hat off to the Jamboree Cigarette Fund, thanks very much.

D Day was no surprise to us but certainly a relief and gave us some satisfaction after all our training. It really was a great show and far beyond the imagination. There was actually a bridge of shipping from England to the invasion coast. This part of

France is all farming; their crops are fair and the people do not seem to have suffered much from the Germans. The farmers just go on with their work and pay no attention to anyone except to look up once in a while as we go by. Of course there are only very old and very young around, none of military age are seen. The villages are very small and old, though they are in ruins now.

We actually live in our tank or under it, as that is the only safe place as Jerry seems to shell us at the most unexpected times.

Things are very quiet for us at present; but we had plenty of excitement to last awhile. Our regiment is due for a rest and, of course we are looking forward to it. It will mean a real wash and general clean up, along with some sleep. Yesterday, attempting to have a bath, in about one-half gallon of water in a gas can, I had to dive into the slit trench three times and each time came out with more mud and dirt on than before. Boy what a sight in my birthday suit. Oh well, such is life in the armored Corps.

We have our ups and downs but all in all we are having a fair time. Give my regards to all. Thanks again for the smokes.

Bill Norton

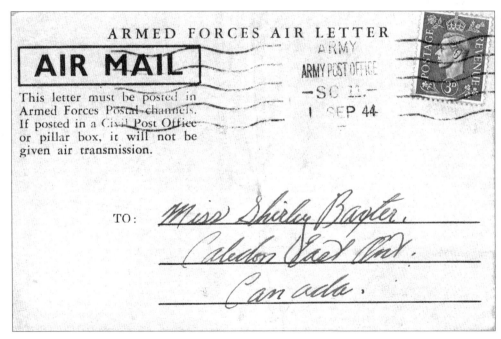

Armed Forces Air Letter to young Shirley Baxter of Caledon East from Lou Hutchinson, September, 1944.

<<< Chapter Twelve >>>
– 1945 –
The World at Peace - The Soldiers Come Home

Trooper "Pasteur" returning soldiers in 1945.
COURTESY VIOLA CORLESS

In the spring of 1945 the Allies were experiencing little serious fighting. The main German force remaining was in the Ruhr River area in western Germany where it was encircled and blockaded. On April 16, 1945 Russia commenced its offensive against Berlin. On April 29, with the sound of guns reportedly heard in Hitler's bunker, it was obvious the end was near. When victory came on May 7, 1945 it was certainly a significant military achievement. On this day General Jodl, representing the German High Command, signed the unconditional surrender at General Dwight David Eisenhower's headquarters in the city of Rhiems, about eighty miles northeast of Paris, France. General Eisenhower was the Commander of the Supreme Headquarters, Allied Expeditionary Forces in Europe.

Our nation erupted in glorious celebrations, taking place in schoolyards, town centres and city streets. Local farmers abandoned their fields for the day to join people in nearby communities. Enthusiastic celebrants followed bands playing lively marches. Local citizens were jubilant and words could not explain the degree of elation felt by Canadians. It was a fact that Canada had made a proud contribution to the total Allied effort during the Second World War and Canadians were well aware of what their country had accomplished. Canada matured as a nation and was recognized accordingly worldwide. As servicemen and women returned to their homes after the Victory in Europe or V-E Day, a rousing welcome awaited each one upon their arrival. The heroes had returned to their families and friends and the outpouring of pride showed on the face of everyone in the happy crowds.

On September 2, 1945 General Douglas MacArthur, Supreme Allied Commander for all land, sea and air forces in the southwest Pacific area, received the formal surrender of Japan on the deck of the battleship Missouri in Tokyo Bay. This marked V-J Day or Victory in Japan and the war was officially at an end. Celebrations were held in a somewhat similar fashion to those following V-E Day, with parades and bonfires taking place in many centres. Dances were held in dance pavilions and community halls. One occurred in a local church basement. The war was officially over and the people of our local communities were relieved and happy.

◇

At three o'clock in the afternoon of May 8, 1945 Winston Churchill addressed Britain and the world -

"Yesterday morning at 2.41 a.m. General Eisenhower's headquarters, General Jodl, the representative of the German High Command, and Grand Admiral Donitz, the designated head of the German State, signed the act of unconditional surrender of all German land, sea and air forces in Europe to the Allied Expeditionary Force, and simultaneously to the Soviet High Command. After five years and eight months, the war in Europe is over".

V-E Day

Like most school days, I remember Friday May 11, 1945 beginning in the usual manner with students entering their classrooms shortly before 9 a.m. However, in time it became far different than others. Mrs. Pearl Newlove's grades six, seven and eight scholars took their places in their room which was located closest to Albert Street in Bolton. About mid-morning a loud noise erupted outside which sounded like someone thumping on a metal object. Ellen (Nellie) Pilson, who sat two rows to my left and near the back of the room jumped from her seat and shouted, "The war is over." Mrs. Newlove said "Oh Nellie, please sit down - how do you know the war is over". Nellie replied "Because my mother said she would make a noise on a tub sitting on our front porch as soon as she heard on the radio that the war was over." Her parents Roger and Violet Pilson lived across the street from the school so the noise was heard quite clearly.

People of the village, indeed everyone among the Allied countries, were living in great anticipation that the war would soon end and an announcement to that effect had been expected for some time. It was therefore wonderful to learn that victory had been achieved and it was only natural for Nellie to be excited. Her two older brothers, Louie in the Lorne Scots and Roger in the Royal Canadian Army Service Corps, were overseas and they would be coming home.

The school principal, Albert Percival Rowe, dismissed all students for the day and they left in great haste jumping on their bicycles and running along the streets to their homes or to the main street of Bolton. Jean (Sheardown) Proctor remembers "the Derbyshire boys (Bob and Ted) who drove a convertible to school had as many students as possible pile into their car and on the running boards and rode around the town waving flags and cheering." According to Ted Derbyshire " this car, owned by their older brother John, was a green 1931 Ford Model "A" convertible with a rumble seat which could be removed to insert a wooden box for haulage purposes."

Bolton Enterprise - May 11, 1945
The community service of thanksgiving was held in the United Church, which was crowded to capacity. Local ministers took part in the fitting order of service. Rev. F.G. Fowler, Rev. J.J. Robbins and Rev. J.M. Boyd participating.

Celebration Marks The Great European Victory

Hitler was burned in Bolton on Tuesday night, as was also that arch crook, Mussolini, before a crowd of hundreds of celebrators of the great European victory. The villains were first shot as they hung on a scaffold and Sergeant Alf McNair, recently returned from overseas, did the honors. A huge torch light procession from the school grounds paraded through the principal streets of the town headed by the Bolton Citizens' Band, under the direction of Bandmaster Bint. William Bell, the veteran color bearer, headed off the procession, followed by veterans, reserve army officers, cadets and citizens. The business places and residences of the town were patriotically decorated for the occasion. A huge bonfire at the foot of the hill on Queen Street was ignited and added to the cheeriness of the occasion. The evening's entertainment was completed with a huge dance in the town hall when those who could crowd their way into the auditorium, were the town's guests.

The news of the surrender of Germany was received very quietly. In fact it seemed citizens were too overwhelmed to do anything at first. Shortly after the word was broadcast, the B.M. Engineering and Howard Furnace plants closed and Principal Rowe let school out. The children were the first to respond to the news. They were soon waving flags and exuberant boys tied cans to their bicycles to add a little noise. Flags and decorations soon appeared and the celebration ushered in.

The victory celebration brought to mind that of the last war, when fireworks and other means were used to mark the occasion. Older residents vividly recall the end of the Boer War - and a celebration it was. The late editor of this newspaper on that occasion had his face burned when letting off a charge of gun powder between two anvils. However, celebrations of past wars were pretty tame when compared with the show on Tuesday night. Everyone seemed to be having a good time and there was an absence of rowdyism, which characterized celebrations everywhere.

◇

Being fourteen years of age at the time, I remember this day in 1945 quite clearly. During the afternoon, dummies of Hitler and Mussolini were being prepared on the ground floor of Bolton Town Hall, located on the northwest corner of King and Chapel Streets. The fire truck had been moved out onto Chapel Street to make space for the several men who seemed delighted to take part in the task. It was obvious they had consumed some "tonic" (Black Horse Ale) and were going about their work with great joy.

With broad smiles, they organized the project in a very deliberate manner. When the dummies were almost completed, a citizen of the village "sailed" through the open King Street door, which brought a chuckle from everyone. This individual began spitting on the dummies and literally kicked the stuffings from each. The workers sat down on chairs somewhat amused while watching the performance and took advantage of the opportunity to partake of more "tonic". After re-stuffing the dummies, this fellow proceeded to take out his frustration on two more occasions, which spanned over most of the afternoon. Surprisingly, the others did not seem perturbed and the dummies became larger with each new stuffing.

Early that evening each dummy was suspended by a wire attached to a wooden framework erected on the west hillside of Queen Street, south of Elizabeth Street. Alf McNair was in charge of shooting the dummies from the structure. In uniform, he positioned himself flat on the highway, raising his rifle toward the targets. With each piercing shot a dummy fell to the ground with loud applause coming from the crowd. They were then taken to Bolton's main intersection, King and Queen Streets, where they were completely burned in a bonfire. It was a great time for celebrations in the area.

Bolton Enterprise - June 1, 1945

V - E D A Y
The streets were gaily decorated
And men with marching stride
Mothers looking anxiously
Little ones at their side.

A little girl looked carefully
Amidst the noisy crowd
When suddenly she turned about
And shouted out so loud.

"Mommy where is Daddy?
I see some soldiers here"!
And mommy looking down at her
Could see a little tear.

Your daddy is so far away
And he will not be here
Today or any other day,
He knew you'd ask my dear.

So please be brave and understand
Like your dad would want you to
For when he went he seemed to know
That it was his job to do.

So the little girl looked up again
And smiled amidst her tears
"If we can't be with daddy now
Will he wait through all the years"?

Her mother smiled and understood
"Of course he'll wait you'll see
And when we meet him once again
We'll be happy once more, we three".

- Anne Woods, Bolton, Ontario

V - J Day

Bolton Enterprise - August 17, 1945.

V - J Day was celebrated in Bolton with a parade, huge bonfire and finally a free dance in the Casino. Hundreds crowded into Bolton for the celebration, marking the war's end with Japan. The Band, under Bandmaster Bint, dispensed plenty of lively music. The arch culprits, Hitler, Mussolini and Togo, were shot ceremoniously and consumed by the flames. It was a bad night for these villains and everyone joined in the fun of the evening. Underneath it all, was a deep spirit of gratefulness that the war has finally ended victoriously.

A most pleasing feature was the hearty welcome extended to four Bolton servicemen recently returned from overseas. Reeve Cecil L. Gott extended a warm welcome on behalf of the municipality to Sergeant L.A. (Bill) Norton, Sergeant Major Harry Nelson, Sergeant Grant Cameron and Corporal Ernest Robertson. The men all spoke appreciatively of the kindness of those at home and expressed gratification at again being in their home circles.

Local Men and Women Return Home

Another significant event occurred in June 1945, that being the return from overseas of Orma's and my brother, John. Our mother had calculated from information contained in his letters and newspaper reports of ships' departure dates from England and arrivals in Canada that he would be arriving at Montreal aboard the Ile de France on a certain date. The Ile de France was a 43,153 ton troopship with steam turbines which discontinued this service in 1947 according to the "Ship's Statistics (1926-1958)". The trip from Montreal to Toronto would be made by train.

We agreed with her calculations because they seemed to make sense. A few days remained before the expected date and I had almost completed painting the blue and white trim of our farmhouse, located near the present west end of Hickman Street in Bolton. My mother hoped it would be finished before his arrival and it was. It rained heavily the day before our trip to Toronto but a "Welcome Home John" sign fringed with coloured crepe was tacked to the facer board of the front verandah and the grass was cut in readiness for his homecoming.

We travelled to the Coliseum building at the Toronto Exhibition Grounds in Otto Hardwick's 1939, two-door Pontiac car, where an anxious crowd awaited the soldiers' arrival. It was early evening and the seats were divided into alphabetical sections with people sitting or standing in eager anticipation. While waiting, Otto smoking a White Owl cigar on this occasion, thought he should meet John at the Union Station, if he was there, because he would not know we were at the Coliseum and therefore might not march in with the others.

Just before we heard the distant sound of the band leading the parade into the building, someone shouted, "There's John" as he entered the south entrance. He was walking quickly towards the "H" section, followed by Otto. My dad jumped over a row of seats and hugged him with tears in his eyes. Others were surprised by John's entrance and wondered if plans had changed. People were requested to remain in their seats until the soldiers arrived at which time they would proceed to their applicable section. Suddenly the band appeared playing a rousing march tune followed by smartly uniformed, briskly marching soldiers. Almost immediately soldiers ran toward the surrounding seats and people stampeded to meet them. Absolute chaos followed. It was a moving event, physically and emotionally, and Toronto's Mayor Robert H. Saunders and other politicians of the day did not make the scheduled speeches.

Otto Hardwick can be credited for his foresight in thinking John might not come to the Coliseum. We later learned it had been his intention to remain in Toronto that night and travel to Bolton by train the next morning. He had been overseas for about 3 1/2 years and I was proud to tell others my age that my brother was a member of the Royal Canadian Air Force and was now home after serving in England, France and Germany.

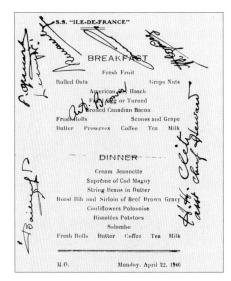

Menu from the "Ile de France", the ship on which many local men and women returned home.

COURTESY TOM BULLOCH

Bolton Enterprise - March 16, 1945

Two local soldiers in two branches of the services were officially welcomed home at a reception held in the Town Hall on Tuesday evening. They were Lieutenant C.F. Daines and Flight Lieutenant E.W. Edwards, the former a Bolton boy and the latter of the Castlederg district.

The returning men were met by the band under the leadership of bandmaster Bint, who featured rousing patriotic numbers. Warden C.L. Gott was the chairman of the evening. The address of welcome was made to Lieutenant Daines by Clerk Herb Elliott. In his reply he expressed his delight at being home again. Wounded some months ago, with bullets in his ankle Lieutenant Daines is able to walk without a cane, and will undergo further treatment, it is understood. He referred to the splendid work of mercy being done by the Canadian Red Cross. From the time he was wounded until his return home, the manifold services of this great organization were manifested on every hand. Blood plasma, excellent hospital facilities in the battle zone and in England, the little amenities like books to read and comforts galore were just evidences of this great organization's heart. In closing, he spoke of the fine work done by local organizations: The Overseas Box Fund with its record of sending boxes of well chosen contents, and the Cigarette Fund who have kept a chain of smokes and gum going overseas.

Reeve R.M.Lavery of Albion, addressed a note of welcome to Flight Lieutenant Edwards, who replied most fittingly. He told of his experiences with the R.A.F., in the Near East, chasing Germany's top ranking general, Rommel, out of North Africa, service in Cypress, Italy and in the Eastern Mediterranean Command. Flight Lieutenant Edwards thanked the Cigarette Fund for their kindness.

It is noteworthy that both Lieutenant Daines and Flight Lieutenant Edwards came up through the ranks for their commissions and are both sons of veterans of the last war. Lieutenant Daines' father passed away a few years ago as the result of war disabilities and Flight Lieutenant Edwards' father, T.E. Edwards, his mother and his wife, were present on the platform Tuesday night, as was Mrs. Daines, mother of Lieutenant Daines.

A member of the audience expressed it aptly when she said, "These two boys have certainly proved themselves the worthy sons of worthy sires".

Rev. J.M. Boyd and Rev. J.J. Robbins had a part in the program and Mrs. Earl Small presided at the piano. Mr. Thomas Crickmore sang two very delightful solos in his usual capable manner.

Reeve Gott dealt briefly with the homecoming of the boys and plans under advisement for the ultimate reception and presentation to the large group of heroes of which we are so proud. Closing prayers were offered, asked for Divine help in the bringing of the great conflict now in its final period in Europe to an early and complete victory.

Bolton Enterprise - August 10, 1945

COURTESY SHIRLEY CANNON

Soldiers Warmly Welcomed by Home Folks at Caledon East

On Friday evening last, a large and enthusiastic audience gathered in the Community Memorial Hall to tender a reception to eight returned servicemen of our community. The Hall and stage were appropriately decorated for the occasion. The program was divided into three sections. The first was Devotional, conducted by Rev. J.S. Veals and Rev. N.H. Noble and consisted of hymns, Scripture lesson and prayer. After the observance of a one minute silence in honor of those who had paid the supreme sacrifice, the Last Post was sounded by Mr. Bernard Clowes.

During the second part of the program, Mr. J.N. Proctor was called to give a history of the Cigarette Club and a summary of its activities. The records revealed that the Club had sent overseas over one-quarter million cigarettes, and that this amount had been duplicated by the local branch of the Canadian Legion 292. Before he called the returned men to take seats on the platform, and presenting them to the audience, a brief outline of the formation, work and aim of our Memorial Reception Committee was given.

Those introduced were Flight Lieutenant Gregg Howard, Corporal Bill Evans, Corporal Morley Hall, Leading Aircraftsman Bert Appleby, Corporal Art Bird, Private Duncan Graham, Private Harry Groves and Private Alex Lynch. A short outline of each man's service consisting of date of enlistment, branch of the service, and nature of his military activities was given. The address of welcome was given by Mr. Roy Lavery, Reeve of Albion, who spoke in glowing terms of the splendid sacrifice and contribution our men had rendered to King and Country. Community singing under the direction of Mr. T.R. McCartney followed, and then each serviceman was called to speak a few words. In their remarks all paid high tribute to the work of the Red Cross and expressed their thanks and appreciation for the packages of cigarettes and other comforts sent to them from the Cigarette Club, the church, and from their many friends.

The remainder of the evening was spent in dancing, with Mr. Orville Baxter as floor manager. Music was supplied by Barbour's Orchestra. Murray Nelson, Chairman of the Committee performed the duties of master of ceremonies for the evening and Mrs. Frank Myers presided at the piano.

◇

Reception At Palgrave

On Friday evening of last week, a large crowd gathered in the Town Hall to welcome home and to tender a Reception to three returned servicemen of this community. The hall was beautifully decorated for the occasion. Mr. Joseph Oliver, acting as chairman, called the boys to take seats on the platform, and gave them a hearty welcome. Mr. Roy Lavery, Reeve of Albion Township, welcomed the boys home and spoke very highly of their splendid contribution to their country. Short addresses were also given by Mr. Willard Taylor and Mr. Gordon Munro. Mrs. H.V. Reynar read the following address:

Dear Bill, Clare and Milton:

We have gathered here this evening to welcome home three of our local boys namely, Bill Smith, Clarence Thompson and Milton Rowley, and also to give grateful thanks for their safe return. At the beginning of the war we heard the troop trains in the night, and as the whistle sounded "war, war, war", we, who kept constant vigil sent our prayers winging after the caravans of those who were destined to thread their way to the far places of the earth. Peace .... and now in the silence of the night we hear the whistle sound once more. Listen, you'll hear them too, "home, home, home", and, as we listen, we again send our prayers winging to the Great Father that he may richly bless every knight of 1939 and 1945, and strengthen all of us to keep untarnished the prize they endured and suffered so much to win for the world; help to make us more worthy of all that they, through their suffering, devotion to all that is good and true, and gallant endurance, have so unselfishly placed at our feet. May we never fail them, and may we never cease to remember the Eternal Garland of Greatness they have placed upon the brow of Canada.

May we all resolve with His help, to strive daily to attain the ideal they held of us through those dark, stormy, lonely historic destiny-fraught days, which now, please God, are behind us. The whistle sounds once more, "Home, home, home, sweet, sweet home", and our prayers follow them on through the silence of the night. There are no words for what we would frame in speech - it is much too big for that - but God who reads the hearts of all, knows that we are truly grateful for the great gift of their giving, - Peace.

◇

The booklet entitled *Nobleton Heritage 1800-1976*, produced by the Nobleton Womens' Institute states in part - "During World War 2 quite a number of boys and girls joined up from Nobleton and district". From available records, it appears that two women from the Nobleton area served. They are Emma Marion Butler and Ruth Hoover. "When these boys and girls returned home to Nobleton, a banquet was held in the Hall for them and they were presented with rings".

Kleinberg Celebrates

Bolton Enterprise - May 24, 1946

Kleinburg really celebrated last week. Twenty-nine of her school's 45 pupils skipped classes at recess, townsmen spent the morning hanging up banners, pennants and flags along the one and only street, women baked cakes, pies and cookies, and boys and girls decorated the village hall.

Shortly before noon more than 120 of the villagers piled into 16 automobiles and drove to Exhibition Park, Toronto, to welcome one of her last sons to return from the war.

Arriving at the Coliseum with more than 400 other returning troops from the Ile de France, 20 year old Private Frank Shaw was immediately singled out by the delegation in the southwest end of the huge arena, and three cheers went up before the city mayor had his chance. It was almost an hour before Frank climbed in his car to lead the procession

Welcome Home

Do you think the trees are lovelier?
The grass more richly green
The birds of summer sweeter
Than they have ever been?

Does the kettle sing more joyously
Are the summer nights star-clad
Do white sheets bring calm slumber
Do you wake refreshed and glad?

You do? Well so do we dears
Since mighty oceans foams
Laid down its magic carpet
For the ships that brought you home.

A soldier comes home.

back to Kleinburg, his right hand hanging limp, his back black and blue, and smoking a cigar with a lighted cigarette in between his fingers.

Frank Shaw's great grandfather settled in Kleinburg in 1841 and opened a hardware shop. His grandfather and his father have operated it ever since. He himself worked in it until he was old enough to enlist in early 1944. Six months later he embarked for Europe as a despatch rider with the R.C.E.M.E. He spent his entire 22 months overseas as a member of that unit from the time he landed in Italy until he left Cleve, Germany, not many days ago. He wouldn't say how many miles he travelled over highways and fields on his motorcycle in front of his workshop unit that repaired everything in the army from a tank to a wrist watch, but he mentioned that he crossed Italy twice, rode from Florence to Marseille, and a few days later began the long trip from there to Nimigen and Arnheim.

Frank isn't old enough to vote yet, but the town was his. In the early part of the evening he sat down to the "biggest and best feed I've had in years". He rolled up his sleeves and helped wash the dirty dishes, went for a bicycle ride down the road to have a look at his garden that he'd started before he went away, which the townsfolk had looked after for him for two years, and inspected the plot of land beside it, on which he wants to build a house one of these days. He has not changed his friends said - just a little sunburned, that's all.

Shortly before dusk the entire village and some 200 people from a couple of neighboring settlements, flocked around the Shaw homestead, waiting for Frank to return from his tour of inspection. The piper's band began playing, Frank fell in behind the big bass drummer, most of the school children followed, and another parade had marched off for the village hall, where Frank entered amid deafening cheers and roars. Frank took his place on the stage with five veterans of this war and half a dozen from the First Great War. The mayor uttered a few warm words of welcome. The big bass drummer sang a Scottish song, the Barnyard Quartet sang a local favorite, someone else did a dance, and after several more numbers the hall was cleared, the band struck up the music, and Frank was dancing with his mother for the rest of the evening, even if he did favor Jean Egan, who sat across from him all through their school days.

"Well, good-night, Frank, and all the best", someone said. "What are you going to do to-morrow?". "Oh, I guess I'll start back in the store," he said. "Good-night".

Yes, Kleinburg sure went to town for one of her sons. "But we've done this for all our eight boys who went overseas and came back," said one of the oldest inhabitants.

Veterans Remember

Four well-known and popular servicemen from the Bolton area have contributed interesting recollections of their experiences during the Second World War, as follows.

Bolton Navy Veteran, Gerald Robinson, Looks Back:

I was growing up in Palgrave, but had gone to Windsor to work and while there, at the age of 17, I joined the Navy and was shortly on my way to Cornwallis to finish basic training. I was called to serve as an anti-aircraft gunner on board a corvette - the "Fennel". We were usually on convoy duty from Newfoundland to Londonderry, Ireland, a trip of approximately 14 days each way.

One eventful day December 24, 1944, a ship - a minesweeper called the "Clayoquot" was hit by a German torpedo from a submarine. This wasn't very far from Halifax and we happened to be in this convoy and were appointed to stay behind to pick up survivors while the rest of the convoy proceeded to Newfoundland. Four sailors went down in the ship and the rest were plucked from the icy cold waters. They were suffering terribly from frozen limbs and we gave them our blankets and rations of rum and then got them back to Halifax and waiting ambulances. We then started back on Christmas day to rejoin the convoy, all the while trying to trace the submarine. The rest of the runs I was on were more or less uneventful except from time to time I would see the floating wreckage of other ships that had sunk.

On VE Day we were docked in Halifax and a big commotion arose during all the hoopla. My recollection of events was that the merchants closed their establishments and then the celebrants broke into them and looted the stores, especially the liquor outlets. A streetcar was set afire and police cruisers overturned and general melee was the order of the day. Martial law came the next day to restore law and order. Part of my job was to confiscate stolen goods that any of our crew were bringing aboard the ship.

The "Fennel" was decommissioned in Scotland and after a couple of weeks wait, I came back to Canada aboard the troop ship "Ile de France". There were 10,000 troops on board and one unfortunate fellow who had served six years as a paratrooper overseas was killed accidentally by a bullet while he slept.

I was at home on leave when the final end of the war came.

◇

Another naval veteran from Bolton, Art Corless recalls being informed in 1943 he was going to be posted overseas. While on his last leave, Art and his girlfriend, Viola Fletcher, decided to get married before he left. During his train trip to the east coast, a two hour delay occurred in Montreal and as a result, Art arrived in Halifax as his ship, Esquimalt, a destroyer, was leaving the dock. About one hour later the ship was torpedoed with three-quarters of Art's division lost along with many others. Whether the train delay in Montreal saved Art's life will never be known. Art says he was confined to barracks for seven days for being AWOL (absent without leave) but after the fifth day he was posted to seagoing tug patrol duty and remained in this capacity until the end of the war.

◇

George Kirby was a Sergeant with the Irish Regiment who saw action in Italy, France, Belgium, Holland and Germany from 1942 to 1946. He recalls:

I was on board a ship leading the way from Eastbourne, England to Naples, Italy, which had just changed positions. Having completed the change, the ship now in the lead was torpedoed. We had gone through the Straits of Gibraltar and could see lights on shore from Morocco when the convoy was attacked. Our ship was strafed by aircraft. After the attack the passengers and crew of the torpedoed ship were picked up by our ship, the only casualty being a nurse who, when climbing a rope ladder on to the rescue ship, fell backward on to a lifeboat and broke her back. When we got underway again our ship was surrounded by destroyers dropping depth charges because it was believed that there were German U-boats in the area. The torpedoed ship was carrying army hospital equipment and the passengers consisted of doctors, nurses and troops. It was towed all that night and the next day by a destroyer and about six o'clock that night the lines were released and I saw the ship sinking. The passengers and crew of the torpedoed ship were taken to a port on the coast of North Africa where they were dropped off, and we proceeded to Italy.

George said his brother, Corporal Allan Kirby also of the Irish Regiment, was on the same ship at this time.

◇

149

Elmer A. Moss, a Sergeant in the Provost Corps, recalls:

After I enlisted I spent a little time taking basic training before going overseas to the UK. The basic training included field gunning and various aspects of signaling. During that time I had the opportunity to train for a commissioned officer. I declined because my long term objective was to join a Canadian police force when the war ended. With that in mind I wanted to get overseas and look for an opportunity to get into the Canadian Provost Corps.

When I arrived in England I was posted to No. 3 Field Gun Company. I was not there very long when I had the opportunity to transfer to the Canadian Provost Corps section at First Canadian Army Headquarters. I attended intensive training in police work and then returned to First Canadian Army Headquarters and No. 11 Company of the Canadian Provost Corps, which had arrived from Canada as the Provost Company for the First Canadian Army Headquarters.

In the UK the Corps was extensively involved in highway patrols to ensure that army troops were obeying the traffic laws. We also patrolled towns and cities in association with local police. The Corps was also responsible during maneuvers to ensure that troops reached the planned destination.

When we embarked for the continent we were then right in the thick of battles. I have vivid memories of the battles for Caen and the Falaise. It was there that I got nicked in the leg by a cannon shell fired from a German war plane. I doctored myself and did not report it to avoid the possibility of getting sent somewhere else for medical attention and not getting back to my company.

We continued through France, Belgium, into Germany and freed Holland from the Germans following which the war ended. My Father died while I was in Holland and I was allowed to return to Canada where, after a leave of absence, I received my discharge. Meanwhile I had been in touch with the Toronto Police and the Ontario Provincial Police. The day I was discharged I saw the Deputy Commissioner of the O.P.P. and while still in uniform I was selected and within a couple of days started my training. My function in the O.P.P. was almost identical to that of the Provost Corps except that I changed uniforms and did not have to deal with military matters.

I had no difficulty in dealing with my military or O.P.P. functions both of which I enjoyed. I progressed through the O.P.P. ranks until I was retired with the rank of Chief Superintendent not to mention about six months of acting assistant commissioner.

I feel very grateful the way life has turned out for me. The most grateful of which was the fact that I married a real gem of a wife. She was an English girl from Epsom, Surrey, England. We have had nothing but a happy married life as well as a family of four girls who are also happily married.

≪≪≪ Chapter Thirteen ≫≫≫
Casualties and Losses

Remembrance Day honours Canadians in all the armed services around the world, who served to maintain freedom and peace. It reminds us of the tragedies of battles, which took the lives of more than 116,000 servicemen and women in wars during this century. Their final resting-places are located in 74 countries. Wreaths are placed at Cenotaphs to remember their achievements and their sacrifices and to show our respect for those who did not return.

In spite of the known dangers, these servicemen and women enlisted because they were dedicated to preserving the well-being of Canada and they fought with iron wills to protect this nation against all harm. They served to protect their families and to keep safe the traditions and customs of this great land. While doing so, they never lost hope that someday they might return to their former way of life to pursue their dreams. It is therefore appropriate that the Government of Canada has acclaimed the first Sunday in June as Canadian Forces Day, the first being June 2, 2002.

Why They Fought

Bolton Enterprise - April 17, 1942
An unfinished letter, its lines filled with the triumphant and unflinching spirit of its author under the shadow of death, has been bequeathed by a 25-year-old Canadian bomber pilot as his last message to a world in which he no longer lives.

> *"I am the lucky one as I have gone to the land where there is no time. It will be only a momentary lapse in the infinite before you are all with me, and so, courage!"*

So wrote Flight Sergeant Reg Robb, before his death on February 26th. He left the unfinished letter in the commanding officer's possession with a message that it should be delivered to his father, Judge W.T. Robb of Orangeville, when the simple arithmetic of death, which he knew so well, would call his number.

> *Dear Dad, Mother and all the beloved Robb family:*
> *I can give this letter no date, as it is possible that it may never be used, but in case anything goes wrong, this will be my last word to you all.*
> *Don't feel sorry for me, as I've gone to something better and the day is not far removed when we will all be reunited. I have lived a happy life and enjoyed it to the fullest - having made a host of friends and (I hope) very few enemies.*
> *Always having been an idealist rather than a realist it was natural that I should answer the call of my conscience to join the service in a crusade against a barbarous enemy who threatens to annihilate mankind. I should never have been able to rest in peace for all the rest of my days had I ignored the call.*
> *The greatest problem I had to solve was the one of the Robb family. I knew that having been brought up as true Canadians, that the whole family would plunge into the conflict, body and soul, and that there would be hearts broken - Those at home who could do nothing but patiently wait. Yes! They also serve! Whatever the end may be you will all be able to proudly walk in any company and explain, "We did our bit." I am the lucky one, as I have gone to a land where there is no time. It will*

be only a momentary lapse in the infinite before you are all with me, and so courage!

Having considered our manner of living, and making an odious comparison with that one which Hitler is trying to push on us, I could arrive at no other decision than to help preserve our civilization. The country that had been so kind to our family was in danger. Was the supreme sacrifice too much to give? No. A quarter of a century ago thousands of our young men were forced to make the same decision. They held up their part bravely and died in the realization of having accomplished their goal. But the goal was not reached — it was only a lull in the storm. To us they threw the torch, and my only hope is that I have the fortitude and ability to be able to handle it in the same proud and unconquerable manner.

One of these nights I will climb into my plane and take off into the black. I shall ascend above the clouds to the peaceful atmosphere only realized by those chosen few who have been given the opportunity of meeting it. How strange it is - so serene, calm and clean. It is like being taken out of a world gone mad for blood, into a land of make-believe. White billowy clouds below, and the moon and stars brightly beaming from above. I will sit back and thank God that He has allowed me this divine pleasure in His sad world. I will take a deep breath of that sweet fresh air - for miles it will be thus - thinking to myself,

"God's in His Heaven, all's right with the world."

Suddenly the realization will sweep over me that all's not right with the world. I will be rudely awakened from my reverie with that peculiar odor associated with aircraft. Fumes of burnt petrol stinging my nostrils - the ominous hum of my motors - I have reached my destination. Alas I must descend to the cruel world once more. Even my kite senses the change. From the calm rocking back and forth it will begin to shudder as I give more power. We will be tossed about by the turbulent clouds - confusion will reign everywhere. Blue pencils of light will stab out, searching frantically of the death-dealing monster that is coming to revenge those people of the horribly scarred English cities. Bomb doors open. There go the messengers of death. One from London - one from Coventry - one from Birmingham - and so on until the monster will be repaid a thousand fold for the destruction of our people.

The Germans will scurry to their little rat holes to get away from us, but the angel of death will be down there, swinging his flaming sword in ever increasing circles, and ever increasing frenzy. I will say a prayer for these people, whose minds have become so distorted, that they believe themselves capable of ruling the world. Pity will reel out of my soul, but after all a mad dog must be exterminated, and below me will be thousands of "mad dogs." Horrible vengeance will be meted out to those who aided the destruction of some of my best friends.

Suddenly there will be an awful crash - we've had it. A lucky hit - or perhaps I should say an unlucky hit. Surprisingly I am not afraid - a peace that I never knew before engulfs me and I wait impatiently to pass through the gates into the unknown.

To you who are left behind is a task - a huge task. A new world order must be created where men can live in peace and plenty without fear or prejudice. It is up to you to see our job finally completed. No more lives must be sacrificed to satisfy the hunger of Mars. Beat your swords into ploughshares earth, good-will toward men. Never again allow the rivers of our world to run with the blood of our youth. I am depending on you to aid in this movement.

The ancient philosopher, Confucius, once wrote: "It is not truth that makes man great, but man that makes truth great." This is the sort of man that must be moulded in the future generations, for if there is great truth on earth then there will be great men, and great men are certainly not those who try to become great at the expense of other people. - Globe and Mail

◇

The following letter was discovered in the papers of Bolton's Robert McAllister, a member of the Lorne Scots (1941-1946) in World War 11. His son James, found the letter following his father's death in 1996 and felt it would touch the hearts of many residents:

Strangely enough, on first thought, I find the question "Why I fight?" most difficult to reply. Certainly not because I must. Whether or not I would, and more, not because I want to - God knows the lust to kill is no normal desire. For a moment perhaps, with the splendor of parades and the roll of drums, thoughts of King and Country come to mind, of Honour, Glory, Crusades of Old. But such, I must confess, are thoughts reserved only for such opportune occasions.

But with me always are the thoughts of what must happen should I and the millions of others with me have neither the courage nor the will to fight.

To think of our own mothers, our fathers, our sisters and brothers, our wives and sweethearts, in short, our people, in the clutches of the beasts who would rule the world, by cunning or by force, to think of the ignominies they would surely suffer, the hardships they would endure, that is surely enough. And should you and I not have the will to fight, terrible indeed would be their fate.

Daily from the vassal states of Europe we have proof of that, facts horrible enough when viewed distantly and impersonally, but terrible beyond expression should the cast be filled with our personal friends. Not that we have ourselves escaped the tolls of war, every bombed home, every war-crippled civilian and soldier, are concrete and insistent reminders of the beasts who worship Mars.

And so I must admit, not for a better world, nor glory for my country, but for my home and family is my will to fight. For given that, shall we not have all? God grant me courage to fight for them alone, to do less I should not be a man.

B51755 Pte. McAllister, R.E.
Lorne Scots
No. 1 C.C.R.U.
Cdn. Army Overseas

Missing and Wounded

Bolton Enterprise - November 26, 1943
Lieutenant Addie Cooney of Lloydtown came through the harrowing experience of being aboard a ship that was torpedoed in the Mediterranean Sea. She was among the many Canadians rescued and taken to North Africa. She is at present serving in Italy. Nursing Sister Cooney, before enlistment, had charge of the operating room in St. Michael's Hospital.

Bolton Enterprise - November 19, 1943
Flight Lieutenant Grant Jackson, is serving in North Africa as a fighter pilot when last heard from. Flight Sergeant Ross Banting Jackson is reported missing after the raid on Kassel on October 25th. The young airmen are sons of Mr. John E. Jackson of Adjala Township.

◇

Acting Lance Corporal William James Halbert, who according to a telegram received by his parents, Rev. and Mrs. Robert G. Halbert, Mono Mills, from the Director of Records at Ottawa on Tuesday October 26th, was officially reported wounded in action October 13th. The telegram went on to say that Lance Corporal Halbert was remaining on duty with his unit, which leads to the belief that his wounds may not be very serious. The young soldier who is 22 years of age, enlisted in the Fusiliers at London, Ontario on April 8th 1942, and commenced his training at Niagara-on-the-Lake. His regiment was sent to the United States to bring up a group of two hundred German Flying Officers to an internment camp in Alberta. Young Halbert took subsequent training at Vernon, British Columbia and on Vancouver Island and while at the latter centre volunteered to go overseas with a reinforcement unit, leaving Canada about September 23, 1942. In a recent letter to his parents, he stated that he was in Italy with "C" Company of the R.C.R. and was going up with General Montgomery's Eighth Army.

Losses

Bolton Enterprise - December 1, 1944

Flight Lieutenant Stanley Herbert Ross Cotterill, D.F.C., 24, is reported missing on a special mission over enemy territory on October 18, according to official word received by his mother, Mrs. Gordon Cotterill of 3 Claxton Blvd. Toronto. His name appeared in an air force casualty list at Ottawa, along with that of Flying Officer Colin Cowans Finlayson, D.F.C. and Bar, of Victoria, British Columbia who was his navigator on the mission.

Flight Lieutenant Cotterill received his Distinguished Flying Cross last September on the night after D-Day when he bagged four German planes in the dark. With "perfect" night vision according to air force tests, he has also built himself a reputation as a robomb destroyer during his nine months overseas. Before being posted to operations, he served in Canada for nearly three years as an instructor.

Born in Beamsville, Ontario, Flight Lieutenant Cotterill attended Beamsville High School and was employed at the Imperial Bank, Bolton, before enlisting. His brother Benedict, is training at the Service Flying Training School in Winnipeg, and expects to get his wings in March. Their father is a member of the Veterans' Guard stationed at Bowmanville.

◇

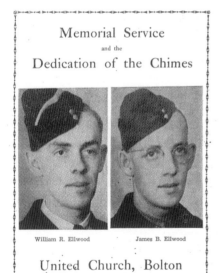

Memorial Service
and the
Dedication of the Chimes

William R. Ellwood   James B. Ellwood

United Church, Bolton

Sunday, June 29th, 1947

Private James Bannerman Ellwood was killed January 17, 1944, age 27, around the town of Arielli, west of Ortona, Italy. It was here that he was last seen storming a height with a section of men. Officers say he was courageously rushing up the hill, gun in hand when the enemy opened up machine gun fire. It is reported but three men returned from the mission. (*Bolton Enterprise*)

Flying Oficer William Ralph Ellwood was killed April 28, 1944, age 30. Halifax aircraft #LL258 was shot down and crashed near St. Trond, Belgium whilst on a night operation against Montzen, Belgium. The Halifax was shot down by Heinz Schnaufer who was one of the top German night fighter pilots. Flying Officer Bomb Aimer William Ellwood was buried at St. Trond, Belgium, exhumed and reburied in the War Cemetery, Heverlee, Brabant, Belgium. (Quoted from *They Shall Grow Not Old*)

With reference to Bill Ellwood's death, Rev. J. Melville Boyd, minister of Bolton United Church from 1943 to 1953 and Palgrave United Church from 1951 to 1953 states in his memoirs: "One night shortly after 11.00 p.m., Roger Pilson, Sr. came to the house, holding a telegram in his hand. At the time, he was an employee of the Canadian Pacific Railway with responsibility at the Bolton Station. It was his task to deliver telegrams and this one was for Lillian Ellwood, wife of William Ellwood. Earlier in the war, Roger had the responsibility of delivering the message to the Ellwood family that their son, James, had been killed in action. Now he had a telegram to inform the family that William was missing, presumed dead. He told me that he just couldn't do it - would I take his place?

Difficult as it was, I agreed. She guessed why I had come with the message that she dreaded might come. We sat and talked well into the morning, drank some coffee and dared to hope that maybe some further word would come to change the picture. We had prayers and took our grief to the ONE who understood."

In memory of Bill and Jim Ellwood, chimes were installed in Bolton United Church on Nancy Street where a dedication service was conducted on Sunday June 29, 1947. Ex-Chaplain Rev. T.V. Hart of Woodbridge was the officiating clergyman. On that day, Bolton Citizens' Band led a parade of ex-servicemen and women, as well as members of local civic bodies, to the church where a large crowd had assembled for the occasion.

When the "hilltop" area of Bolton was developed on the south hill, a street was named Ellwood Drive in memory of the Ellwood brothers. In September 1960, a new four-room school opened on that street which was called Ellwood Memorial Public School and later, Ellwood Memorial Senior Public School.

Bill and Jim Ellwood were the only soldiers from Bolton to lose their lives during the Second World War. The news of their deaths within a period of about three months stunned the entire village. It was a terrible tragedy, taking place at a time when all residents of Bolton knew every inhabitant of the community. As the war raged on, there was great respect for all soldiers. Citizens held all the servicemen and women in high regard and were proud of them.

The Ellwood brothers were fine young men, pleasant and kind in their own distinct ways. I recall seeing Bill on his last leave before going overseas. He was walking into his parents' residence, adjacent to their store, Carload Groceteria, on Queen Street just south of Mill Street, with his wife Lillian carrying their daughter, Beverly, in her arms. There was a light rain falling on a misty afternoon as I made my way home from school. Bill looked very striking in his officer's uniform of the Royal Canadian Air Force. My last recollection of Jim was during a skating carnival in the Hickman Street Arena (near Glasgow Road). Wearing his Army uniform, he was assisting George Robertson, while they steadied a structure through which a speeding skater jumped and landed on the ice to the enjoyment of the excited spectators.

Bill and Jim Ellwood are gone but they are certainly not forgotten.

◇

Details of the death of William Robert Moore were sent by his padre, Captain K.A.J. Sunstrum. The following excerpts were taken from his letter to Mr. & Mrs. Moore:

Regina Rifle Regiment
C.A.O.

William Robert Moore was killed in action on April 30th. We were still very much at war. Regina Rifles were engaged in mopping up enemy resistance on the outskirts of the city Leer, just over the Ems River in the north west Germany. B Company, of which he was a member, was attacking a German barracks that was putting up stiff resistance. He had been a company "runner", but was driving the company, "Jeep" that day. This Jeep under protection of the Red Cross flag is used in action for the evacuation of casualties. One of our platoons had come under heavy enemy machine gun fire and had suffered casualties. He drove to their platoon area to get them. It was while running across open ground to assist his wounded comrades that he was hit by enemy fire. He died instantly.

His loss is keenly felt in our company. He had been with B Company, steadily since the start of the invasion of Europe, that is with the exception of the time he spent in hospital after being wounded on the Leopold canal 1st October.

He was rated one of the originals, having come in with the unit on "D" Day last June. He was liked, appreciated and trusted by all who knew and came in contact with him. He was a very good boy. I say "boy" because of his youthful appearance, as a soldier he was one hundred per cent "man".

William Robert Moore is buried in grave VIII.E.II., Holten Canadian War Cemetery, Overijssel, Netherlands (Bolton Enterprise)

LOCAL SERVICEMEN WHO LOST THEIR LIVES IN THE SECOND WORLD WAR

JOHN DAVID ARMSTRONG

ALAN CAMERON BONE

JOHN B. BROWNLEE

WILLIAM PATERSON CONNELL

JOHN ROBERT COOPER

STANLEY HERBERT ROSS COTTERILL

ALBERT E. CROCKER

MICHAEL TERRANCE JOSEPH CRONIN

GEORGE ALVIN DAVIS

ALBERT GORDON EDWARDS

JAMES BANNERMAN ELLWOOD

WILLIAM RALPH ELLWOOD

HOWARD RICHARD EZEARD

JAMES EDWARD GROGAN

WILLIAM JOHN HESP

FREDERICK GRANT JACKSON

ROSS BANTING JACKSON

WILLIAM ROBERT MOORE

RICHARD HERBERT ORR

GEORGE REID

REGINALD FRANCIS ROBB

C. GRAHAM SANDERSON

NORMAN EDWARD SANDFORD

RAYMOND ROBERT ALEXANDER SPEIRS

WILLIAM PETER STOREY

GORDON ELMER CLIFFORD WALKER

HARRY WARD WILLIAMSON

STANLEY ALBERT WOOD

⋘ Chapter Fourteen ⋙
Honours and Medals

The Second World War involved a different type of warfare compared to the First World War. This time a heavier concentration of Air Force and Navy strength joined with the Army to present a united attack on several fronts. Bravery was just as prominent in this war, but with the aid of better equipment and advanced technology, more effective and faster progress was achieved. Among those who contributed to this success are seven distinguished servicemen and one distinguished servicewoman from this area.

◇

"The Canadians in Italy" by Lt. Col. J.W.L. Nicholson gives an interesting account of Sergeant Norman John McMahon who was awarded the Distinguished Conduct Medal at the time of the Battle of the Rimini Line (September 3 - 22, 1944) as follows:

The day's fighting produced a noteworthy example of the good work done by junior infantry leaders throughout the Italian campaign. Corporal N. J. McMahon of the Royal Canadian Regiment was in command of the foremost section in the leading platoon of the company attacking towards the Rimini airfield. When machine-gun fire from a nearby house held up the advance, on his own initiative he led his men across fire-swept ground to assault the enemy post. In a hand-to-hand fight they killed twelve of the defenders, estimated at a platoon in strength, captured two and put the remainder to flight. Then McMahon, who had personally accounted for five or six Germans, pushed on with his section to seize the company objective. His bravery and initiative brought him the D.C.M.

Bolton Enterprise - December 15, 1944
Squadron Leader D. C. Graham, Senior Medical Officer, Posted Overseas

The station hospital in particular, and the station as a whole, suffered its second great loss, within two weeks, this time, the powers that be, going straight to the top and posting its Senior Medical Officer, S./L. D.C. Graham, overseas.

S./L. Graham took the Hippocratic Oath in 1938, completing his course in medicine at the University of Toronto. As an under graduate, he was an outstanding member of his class, combining athletic proficiency with scholastic ability, achieving distinction in both these fields. As he was a member of Toronto's intercollegiate rugby team, and on the side was elected to an honorary medical facility, reserved for the intelligentsia.

Of Scottish decent, and following in the footsteps of his father, who was a medical officer in the last war, S./L. Graham enlisted early in this war in the Royal Canadian Medical Corps and voluntarily joined the medical branch of the R.C.A.F. at the time of its conception four years ago. During the past four years he has unstintingly given his talent, which combined medical and administrative ability to the betterment of the service.

While at "Mountain View", he has continued to partake in sports of all forms, these past two summers being particularly active in managing the station baseball team. While on the station, he has also served his term as president of the Officers Mess.

However, undoubtedly his greatest and most lasting contribution to the continual welfare of the station is the fact that during his period as Senior Medical Officer, our hospital has been enlarged. At his insistence a new wing to the hospital was added in the spring of 1943. As a result of this, hospital facilities here are second to none on any station of comparable size in the RCAF.

After returning from Newfoundland in September 1942, S./L. Graham has given our station two years of most excellent service.

At his long sought for posting overseas, we say goodbye with regret and wish him the very best. (*Mountain View, RCAF paper*)

Doctor and Mrs. Graham presently reside in a retirement residence in Richmond, British Columbia.

Bolton Enterprise - January 26, 1945

Squadron Leader John W. Perry has been awarded the Distinguished Service Order on completion of two tours of operations as a pilot during which his achievements were "a splendid tribute to his outstanding ability, great personal courage and iron determination".

Squadron Leader Perry attended Linton Public School and his many friends in King Township are offering congratulations on the honors he has received. He recently reported for duty at Trenton, Ontario, Air Training Headquarters.

◇

The following information pertaining to John Perry has been supplied by his wife, the former June Campbell, whose father Brigadier Colin A. Campbell served overseas for six years during World War II.

Lancaster bomber.

COURTESY MURRAY HESP

A Squadron Leader at the age of 21, a member of the famed Pathfinder Squadrons and winner of the D.S.O and D.F.C., one of the few Canadian airmen to receive both decorations, John Perry was fresh out of high school when he enlisted. As Master Bomber on a Lancaster aircraft, he M.C.'d the raid, remaining over the target, directing the others. He did two tours – most stop after one (30 trips). He was called the "Pepsi Cola Kid" which was painted on his aircraft. To ease tension, he would call on the intercom system to the other aircraft - "Black Tie one to Black Tie two, Pepsi Cola is the drink for you" followed by the noise of bubbles. Eventually headquarters told him to stop as the Germans were interfering on radio, imitating his noise and trying to re-route the bombers. After John Perry's discharge, he chose pharmacy as a profession in civilian life and served his apprenticeship at the R.G. Henderson Drug Store in Woodbridge".

Squadron Leader Perry's Citation for the Distinguished Flying Cross reads - "This officer is a very keen and capable captain. He is a first class pilot with a high sense of devotion to duty and an unquenchable spirit which has acted as an incentive to all members of his crew. On one occasion his aircraft was attacked by an enemy fighter and badly damaged but this did not in any way deter him from completing his mission successfully and returning to base against fearful odds. The fine leadership and personal example set by this officer is most commendable".

Squadron Leader Perry's Citation for the Award of the Distinguished Service Order reads – "Squadron Leader Perry is a highly efficient Pilot and Captain who has now completed two tours of operations. He is an outstanding organizer and leader whose personal example of fearlessness and extreme devotion to duty has had a most inspiring effect on all aircrew in the Squadron. Since 22.5.44 this officer has been Master Bomber and nearly every occasion on which he has operated under adverse conditions involving great personal danger to himself, he has pressed home his attacks to a successful conclusion and has undoubtedly contributed considerably towards the successes attained. On ground duties as a Flight Commander he has displayed the same insatiable zeal and keenness, thereby setting an example to his fellow aircrew members which it will be difficult to surpass".

Bolton Enterprise - February 9, 1945
In a recent list of awards to members of the Canadian Army, word comes that Private J.B. Studholme, Bolton has been awarded the Canadian Efficiency Medal. He was a member of the Lorne Scots before the war and is still serving with this regiment in Italy.

Bolton Enterprise - February 16, 1945
Mr. G.A. Stewart and Mrs. R. Longstreet, Palgrave have received word that their nephew, Squadron Leader W.A. Stewart and Mrs. Stewart, and Heather arrived at Indian Head, Saskatchewan. Squadron Leader Stewart volunteered for duty in the R.C.A.F. in February 1940, went overseas in 1941, spent 19 months in England and was transferred back to Canada and has been instructing in S.B.S. flying and instrumental flying, also was Chief Flying Instructor at No. 1 instrument school, Deseronto, Ontario. For a time he was acting Wing Commander. Squadron Leader Stewart has obtained an honorable discharge and will take up farming on his father's estate of 320 acres. We wish him every success.

Bolton Enterprise - June 8, 1945
A military promotion of local interest was that of Lieutenant Colonel C.R. McCort, Westmount, Royal Canadian Engineers, who has been promoted to that rank and appointed as Assistant Quartermaster General at National Defence Headquarters, Ottawa. Colonel McCort is a son of the late Alex McCort of Bolton and Mrs. McCort, Weston. A brother, Howard T. McCort, resides near here, on the family homestead.

Bolton Enterprise - December 21, 1945
Lieutenant Mary Adelaide Cooney, formerly of Lloydtown, has been awarded the Royal Red Cross, second class. Lieutenant Cooney was one of 99 Canadian nurses, saved in the torpedoing of an Allied ship in the Mediterranean in 1943. A daughter of Mr. & Mrs. E. Cooney, she was operating-supervisor at St. Michael's Hospital and later at the Medical Centre, New York, before enlisting in the R.C.A.M.C. in 1942. Nursing Sister Cooney served in England and Italy. She is at present on the staff of Toronto East General Hospital.

WORLD WAR II MEDALS AWARDED LOCAL MEN AND WOMEN FOR DISTINGUISHED SERVICE

IN ORDER OF AWARD STANDING

SQUADRON LEADER JOHN WYCLIFFE PERRY	DISTINGUISHED SERVICE ORDER DISTINGUISHED FLYING CROSS	KING TWP.
LIEUTENANT MARY ADELAIDE COONEY	ROYAL RED CROSS MEDAL	KING TWP.
CAPTAIN REGINALD GEORGE FITZGERALD	MILITARY CROSS	PALGRAVE
FLIGHT LIEUTENANT BILLY PROCTOR	DISTINGUISHED FLYING CROSS	CALEDON EAST
SERGEANT NORMAN JOHN MCMAHON	DISTINGUISHED CONDUCT MEDAL	CALEDON TWP.
CORPORAL JESSE TURTON	BRITISH EMPIRE MEDAL	NOBLETON
MAJOR EVERETT DOUGLAS HERSEY	MENTION-IN-DESPATCHES	BOLTON
FLIGHT LIEUTENANT JOHN T. MAW	MENTIONED IN THE 1945 KING'S NEW YEAR'S HONOUR LIST FOR OUTSTANDING SERVICE WITH THE ROYAL CANADIAN AIR FORCE	NASHVILLE

Distinguished Service Order   Royal Red Cross Medal   Military Cross   Distinguished Flying Cross   Distinguished Conduct Medal   British Empire Medal

"While no medal was issued for Mention-In-Despatches, it is highly regarded in military circles as it signified exemplary conduct in battle. In some cases an oak leaf emblem was awarded for Mention-In-Despatches, to be worn on a medal previously issued to the individual" as quoted from information supplied by Captain (Ret'd) Douglas F. Hersey, CD, RC Sigs.

⋘ Chapter Fifteen ⋙
Medals, Military Ranks
and Decorations

Medals are awarded to recognize a serviceman or woman for distinguished service in carrying out a specific exercise under dangerous and difficult circumstances. To pay tribute in this manner is a distinct honour for the recipient. A Bar is a mounting or ribbon attachment signifying a second award to a medal.

Campaign Medals or Stars are awarded for taking part in a campaign or for service in time of war. Clasps are often added to the medal mounting or to the ribbon and inscribed with the name of the battle or campaign for which it was awarded. A Bar is a mounting or ribbon attachment signifying a second award to a decoration.

Decorations are presented to those exhibiting exemplary conduct in combat, showing an unremitting effort to carry out duties in the best possible manner and for serving in the military for a long period of time. Mention-In-Despatches is a worthy award in this category.

Medals

1914 Star

1914-1915 Star

War Service Medal 1914-1918

British War Medal 1914-1920

The Great War for Civilization Medal 1914-1919

Territorial Force War Medal 1914-1919

Victory Medal 1918

Mercantile Marine War Medal 1914-1918

Canadian Expeditionary Force for Service at the Front 1919

The 1939-1945 Star

The Atlantic Star

The Air Crew Europe Star

The Africa Star

The Pacific Star

The Burma Star

The Italy Star

The France and Germany Star

The Defence Medal

The Defence of Britain Medal

The Canadian Volunteer Service Medal

Canadian Efficiency Decoration superseded by Canadian Forces Decoration in 1951

The 1939-1945 War Medal

The 1939-1945 India Medal

World War II Comparative Military Ranks

ARMY	AIR FORCE		NAVY
			Stoker 2
Private, Sapper, Signalman	Aircraftsman 2		Ordinary Seaman
Trooper, Fusilier, Rifleman	Aircraftswoman 2		Ordinary Wren
			Stoker 1
	Aircraftsman 1		Able Seaman
	Aircraftswoman 1		Ordinary Wren
Craftsman (Cfmn)			
Lance Corporal	Leading Aircraftsman		Leading Seaman
Lance Corporal	Leading Aircraftswoman		Leading Wren
Corporal	Corporal		Leading Seaman
Corporal	Corporal		Leading Wren
Sergeant	Sergeant	male & female	Petty Officer
Sergeant Major/Warrant Officer 2	Flight Sergeant	male & female	Petty Officer
Sergeant Major/Warrant Officer 1	Warrant Officer 2nd		Chief Petty Officer
Sergeant Major/Warrant Officer 1	Warrant Officer 2nd		Chief Wren
	Warrant Officer		Chief Petty Officer
			Chief Wren
2nd Lieutenant	Pilot Officer	male	Sub Lieutenant
2nd Lieutenant	Assistant Section Officer	female	Third Officer
Lieutenant	Flying Officer	male	Lieutenant
Lieutenant	Section Officer	female	Third Officer
Captain	Flight Lieutenant	male	Lieutenant
Captain	Flight Officer	female	Second Officer
Major	Squadron Leader	male	Lieutenant Commander
Major	Squadron Officer	female	First Officer
Lieutenant Colonel	Wing Commander	male	Commander
Lieutenant Colonel	Wing Officer	female	Chief Officer
Colonel	Group Captain	male	Captain
Colonel	Group Officer	female	Superintendent
Brigadier	Air Commodore	male	Commodore 2nd and 1st
Brigadier	Air Commandant	female	Deputy Director
Major General	Air Vice Marshal	male	Rear Admiral
Major General	Air Chief Commandant	female	Director, Wrens
Lieutenant General	Air Marshal	male	Vice Admiral
Lieutenant General	Air Marshal	female	Chief Commandant
Brigadier General male & female			
General	Air Chief Marshal	male & female	Admiral
Field Marshall	Marshal	male & female	Admiral of the Fleet

Branches of the Service

ABBREVIATIONS:

CAC	Canadian Armoured Corps
CADC	Canadian Army Dental Corps
CAMC	Canadian Army Medical Corps
CAO	Civil Affairs Organization - Combat Air Operations - Counter Air Operations
CASC	Canadian Army Service Corps
CAVC	Canadian Army Veterinary Corps
CIC	Canadian Intelligence Corps
CIC RIFLES	Canadian Infantry Corps Rifles
CITC	Cadets In Training Corps
CPC	Canadian Pay Corps - Canadian Postal Corps
CWAC	Canadian Womens Army Corps
ITC	Infantry Training Corps (Centre) - Integrated Training Command
RAF	Royal Air Force
RAFC	Royal Army Flying Corps
RCA	Royal Canadian Artillery
RCAC	Royal Canadian Armoured Corps
RCADC	Royal Canadian Army Dental Corps
RCAF	Royal Canadian Air Force
RCAMC	Royal Canadian Army Medical Corps
RCAPC	Royal Canadian Army Pay Corps - Royal Canadian Army Postal Corps
RCASC	Royal Canadian Army Service Corps
RCATC	Royal Canadian Army Transport Corps
RCCS or RCSIGS	Royal Canadian Corps of Signals
RCDC	Royal Canadian Dental Corps
RCE	Royal Canadian Engineers
RCEME	Royal Canadian Electrical & Mechanical Engineers
RCIC	Royal Canadian Infantry Corps
RCN	Royal Canadian Navy
RCNVR	Royal Canadian Naval Volunteer Reserve
RCOC	Royal Canadian Ordnance Corps
RCR	Royal Canadian Regiment
RIF	Royal Inniskilling Fusiliers - Rifles
WRCNS	Womens Royal Canadian Naval Service

Decorations

Victoria Cross

George Cross

Order of the Bath

Croix de Guerre 1914-1918

Croix de Guerre 1939-1945

Order of Merit

Order of St. Michael and St. George

Order of the British Empire

Commander of the Order of the British Empire

Officer of the Order of the British Empire

Member of the Order of the British Empire

Distinguished Service Order

Royal Red Cross

Distinguished Service Cross

Military Cross

Distinguished Flying Cross

Air Force Cross

Distinguished Conduct Medal

Conspicuous Gallantry Medal

George Medal

Distinguished Service Medal

Military Medal

Distinguished Flying Medal

Air Force Medal

Albert Medal

British Empire Medal

Mention-in-Despatches

King's Commendation for Brave Conduct

King's Commendation for Valuable Service

ALPHABETICAL LIST OF
THOSE WHO SERVED IN WORLD WAR II

Where available, this list includes the following information in order:
Rank, Name, Decorations, Reg.#, Service Branch, Enlistment/Discharge Dates.

Private, **Thomas James Allan**, B52407, Lorne Scots, Jan 13 1942, husband of Dorothy Ann Allan, Bolton

Sergeant, **Stanley Allengame**, R70233, RCAF, Aug 29 1940-May 1945, son of Mark Allengame & Josephine A. Goverd, Caledon East

Flight Lieutenant, **Andrew Borden Allison**, Non Permanent Active Militia, Oct 1932, Machine Gun Corps, 1940, C10861, RCAF, Jan 30 1942-Oct 26 1945, son of Andrew Allison & Nellie O'Connor, Caledon East, Canadian Volunteer Service Medal, The 1939-1945 War Medal

Private, **Jim Allison**, 1939-1945, son of Samuel Allison & Violet Speers, Caledon East

Trooper, **Ernest Anderson**, B63062, Algonquin Rifles, July 20 1942, son of Helen Anderson, Caledon Twp.

Trooper, **Gordon Anderson**, C70758, Dragoons, son of Peter Anderson & Helen Smith Munro, Albion Twp.

Private, **Dave Andrews**

Leading Aircraftsman, **George Berney Appleby**, R145502, RCAF, Dec 1941-Sept 4 1945
son of Albert Appleby & Letitia Berney, Caledon East, Canadian Volunteer Service Medal, The Defence Medal, The 1939-1945 War Medal, Airframe Repair Medal

Harold Arden, prisoner of war, Mono Mills

Daniel Armstrong, born in Durham Ontario, employed by Russell Snider, King Twp. farmer

Ed Armstrong, King Twp.

Private, **Eric Harry Armstrong**, B89522, RCASC, Oct 1940, son of George Armstrong & Florence Edwards, Albion Twp., Castlederg, Canadian Volunteer Service Medal

Squadron Leader, **John David Armstrong**, J5707, RCAF, Sept 20 1940, son of Claude H.B. Armstrong & Winnifred Russell, Toronto, husband of Hilda Charman, Victoria, British Columbia, employed by Imperial Bank in Bolton, was killed in action March 7, 1945 at age 31. #128 Squadron, Mosquito aircraft returned from operations over Berlin, Germany with one engine shut down. Overshot a down wind landing and crashed at Gilze, Rijen, Holland. Squadron Leader Armstrong is buried at Canadian War Cemetery, Bergen-Op-Zoom, Holland, grave 8.D.12, (Quoted from book *They Shall Grow Not Old*)

Alfred Atkinson, B64714, son of George Atkinson, Caledon East

Sergeant, **Bill Atwell**, B8566, RCOC, Sept 16 1941, son of William Atwell, Caledon East

Private, **Nelson Elmer Baird**, B162304, Royal Regiment, June 15 1944, son of Isabel Baird, Mono Road

Lance Corporal, **Clifford William Baker**, B76038, Toronto Scottish Reg., Sept 9 1939, son of Mrs. T.W. Baker, Caledon

Private, **Frank Ward Barker**, B2970, RCOC, Aug 6 1942, son of M.W. Barker, Albion Twp.

Private, **John Oswald Barker**, B2127, RCOC, Aug 6 1942, son of M.W. Barker, Albion Twp.

Private, **Clifford Barnes**, RCE, raised by William & Laura Slack, Sand Hill

Private, **William Ernest Barnes**, B74320, 48th Highlanders & Calgary Tank Regiment, May 27 1940 after the death of his mother, Wm. Ernest Barnes was raised by Mrs. William Lougheed of Sand Hill

Charles Barthorpe, RCNVR, lived in Tullamore area

Francis G. Bartlett, U.S. Navy Air Force, Aug 1939, son of E.G. Bartlett, Mono Road

Corporal, **Donald Banting Barton**, R72197, RCAF, Sept 1940, son of Norman Barton & Norma Banting, Palgrave

Patrolman, **John William Barton**, V72798, RCNVR, Sept 1 1943, son of Norman Barton & Norma Banting, Palgrave

Private, **Leonard Beamish**, B78444, Cadets in Training Corps, 1945-1946, son of Francis Beamish & Otta Barry, Toronto, formerly of Bolton

Able Seaman, **Frank Belcher**, V51585, RCNVR, Mar 1943-Nov 1945, of Bolton area, son of Hugh Belcher & Hazel Davis, Toronto, Able Seaman Belcher trained at HMCS York in Toronto, Digby, Nova Scotia at Cornwallis and then to Victoria, B.C. with the frigate, Beacon Hill. He sailed to Newfoundland to Londonderry, Ireland and was at sea for six week periods. On two occasions the ships that replaced them were sunk by German torpedoes. He was scheduled to be trained as an officer but the war in Europe ended before the class was organized. (This information was supplied by Velma (Norris) Belcher.)

Private, **Joffre Bellchamber**, B612693, Brockville Rifles, June 14 1942, son of Harry Bellchamber & Agnes Hunt, Bolton

Sergeant, **James Henry Bennett**, RCE, son of Vincent Bennett & Constance Edgson, husband of Marie Nash, Caledon East

Technical Sergeant, **Leighton William Bernath**, U.S. Army Medical Corps, 1942-1946, son of James Bernath & Mary Devins, Nashville, Sgt. Bernath trained in Arkansas and Illinois, U.S.A. He served in Australia, New Guinea and in 1944-1945 was part of General McArthur's army fighting to liberate the Philippines. (This information was supplied by his niece, Jean (Black) Stewart.)

Leading Aircraftsman, **Lloyd George Berney**, R266065, RCAF, July 12 1943, son of George E. Berney & Mable McCaffrey, Caledon East

Private, **Arthur Francis Bird**, B93223, RCAMC, Apr 7 1941, husband of Stella McCaffrey, Caledon East

Warrant Officer 2, **Leonard Bishop**, R97065, RCAF, on surveillance patrol for enemy submarines and protective circling of allied convoys in north Atlantic Ocean region, Feb 1940-Mar 1944, son of William Henry Bishop & Ada May Jones, Nobleton, Canadian Volunteer Service Medal, The 1939-1945 War Medal

Lieutenant, **John Black**, B21294, RCA, June 8 1942-May 3 1946, son of William Black & Mary Quigley, Bolton, Canadian Volunteer Service Medal

Lance Corporal, **Annie Muriel Blake**, CWAC, Bolton

Norman Boak, Cameron Highlanders, was briefly hidden in a haymow by a Dutch family to avoid capture by German forces, son of John Boak & Edith Stewart, King Twp.

Leading Aircraftswoman, **Thelma Bolton**, RCAF, Sept 1942, daughter of Walter Bolton, Summerland, British Columbia, formerly of Bolton

Sergeant Pilot, **Alan Cameron Bone**, R85712, RCAF, Dec 18 1940, son of James Harvey Bone & Nadine Middlebro, (Forest Hill) Toronto, employed by Imperial Bank in Bolton, was killed December 12, 1941, age 23, Spitfire #R6829 and Spitfire #7062 collided in mid air and crashed at Rhosemor, Flintshire, Wales. Sergeant Pilot Bone is buried at St. Deinoil Churchyard, Hawarden, Flintshire, Wales. (Quoted from book - *They Shall Grow Not Old*)

Private, **Harry Boyce**, son of Aubrey Boyce & Alberta Swinton, Caledon East

Private, **Irwin Boyce**, B84214, RCASC, son of William C. Boyce & Lucy Ann Norris, Bolton

Lieutenant, **Keith Aubrey Boyce**, RCAC, Mar 1 1943, son of Aubrey Boyce & Alberta Swinton, Caledon East

Leading Aircraftsman, **Louis Wilbert Boyce**, 152006, RCAF, Dec 20 1941, son of Aubrey Boyce & Alberta Swinton, Caledon East

Corporal, **Clarence Bracken**, B155516 & B438530, RCCS, June 25 1942, son of R.H. Bracken, Caledon Twp.

Signalman, **Herbert Charles Bradley**, B31125, RCCS, 1939-1940, of Bolton, son of William Bradley & Sarah Elizabeth Crown, Toronto, husband of Evelyn V. Milligan, father of Evelyn, Beryl, Margaret, Eleanor, Beverley & Herbert Jr., Bolton

Leading Aircraftsman, **Walter Nevill Bradley**, R277748, RCAF, Sept 21 1943-Jan 15 1945 and Corporal **Walter Nevill Bradley**, B78459, RCAPC, Feb 21 1945-Aug 29 1947, son of George Bradley & Dora Nevill, Bolton, Canadian Volunteer Service Medal, The 1939-1945 War Medal

Aircraftsman 2, **Kenneth Brewster**, B285541, RCAF, Oct 18 1943, son of James Brewster & May Bosley Spencer, Caledon Twp.

Alexander Brooks, army, born in Scotland, employed on farms in the 8th line area of King Twp.

Alfred Brown, Caledon East

Gunner, **David Brown**, B22388, RCA, Feb 19 1942, came to Canada as an orphan at a young age from Tarbert, Sterlingshire, Scotland and was employed by Albert E. MacCarl, Caledon East

Private, **Harry Brown**, B149349, Infantry, July 15 1943, foster son of Mrs. Mabel Wilson, Sand Hill

Sergeant, **Ken E. Brown**, Argyll & Sutherland Highlanders, Infantry Armoured Division, Mar 1942-1945, son of Jack Brown & Margaret Smith, Nobleton

Flight Lieutenant, **John B. Brownlee**, C5894, RCAF, 1942, son of Archibald Brownlee & Isabella McCallum, Nashville, died by natural causes at age 36, Aug 23 1943, Flight Lieutenant Brownlee is buried at Brookwood Military Cemetery, Woking, Surrey, England. grave 45.F.8. (Quoted from book - *They Shall Grow Not Old*)

Major, **Robert C. Bulloch**, RCASC, 1941-1946, born in Crystal City, Manitoba, son of Thomas Charles Bulloch & Mattie Brown, husband of Elsie Gibbs, father of Tom & Bob, Bolton, Canadian Volunteer Service Medal & Clasp, The 1939-1945 Star, The France & Germany Star. Major Bulloch purchased Cold Storage Lockers, located at the south east corner of Queen and Mill Streets in Bolton, from Otto J. Hardwick about 1947. At this location he later built an expanded facility to house one of the first three IGA grocery stores in Ontario, according to his son Tom. Following this, he moved to a much larger IGA store business constructed in the Hilltop Plaza at the corner of Queen Street and Wilton Drive which he and his wife successfully managed until his death on May 30 1965. Elsie Bulloch then assumed full charge of the business. Major Bulloch was a Village of Bolton Council member for seven years and Reeve for two years.

Lance Bombardier, **Roye George Burnfield**, B116946, RCA, 1943-Aug 1946, son of Robert Burnfield & Hazel Atkinson, Nobleton, Canadian Volunteer Service Medal, The Defence Medal, The 1939-1945 War Medal, The European Campaign Medal

Lance Corporal, **Emma Marion Butler**, CWAC, 1942, daughter of Frank Butler & Nellie Irving, Nobleton

Corporal, **Charlie A. Butler**, B74197, 48th Highlanders, Mar 1940, son of Frank Butler & Nellie Irving, Nobleton

George Butler, B66802, 48th Highlanders, 1940, son of Frank Butler & Nellie Irving, Nobleton, was captured at Dieppe and was a prisoner of war in Germany

Private, **Charles Wilfred Byrne**, B73822, 48th Highlanders, Feb 1940, son of James P. Byrne & Alice Pickerell, Bolton

Leading Aircraftsman, **George W. Byrne**, R167279, RCAF, tail gunner, May 27 1942-Oct 1945, son of James P. Byrne & Alice Pickerell, Bolton

Corporal, **Charles James Calladine**, B74668, 48th Highlanders, 1940, Vaughan Twp.

Private, **Grant Cameron**, B51754, Lorne Scots, Apr 25 1941 and Sergeant Pilot Grant Cameron, R225250, RCAF, Oct 29 1942-Sept 26 1945, son of Stewart Cameron & Ethel Boyce, Bolton
Canadian Volunteer Service Medal, Air Bomber's Badge

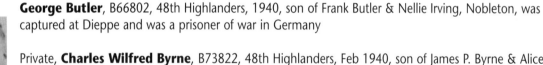

Private, **Willis Cameron Card**, son of Albert Card & Myrtle Cameron, Nashville

Lance Corporal, **Sidney William Carman**, B9516, RCA, Aug 27 1941, born in England, employed by George P. Hansford, Caledon East

Gunner, **Thomas Carney**, B11490, RCA, 1942, born in England, employed by John Stokes, Tullamore

Driver, **Verner Carr**, B11494, RCASC, Aug 13 1942, son of William M. Carr & Annie E. Riddell, King Twp.

Private, **John Austin Chamberlain**, B635232, National Resources Mobilization Act (1940) July 6 1944-Sept 10 1945, son of John Chamberlain & Myrtle Maw, King Twp.

Private, **William J.R. Chamberlain**, L2621 Saskatoon Light Infantry, July 12 1940, son of Russell Chamberlain & Myrtle Clark, Albion Twp., Castlederg

Private, **B.C. Chapman**, B88098, RCASC

Sergeant, **J. Arthur Cherry**, B74284, 48th Highlanders, Mar 1940, son of James Cherry & Annie Atkinson, Nobleton

Flight Sergeant, **William Paterson Connell**, R60557, RCAF, son of Allen Connell & Jeanie L. Paterson, Bolton was killed at age 29, Feb 16 1942. #77 Squadron, Whitley aircraft #Z9229 had the port engine fail before it crashed at Sharbourne, Warwickshire, England. Flight Sergeant Connell is buried at Stratford-On-Avon Cemetery, Evesham Road, Warwickshire, England grave 4016 (AQuoted from book - *They Shall Grow Not Old*)

Lieutenant, (Nursing Sister), **Mary Adelaide Cooney**, Royal Red Cross, RCAMC, 1942-1945, daughter of J. Edward Cooney & Mary E. Deacon, Lloydtown, Royal Red Cross Medal

Flight Sergeant, **John Robert Cooper**, R72104, RCAF, wireless operator/air gunner, Sept 10 1940, son of Robert Cooper & Margaret Knight, Mono Road, Canadian Volunteer Service Medal, The Defence Medal, The 1939-1945 War Medal, The 1939-1945 Star, The Air Crew Europe Star, was killed at age 21, June 5, 1942. #150 Squadron, Wellington aircraft #X3674 lost during a trip over enemy held territory. Flight Sergeant, Wireless Operator Air Gunner Cooper is buried in the Oud Leusden Cemetery, Amersfoort, Utrecht, Holland. Plot 13, Row 3, Grave 33 (Quoted from book -*They Shall Grow Not Old*)

Stoker 1, **Arthur Corless**, V68776, RCNVR, Sept 8 1943-Feb 18 1946, son of Edward Corless & Alma Ireland, husband of Viola Fletcher, Bolton

Leading Aircraftsman, **John W. Corless**, R285701, RCAF, Oct 22 1943- Mar 11 1946, son of Edward Corless & Alma Ireland, Bolton

Flight Lieutenant, **Stanley Herbert Ross Cotterill**, DFC, J4874, RCAF, Sept 25 1940, son of Gordon & Mary Angela Cotterill, Toronto, employed by Imperial Bank, Bolton, Distinguished Flying Cross, was killed at age 22, Oct 18 1944. #418 City of Edmonton Squadron. Target, eastern Austria. Mosquito aircraft #HR351 lost. Flight Lieutenant Cotterill is buried in the Belgrade British Military Cemetery, Yugoslavia. grave 6.D.3. (Quoted from book -*They Shall Grow Not Old*)

Private, **Harry Charles Courtney**, B94316, RCOC, Nov 24 1939-Feb 26 1944, son of Jonathon Courtney & Emily Ann Palmer, Schomberg, husband of Letticia Fry and father of Elizabeth, Jessie, Carl, Douglas, Norma and Hazel, Toronto, Canadian Volunteer Service Medal with Clasp, The Defence Medal, The 1939-1945 War Medal

Sergeant, **Arthur Walter Cox**, B19970, RCE, 1942-1945, born in Surrey, England, employed by Leonard Clarkson, Albion Twp., Castlederg

Rifleman, **Albert E. Crocker**, B79703, Queen's Own Rifles, Jan 27 1942, born at Niagara-on-the-Lake. After his mother's death, Albert Crocker lived with Mrs. William Lougheed at Sand Hill and was later employed by Henry & James Harper, farmers on highway 50, north of Bolton, killed in France June 11 1944, grave IV.B.15., Beny-Sur-Mer Canadian War Cemetery, Reviers, Calvados, France

Sapper, **Edward Albert Cronin**, B25540, RCE, 1941, son of John Richard Cronin & Elda Margaret Rooney, Albion Twp.

Private, **Michael Terrance Joseph Cronin**, B38339, Royal Hamilton Light Infantry, May 13 1941 son of John Richard Cronin & Elda Margaret Rooney, Albion Twp., killed at Dieppe Aug 19 1942, grave 19. Plot 12. Row E., Boulogne Eastern Cemetery, Pas de Calais, France

Private, **Leo Patrick Cronin**, B55144, Algonquin Regiment, July 29 1940, son of John Richard Cronin & Elda Margaret Rooney, Albion Twp.

Sergeant, **Gordon Cunningham**, RCCS, 1939-1945, son of John Cunningham & Mabel Somerville, Mono Road, Canadian Volunteer Service Medal

William Curry, B11989, RCASC, Albion Twp., Castlederg

Captain, **Calvert Frederick Daines**, B51889, Lorne Scots, Oct 3 1939-June 1946, son of Frederick Ernest Daines & Edith Anne Allan, Bolton, Canadian Volunteer Service Medal & Clasp, The France and Germany Star, The Defence of Britain Medal, The 1939-1945 Star. Cal Daines was Bolton's Postmaster from February 4 1947 to February 4 1975.

Gunner, **Joseph Arthur D'Angio**, B138490, RCA, Jan 13 1943, son of Louie D'Angio & Florence Emily Tatum, Albion Twp.

Flying Officer, **Robert Vincent D'Angio**, J88652, RCAF, Mar 5 1941-Dec 7 1945, son of Louie D'Angio & Florence Emily Tatum, Albion Twp., Canadian Volunteer Service Medal & Clasp, The Defence Medal, The 1939-1945 Star, The Africa Star, The Italy Star, Operational Wings, Air Gunner's Badge

Sergeant Pilot, **George Alvin Davis**, R85636, RCAF, Nov 1940, son of Rev. Douglas Gordon Davis & Macil Alice Boyce, King Twp. was killed at age 21, Feb 11 1942. #52 Operational Training Unit. Sergeant Davis was killed when his Spitfire aircraft crashed at New Grange Farm near the railroad station at Dymock, Gloucestershire. Sergeant Pilot Davis is buried in the Chalford Tabernacle Graveyard, grave 2, Gloucestershire, England. (Quoted from book *They Shall Grow Not Old*)

Leading Aircraftsman, **Albert W. Dean**, R153835, RCAF, Feb 1942, son of Charles Dean & Ida May Robinson, Mono Road

Charles Debenham, Mono Road

Corporal, **Clifford R. Defoe**, son of Melvin Defoe & Myrtle McLaughlin, Kleinburg

Private, **William W. Defoe**, 47th Armored Service Corps, Aug 10 1942, son of Melvin Defoe & Myrtle McLaughlin, Kleinburg

Gunner, **Bill Dick**, RCA, July 1942 and Leading Aircraftsman Bill Dick, R213406, RCAF, 1943-1945, son of William R. Dick & Charlotte Strong, Bolton, Canadian Volunteer Service Medal

Trooper, **Gordon Dinwoodie**, B148423, Armoured Corps, June 19 1943-Mar 12 1946, Bolton, son of William Dinwoodie & Annie Byng, Toronto, Canadian Volunteer Service Medal, The 1939-1945 Star, The France and Germany Star

Private, **John Thomas Doherty**, B143998, Lorne Scots, Mar 1943, son of William Doherty & Nellie McNamara, Albion Twp.

Private, **Fred Douglas**, B122805, Canadian Infantry Corps, Feb 1945-Sept 1945, son of Frederick W. Douglas & Rose M. Jarvis, King Twp.

Private, **George Downey**, B56076, RCASC, Sept 14 1942-Dec 7 1943, son of Wilton Downey & Gertrude Verner, Albion Twp.

Major, **Frederick Drayton**, 21st Company, Canadian Forestry Corps, son of Herbert Drayton & Caroline Brooks, Shropshire, England, husband of Catherine Kaiser, father of Catherine, Mono Road

Private, **John R. Drew**, B68260, Caledon East

Signalman, **Donald Roy Drummond**, B119075, RCCS, Nov 8 1943, husband of T. Elizabeth Drummond, Mono Mills

Frank Dudley, Caledon East

Private, **Lex Duff**, RCASC, 1945-1945, son of Cameron Duff & Lila McEwan, Caledon East and Bolton

1st Lieutenant, **Mac Duff**, Royal Canadian Artillery & Royal Hamilton Light Infantry, 1941-Dec 1945, son of Cameron Duff & Lila McEwan, Caledon East and Bolton, Canadian Volunteer Service Medal

Private, **Howard Dunn**, B122587, Canadian Infantry Corps Rifles, Mar 12 1945, foster son of Mrs. Mabel Wilson, Mono Road

Corporal, **George Dyce**, R266795, RCAF, Oct 1943, born in Scotland, husband of Betty Rambo (Switzer), Caledon East

Flight Lieutenant, **Albert Gordon Edwards**, 136142, R156042, J13417, RCAF, Nov 18 1941, son of Edward Thomas Edwards & Leveno Armstrong, Castlederg, Albion Twp., husband of Norma Rosetta Edwards, Nanaimo British Columbia, was killed at age 23, Mar 15 1945. #431 Iroquois Squadron. Lancaster aircraft #KB815 missing during a night operation, a raid against Hagen, Germany. Flight Lieutenant Navigator Edwards is buried in the Communal Cemetery, Perwez, Brabant, Belgium. grave 5. Mil. Plot. Row A. Coll. (Quoted from book - *They Shall Grow Not Old*)

Flight Lieutenant, **Edward Williams Edwards**, R88802, RCAF, Dec 1940, son of Edward Thomas Edwards & Leveno Armstrong, Castlederg, Albion Twp., husband of Dorothy Head

Lieutenant, **Helen Mabel Egan**, Red Cross Territorial Transport Service, Aug 1939-Mar 1946, daughter of William R. Egan & Ida Mabel Hicks, Bolton

Private, **James Bannerman Ellwood**, B130724, Perth Regiment, Aug 3 1942, son of A. Ralph Ellwood & Sybil Louise Irving, husband of Edith Mary McCauley, Bolton, Canadian Volunteer Service Medal, The Defence Medal, The Defence of Britain Medal, The 1939-1945 Star, The Italy Star, was killed Jan 17 1944. Information issued by the Commonwealth War Graves Commission states Private James Ellwood is buried at the Moro River Canadian War Cemetery, Italy, grave 111.H.12.

Flying Officer, **William Ralph Ellwood**, R167119, J25698, air bomber with the #434 Bluenose Squadron, RCAF, Apr 1942, son of A. Ralph Ellwood & Sybil Louise Irving, husband of Lillian R. Armstrong, father of Beverly, Bolton, Canadian Volunteer Service Medal, The Defence Medal, The 1939-1945 War Medal, The 1939-1945 Star, The Air Crew Europe Star, was killed Apr 28 1944.

Corporal, **Doris Jane Evans**, W2508, CWAC, July 1 1942-July 26 1946, daughter of George Arthur Evans & Edith Mildred Holdnall, Caledon East, Canadian Volunteer Service Medal with Clasp, The 1939-1945 War Medal

Leading Aircraftsman, **George Beamish Evans**, R146679, RCAF, Dec 10 1941, son of Thomas Richard Evans & Frances Louella Beamish, Caledon East, Canadian Volunteer Service Medal with Clasp, The Defence of Britain Medal, The 1939-1945 War Medal

Sergeant, **Stuart Ross Evans**, R293516, RCAF, Jan 17 1944-June 27 1945, son of George Arthur Evans & Edith Mildred Holdnall, Caledon East, The 1939-1945 War Medal

Corporal, **William Thomas Evans**, B92639, RCASC, Apr 1941, son of Thomas Richard Evans & Frances Louella Beamish, Caledon East, Canadian Volunteer Service Medal with Clasp, The 1939-1945 Star, The Defence of Britain Medal, The 1939-1945 War Medal, The Italy Star

Private, **Howard Richard Ezeard**, B119611, 4th Princess Louise Dragoon Guards, Nov 25 1943, son of Robert E. Ezeard & Matilda Watt, Kleinburg, killed in Italy Sept 1 1944, grave 111.J.17. Montecchio War Cemetery, Italy

Aircraftsman 2, **Holly Mac Fagan**, R219856, RCAF, Feb 8 1943, son of Holly & Cora Fagan, Mono Mills

Private, **William Thomas Fanning**, 3628270, RCE, Apr 1944, next of kin, Mr. & Mrs. Albert O'Donnell, Mono Road

Captain, **Reg. George Fitzgerald**, MC, RCA, husband of Marjorie Barton, Palgrave, was awarded the Military Cross following the battle of Ortona in Italy in which he received serious abdominal wounds. (Quoted from The Bolton Enterprise)

John Flanagan, army, son of William Flanagan, King Twp.

Private, **Cecil Flatt**, Canadian Infantry Corps, 1944-Sept 1945, son of Joseph Henry Flatt & Gladys Ireland, Nobleton

Dalton Flatt, RCE, 1941-1945, son of Joseph Henry Flatt & Gladys Ireland, Nobleton

Lance Corporal, **Tasman (Ted) Foster**, B24184, RCEME, Feb 1940-1945, born in New Zealand, husband of Mary White Hunter, father of Ada, Marjorie, Bob & Rhea, Bolton, Canadian Volunteer Service Medal, The France and Germany Star

Samuel Fraser, raised by Mr. & Mrs. Stanley Scott, Mono Road

Corporal, **Arthur Edward Fry**, B148191, July 1 1943, son of Arthur Fry & Emmaline Cooper, Caledon East

Sergeant, **Austin E. Fuller**, R250111C, RCAF, Oct 15 1941-Oct 1 1945, son of James Fuller & Queenar McKinley, King Twp., Hammertown, Canadian Volunteer Service Medal, The 1939-1945 War Medal

Jack Gardiner, B60799 Ontario Tank Regiment, son of Mrs. Nellie Gardiner, Mono Road

Gunner, **William Bruce Gardner**, B16936, RCA, June 1941-1945, son of William Albert Gardner & Mary Martha Farnell, Bolton, Canadian Volunteer Service Medal, The Defence Medal, The France and Germany Star, The 1939-1945 Star, The 1939-1945 War Medal

Corporal, **William Gordon Gibson**, B3638, RCASC, June 29 1942, son of Wesley Gibson, Caledon East

Ken Goodfellow, RCAF, 1940-1945, son of Adam Goodfellow & Mary Beatty Cherry, Nobleton

Glen Orian Gould, B74301, 48th Highlanders, son of Rae Gould, Mono Road

Private, **James Wilbert Gould**, B20547 Canadian Forestry Unit, Aug 1 1940, son of David Gould & Lillie Barker, Albion Twp., Castlederg, Albion Twp.

Aircraftsman 2, **Lorne Alexander Gould**, R173180, RCAF, Jan 1942, son of David Gould & Lillie Barker, Albion Twp., Castlederg

Squadron Leader, **Donald C. Graham**, C3953, RCAF, June 24 1940-Dec 1 1945
son of Dr. John Graham & Olivia Carter, Bolton, Canadian Volunteer Service Medal, The France and Germany Star, The Defence of Britain Medal, The 1939-1945 Victory Medal. Promoted to the rank of Wing Commander, Donald C. Graham was the Officer Commanding of the RCAF Auxillary Medical Branch 4005 from 1951 to 1956.

Private, **Duncan Alexander Graham**, B112202, 48th Highlanders, Mar 1942, son of Peter Graham, Caledon East

Elizabeth Mary Graham, Canadian Red Cross, Voluntary Aid Detachment, 1943, daughter of Peter Graham, Caledon East

Private, **James Edward Grogan**, B438619, Royal Canadian Infantry Corps, son of J. Frank Grogan & Kate McCormick, Albion Twp., died Feb 13 1941 at Christie Street Hospital, Toronto, interred at St. John's Roman Catholic Cemetery, 4th line, Albion Twp.

Michael Grogan, Army, son of Bennett Grogan & Bridget Keenahan, Albion Twp.

Private, **Vincent John Grogan**, B98758, RCASC, Apr 8 1942, son of John Grogan & Olive White, Albion Twp. husband of Anne Roden, Bolton

Private, **Harry Groves**, B58759, RCOC, Mar 16 1942, his guardian was Mrs. James Elliott, Mono Road

Corporal, **William James Halbert**, Royal Canadian Regiment, Apr 8 1942, son of Rev. Robert G. Halbert, Mono Mills

Corporal, **Morley Hall**, Caledon East

Alphonse Hamilton, Lorne Scots, son of William Hamilton & Jane Sullivan, Owen Sound, lived in Albion Twp. area

Private, **John Arthur S. Hanna**, B74698, Lorne Scots, Jan 4 1940-1946, son of Thomas Henry Hanna & Elizabeth McInnis, Mono Road

Gunner, **Gilbert R. Hardman**, B627674, Royal Canadian Artillery, Dec 1942, son of R. Hardman, Caledon East

Private, **Ernest Hart**

Flight Sergeant, **Edward Albert Hartt**, R69911, RCAF, July 23 1940-May 8 1943, husband of Eileen Violet Smith, Bolton

Craftsman (Cfmn.), **Henry Hawman**, son of William Hawman & Elizabeth Ann Breedon, Nobleton

Gunner, **Hershall Hawman**, son of William Hawman & Elizabeth Ann Breedon, Nobleton

Sergeant, **Marshall Hawman**, RCAF, son of William Hawman & Elizabeth Ann Breedon, Nobleton

Private, **John Francis Hayes**, B46992, Lorne Scots, Apr 3 1943-1945, son of Joseph Hayes & Bridget McNamara, Albion Twp.

Signalman, **Vincent Joseph Hayes**, B58821, Canadian Signal Corps, Apr 1942-1945, son of Joseph Hayes & Bridget McNamara, Albion Twp.

Private, **Edwin Ralph Hayhoe**, B164540, RCAMC, Aug 26 1944, husband of Orma R. Forsyth, Bolton, formerly of Woodbridge

Sergeant, **Norton Campbell Heard**, R182124, RCAF, Sept 1942, son of John Heard & Katie Christina Campbell, Caledon East

Leading Aircraftswoman, **Evelyn Bernice Hearn**, W307235, RCAF, Aug 1942-May 2 1946, daughter of Ernest Hearn & Bernice Drummond, Caledon East, Canadian Volunteer Service Medal, The Defence Medal

Lieutenant, **Lloyd B. Herman**, Signal Corps, son of Rev. Frank Herman, Bolton

Major, **Everett Douglas Hersey**, MiD, Royal Canadian Regiment, born in Fredericton, New Brunswick, son of E. Frank Hersey & Laura McCorquindale. Major Hersey came to Bolton in 1960 after 30 years service in the Canadian Army. He rose from Private to Regimental Sergeant Major by 1939. Commissioned in 1941, he went overseas with the West Nova Scotia Highlanders to serve in the Italian campaign where he was twice wounded in action and Mentioned in Despatches. Major Hersey was the Clerk-Treasurer of the Village of Bolton from 1962 to 1973 and Treasurer of the Town of Caledon from 1973 until his death on September 16 1975. Mention-In-Despatches, Canadian Volunteer Service Medal & Clasp, The 1939-1945 Star, The Italy Star, The 1939-1945 War Medal, Canadian Medal for Long Service and Good Conduct, I.C.S.C. (International Commission for Supervision and Control (Indo China). This information has been supplied by Major Hersey's sons, Captain (Ret'd) Douglas F. Hersey, CD, RC Sigs of Bolton and Colonel (Ret'd) Robert C. Hersey, CD, RCR of Brockville.

Private, **Mark Ernest Heseltine**, B57123, RCOC, Aug 18 1942, employed in the Mono Road area, son of Ruben Heseltine, Yorkshire, England

Leading Aircraftsman, **John Henry Hesp**, R133546, RCAF, Sept 11 1941-Aug 21 1945, son of William Roy Hesp & Mary Ellen Barry, Bolton, Canadian Volunteer Service Medal & Clasp, The 1939-1945 Star, The France and Germany Star, The Defence Medal, The 1939-1945 War Medal

Flight Sergeant, **William John Hesp**, R86357, RCAF, son of John Hesp & Annie Newton, Winnipeg, Manitoba, formerly of King and Albion Townships, Canadian Volunteer Service Medal & Clasp, The 1939-1945 Star, The Air Crew Europe Star, The 1939-1945 War Medal, Operational Wings, was killed in action at age 27, Aug 29 1942. #115 Squadron (Despite The Elements) Markham, Norfolk, England. Wellington aircraft #X3647 missing during night operations against Saarbrucken, Germany. Flight Sergeants J.F. Tuck, W.S. Allen (RAF), and Sergeant E. Hepworth (RAF) were also killed. Flight Sergeant Pilot Hesp is buried in the Communal Cemetery, grave 1, Attigny, Ardennes, France. (Quoted from the book - *They Shall Grow Not Old*)

Ross Charles Hill, army, son of Charles Hill & Jemima Chamberlain, Nobleton

Gunner, **Stephen George Hill**, B44327, RCA, Sept 28 1942, Caledon East

Private, **Frank Hodgson**, B36028, Veterans' Home Guard, born in Kendal England, husband of Etta Irene Curtis, Mono Road

Sergeant, **Gerald Holder**, B53001, RCOC, July 31 1941, son of Frederick John Holder & Charlotte Jackson, Mono Road

Wren, **Ruth Hoover**, WRCNS, 1944- Feb 1946, daughter of Melville Hoover & Bernice Archibald, Nobleton

Private, **(Frank) Francis James Horan**, Permanent Militia, June 29 1935, P13203, Royal Canadian Regiment, July 3 1935 - Mar 3 1957, son of John Francis Horan & Lydia Bridget Mary Gilmore, Albion Twp., Canadian Medal for Long Service and Good Conduct

Wing Commander, **Verton Shirreff Houston**, RCAF, Sept 1939, son of Alexander Houston & Maude Shirreff, husband of Sally Ann Taylor, Nashville area

Wren, **E. Marjory Howard**, WRCNS, *HMCS Stradacona*, daughter of Joseph Howard & Lillian Anderson, Orangeville

Flight Lieutenant, **Gregg Howard**, R105220, RCAF, May 23 1941-Nov 1947, son of Joseph Howard & Lillian Anderson, Orangeville, husband of Helen Ward, Caledon East, prisoner of war for three years, Canadian Volunteer Service Medal, The Defence Medal, The 1939-1945 War Medal, The 1939-1945 Star, The Air Crew Europe Star

Lieutenant Colonel, **James Willis Howard**, ED, Argyle Light Infantry, May 20 1940-May 10 1946 son of Joseph Howard & Lillian Anderson, Orangeville. Born in 1899, J.W. Howard served briefly in the R.F.C. near the end of the First World War. He was active in the Militia in Belleville for many years, attended officer training courses and was in charge of the Belleville Collegiate Cadet Corps. Later, he was appointed to a commissioned rank in the (active) Canadian Army. Lieutenant Colonel Howard acted in the capacity of psychologist in the Directorate of Personnel Selection at National Defence Headquarters in Ottawa. He then took complete charge of the Directorate of Personnel Selection in London England. Canadian Efficiency Decoration, Canadian Volunteer Service Medal & Clasp, The Defence Medal. This information was supplied by Joseph (Jay) H.G. Howard, son of Lieutenant Colonel Howard.

Trooper, **Peter Huson**, B118556, 1941, son of Peter Huson & Laura Clarissa Wallis, Bolton

Lance Corporal, **Forest Hutchison**, B61391, Canadian Armored Corps, Apr 23 1941-Dec 4 1945, son of Samuel Hutchison & Ellen Brinkman, husband of Edna Young, father of Pat, Bolton, Canadian Volunteer Service Medal & Clasp, The Defence Medal. Following the war, Forest and Edna Hutchison operated a grocery store business at the south-west corner of King and Queen Streets in Bolton.

Driver, **Louis Mercer Hutchinson**, B56213, RCASC, May 10 1942-1946, son of George A. Hutchinson & Greta Mercer, Caledon East, Canadian Volunteer Service Medal, The Defence Medal

William Norman Hutchinson, DCM, MM, Veterans' Home Guard, 1943-1945, son of William J. Hutchinson & Elizabeth Ann Drummond, husband of Leola Hutchinson, father of Carl, Daisy, Patricia, Doreen, Leola, Norma & June, Caledon East, Distinguished Conduct Medal, Military Medal, The 1914-1915 British Star, The British War Medal, The Victory Medal 1914-1918

Leading Aircraftsman, **Edward Arthur Hyde**, R148601, RCAF, Jan 5 1942, son of Arthur C. Hyde & Martha K. Smith, Albion Twp.

Private, **Horace Victor Hyde**, B148588, RCASC, June 22 1943, son of Arthur C. Hyde & Martha K. Smith, Albion Twp.

Gunner, **A. Harry Ingle**, B600379, RCA, 1943, son of Norman E. Ingle & Mabel Ewart, Bolton

Private, **Ross George Innis**, B1295, Cadets in Training Corps, Feb 1945, son of Robert James Innis & Elva Reta Watson, Caledon East

Garfield Lindsey Ireland, wounded in leg and captured at Dieppe on August 19 1942 and remained a prisoner of war until 1945, son of John Ireland & Agnes McKay, King Twp.

Corporal, **Robert Henry Ireland**, B35131, June 8 1940-Jan 15 1947, son of Alfred Ireland & Frances Clubine, Albion Twp., Canadian Volunteer Service Medal, War Service Badge. Robert Ireland was in the Veterans' Guard first, then later in the Provost Corps. In the Guards, he escorted Japanese citizens by train to northern camps. Later in the Corps, he drove army officers around the country by army car in Canada. This information was supplied by Bruce Ireland, son of Robert Ireland.

Flight Lieutenant, **Frederick Grant Jackson**, J6209, RCAF, son of John Edgar Jackson & Esther Banting, Ballycroy, was killed Aug 4 1944. #353 Squadron Dakota aircraft #FZ587 flew into a heavy storm, dived into the ground and exploded. Three RAF members of the crew, and eleven soldiers, not Canadians, were also killed. Flight Lieutenant Pilot Jackson is buried in the War Cemetery at Ranchi, India. grave 5.E.8.Sp. Mem."C" (Quoted from the book - *They Shall Grow Not Old*)

Private, **Mathew Jackson**, C97900, RCAPC, Jan 5 1942-June 15 1946, son of Edward Jackson & Mary Graham, Albion Twp., Canadian Volunteer Service Medal

Pilot Officer, **Ross Banting Jackson**, J19031, RCAF, son of John Edgar Jackson & Esther Banting, Ballycroy, was killed in action at age 20, Oct 22 1943. #408 Goose Squadron (For Freedom). Target - Kassel, Germany. Lancaster aircraft #DS 778 was shot down over Lavelsloh, Germany during a night trip to Kassel, Germany. Pilot Officer Air Gunner Jackson was buried in the Parish Cemetery at Lavelsloh, Germany, exhumed, reburied in the Limmer British Cemetery at Hanover, Germany. grave 15. G.2-7. Coll. (Quoted from the book - *They Shall Grow Not Old*)

Private, **William Jackson**, C97851, RCAPC, Nov 17 1941-Feb 4 1944, son of Edward Jackson & Mary Graham, Albion Twp., Canadian Volunteer Service Medal

Private, **J. Jeoffrey**, R41517, RCASC, son of Frank Jeoffrey, Bolton

Flight Sergeant, **Arthur J.E. Johnston**, 105361, RCAF, May 29 1941-1945, son of Arthur E. Johnston & Mary I. Black, Nashville

Private, **Robert Johnstone**, B159638, Rifles Regiment, Feb 29 1944, employed by Edward Thomas Edwards, Castlederg, Albion Twp.

Private, **Clifford Johnston Jordan**, B90234, Feb 28 1945, husband of Estella Jordan, Palgrave

Private, **Gordon Dalton Kearns**, B16175, Canadian Reinforcement Unit and RCAPC, May 15 1944-July 17 1946, son of Dalton Kearns & Helena Rawn, Albion Twp., Canadian Volunteer Service Medal & Clasp, European Theatre Medal

Sergeant, **Leo Kehoe**, RCA and RCAF, son of Michael Kehoe & Caroline Fuller, King Twp.

Leading Aircraftsman, **Edward (Ted) A. Kerr**, R203470, RCAF, Apr 1942-1946, son of Albert Kerr & Edna Cain, King Twp., Canadian Volunteer Service Medal, The 1939-1945 War Medal, The Defence Medal, The 1939-1945 Star, The France & Germany Star

Gunner, **Stanley A. King**, B45179, RCA, 13th Canadian Field Regiment, son of Harry King & Maybelle Johnston, Vaughan Twp. and later on highway 50 south of Palgrave

Corporal, **Allan J. Kirby**, B107007, Irish Regiment, July 1942-Mar 1 1946, son of James Percy Kirby & Ellen Robertson, Bolton, Canadian Volunteer Service Medal, The Defence Medal, The Defence of Britain Medal, The France and Germany Star, The 1939-1945 Star, The Italy Star

Sergeant, **George Kirby**, B130728, Irish Regiment, Aug 3 1942-Mar 1 1946, son of James Percy Kirby & Ellen Robertson, Bolton, Canadian Volunteer Service Medal, The Defence Medal, The Defence of Britain Medal, The France and Germany Star, The 1939-1945 Star, The Italy Star

Private, **Ed Koury**, husband of Norma V. McCabe, Bolton

Joe Kuniski, army, son of Alexander Kuniski & Theresa Ryza, King Twp.

Private, **Ivan Lavery**, B131201, Infantry, Aug 14 1942, son of Robert Lavery & Elizabeth McMahon, Palgrave

Leading Aircraftswoman, **Anne Lindsay**, RCA.F, 1941-1944, daughter of William Lindsay & Jennie Black, Albion Twp.

Captain, **Peter Bryson Lindsay**, RCAMC, son of Nelson S. Lindsay & Annie Mitchell, Toronto Gore Twp. After World War II, Dr. Lindsay operated a medical practice at the south west corner of King and David Streets in Bolton

Archibald Lippe, Nobleton - King Twp.

Private, **Irwin E. Little**, B103183, Mar 30 1942, son of Elmer Little & Ida Elsie Boyce, Albion Twp.
Art Lloyd, Caledon East

Art Lloyd, Caledon East

Leading Aircraftsman, **Allan Lockhart**, R276477, RCAF, Aug 20 1943, son of Robert Lockhart & Harriett Cross, Bolton

Trooper, **Earl Lockhart**, B61265, RCAC, Apr 8 1941, son of Robert Lockhart & Harriett Cross, Bolton

Corporal, **Thomas Lockwood**, B46818, Lorne Scots, Apr 8 1942, son of William R. Lockwood & Evelyn Phillips, husband of Ruth McCabe, Bolton

Private, **Alexander Lynch**, B35188, Veterans' Home Guard, June 14 1940, son of A. Lynch, Montreal, husband of Mary Conway, Caledon East

Trooper, **Jerry Lynch**, B29116, RCE

Signalman, **James MacCallum**, B31252, No. 2 Company, Signallers, CASF, employed by Elmer Little, Albion Twp.

Lieutenant, **John Fletcher MacLean**, Provost Corps, Mar 3 1941, son of H. MacLean, Minedosa, Manitoba, husband of Marguerita Rogers, father of Dorothy, Norma & Hugh, Bolton.

Walter Manson

Corporal, **Gordon N. Martin**, B78810, CAO, brother to Ruth Martin who married Roy Davidson, Bolton

Private, **Richard Martindale**, B29808, RCE, Aug 22 1941, born in England, step-son of Mr. & Mrs. Dolphus Raymond, Palgrave

Leading Aircraftsman, **Kenneth P. Mashinter**, R193185, RCAF, Oct 5 1942-Aug 18 1945, son of Leonard Mashinter & Sarah Ann Piercey, Albion Twp., Canadian Volunteer Service Medal

Trooper, (Bandsman), **Jim Maw**, B62851, RCAC, Oct 21 1942-June 1945, son of Wilfred Henry Maw & Annie Kathleen Woodill, Bolton

Flight Lieutenant, **John T. Maw**, C4269, RCAF, 1940-1946, son of John Thompson Maw & Caroline Culham, Nashville, mentioned in the 1945 King's New Year's Honour List for outstanding services with the Royal Canadian Air Force

C.G. Miller

Private, **James Oswald Mitchell**, B51712, Lorne Scots, Sept 2 1940, son of John George James Mitchell, Mono Mills

Kenneth Moffatt, son of John Henry Moffatt & Annie Lindsay, Caledon East

Wilmer Moffatt, R206059, flight engineer, RCAF, son of John Henry Moffatt & Annie Lindsay, Caledon East

Bob Moore, army, employed by Lorne Ellis, King Twp.

Rifleman, **William Robert Moore**, K48851, Regina Rifle Regiment, Dec 1942, son of Wilford R. Moore & Caroline P. Purchase, Albion Twp., killed at age 22 Apr 30 1945.

Gunner, **Leo Morrison**, F2596, RCA, Feb 3 1943-Apr 9 1946, Bolton, son of Heman Morrison & Gertrude Davis, Lower Economy, Nova Scotia, Canadian Volunteer Service Medal with Clasp, The 1939-1945 War Medal

Driver, **William Morton**, 1941-1947, son of Charles Morton & Florence Mills, Vaughan Twp.

Sergeant, **Elmer A. Moss**, B89518, Provost Corps, Oct 7 1940-Sept 6 1945, son of Richard Moss & Ethel Rowley, Albion Twp., Canadian Volunteer Service Medal and Clasp, The Defence Medal, The 1939-1945 Star, The France and Germany Star. Following his discharge, Elmer Moss joined the Ontario Provincial Police where he progressed to the rank of Chief Superintendent.

Warrant Officer, **Ernest Munro**, RCAF, 1939-1945, son of James Munro & Zella Nelson, Albion Twp. Ernest Munro was a prisoner of war for 28 months

Staff Sergeant, **James Clifford Munro**, B28549, RCE, June 1940-1945, son of James Munro & Zella Nelson, Albion Twp., Canadian Volunteer Service Medal, The Defence of Britain Medal, The 1939-1945 Victory Medal, The France and Germany Star, The Italy Star, The 1939-1945 India Medal

Sergeant, **Norman Munro**, B4410, Tank Corps, son of James Munro & Zella Nelson, Albion Twp.

Private, **George Ross Murray**, B103522, CIC, Mar 5 1945, son of George & Elizabeth Jane Murray, Mono Mills

Private, **James Ritchie Murray**, B127513, 1st Battalion, Midland Regiment, June 1 1942, son of George & Elizabeth Jane Murray, Mono Mills

Leading Aircraftsman, **Spence Arthur Murray**, R167208, RCAF, son of George & Elizabeth Jane Murray, Mono Mills

Private, **Robert E. McAllister**, B51755, Lorne Scots, Apr 25 1941-Dec 12 1946, son of Thomas E. McAllister & Emily Edwards, King Twp., husband of Agnes Dixon, Wales, United Kingdom, Canadian Volunteer Service Medal & Clasp, The Defence Medal, The 1939-1945 War Medal, General Service Badge

Flight Sergeant, **Walter Clinton McBride**, R209032, RCAF, Nov 25 1942-Apr 14 1945, son of William George McBride & Gertrude Frances Marks, Palgrave, Canadian Volunteer Service Medal, Defence Medal

Corporal, **William Henry McBride**, R118825, RCAF, July 19 1941-Feb 5 1946, son of William George McBride & Gertrude Frances Marks, Palgrave, Canadian Volunteer Service Medal, Defence Medal, The Defence of Britain Medal, The 1939-1945 War Medal

Lieutenant, **Alice J. McCabe**, RCAMC, Feb 15 1943, daughter of Thomas J. McCabe & Annie York, Caledon East

Fusilier, **Henry McCabe**, B625559, Irish Fusiliers, Sept 30 1942, son of Egerton McCabe & Hazel Allan, Bolton

2nd Lieutenant, **Mary Louise McCabe**, Nov 1 1941, daughter of Thomas J. McCabe & Annie York, Caledon East

W. James McCabe, RCNVR, medical research unit, May 21 1942-Feb 1946, son of Dr. William James McCabe & Ethel Alma Culbert, Bolton

Corporal, **Harold V. McCaffrey**, son of Patrick J. McCaffrey & Alice McKenna, Caledon East

Corporal, **Leonard McCaffrey**, son of Patrick J. McCaffrey & Alice McKenna, Caledon East

Leading Aircraftsman, **Bernard McCarthy**, B148520, RCAF, husband of Mary Jane Stewart, Caledon East, formerly of Cooksville

Lieutenant, **Jack Gordon McCartney**, B91197, 22nd Company, CDC, May 21 1942, son of T. Roy McCartney & Irene Gott, Caledon East

Private, **Albert McCluskie**, B132149, Provost Corps, Aug 30 1942, son of Albert McCluskie & Alice Hardwick, Bolton

Gunner, **Lorne McCordick**, RCA, 1940, son of Harvey McCordick, Newmarket, employed at Leggett's Drug Store, Bolton

Gunner, **Allan McCort**, B626397, Army, 1943-1944, son of Cecil J. McCort & Nellie Mabee, Bolton

Lieutenant Colonel, **Cecil Roy McCort**, Royal Canadian Engineers, Oct 1940, son of Alexander McCort & Harriett Burgess, Albion Twp.. In 1945 Lieutenant Colonel McCort was promoted to Assistant Quartermaster General at National Defence Headquarters in Ottawa.

Leading Aircraftsman, **Doherty McDevitt**, R194000, RCAF, Oct 1 1942-1945, son of Frank McDevitt & Honora Horan, Albion Twp.

David McDuff, lived in Tullamore area

Leading Writer, **A. David McFall**, V64886, RCNVR, Dec 1 1943-Jan 28 1945, son of Arthur A. McFall & Eva Hughes, Bolton

Driver, **Edward McGlasson**, B83919, RCASC, 1941, son of William McGlasson, Roseburghshire, Scotland, husband of Netta Marshall, Caledon East, employed by Albert E. MacCarl, Caledon East

Jack McIntyre, raised by Craig & Mabel Wilson, Sand Hill

Aircraftswoman 1, **Margaret McKee**, RCAF, wireless operator, July 1943-Sept 1945, daughter of Alexander McKee & Emma McGlinn, Minesing. After World War II Margaret McKee married William F. Richardson, Bolton

Gunner, **Walter Carson McKee**, C14351, RCA, 1940, son of James McKee & Margaret Jane Carson, husband of Dorothy Ruth Vinton, Sand Hill

Gunner, **Jack McKellar**, B9903, RCA, Nov 19 1941, born in Scotland, employed by Albert E. MacCarl, Caledon East

Private, **Joseph Perry McKinley**, B130559, CPC, July 23 1942, son of William J. McKinley & Elizabeth Catherine Brooks, husband of Beryl V. Howitt, Caledon East

Ordinary Seaman, **William Earl McKinley**, V89805, RCN, July 1944, son of Wilfred McKinley & Myrtle McMullin, Caledon East

Private, **Earl Leonard McLean**, B164163, Aug 16 1944, son of Neil McLean & Mae Carter, Palgrave

Private, **Francis McLeod**, B148956, Infantry, July 3 1943, son of John McLeod & Eliza Jane Martin, Bolton

Private, **Kenneth McMahon**, B627736, RCOC, Oct 12 1941-May 1946, son of James McMahon & Pearl Lundy, husband of Evelyn Watson, Palgrave

Sergeant, **Norman John McMahon**, DCM, B132561, Royal Canadian Regiment, Sept 1941-June 1945, son of James Russell McMahon & Myrtle Mary Ford, Caledon Twp., Distinguished Conduct Medal, The Italy Star, The France and Germany Star, The Defence of Britain Medal, The Canadian Volunteer Service Medal

Sergeant, **Alf McNair**, B76401, Toronto Scottish Regiment and 328654, 47th Canadian Infantry, Nov 1939-1945, son of William McNair & Emma Place, Bolton, The 1939-1945 Star, The France and Germany Star, The Defence Medal, The Canadian Volunteer Service Medal, The 1939-1945 War Medal

Petty Officer, **Herb McNair**, V80174, RCNVR, -1945, son of William McNair & Emma Place, Bolton

Able Seaman, **John Norton Naylor**, V63286, RCNVR, Sept 1942, son of Joseph R. Naylor & Elise Mant, Caledon East

Leading Aircraftsman, **Walter Naylor**, R175458, RCAF, Mar 1942, son of Joseph R. Naylor & Elise Mant, Caledon East

Private, **Christopher Charles Neilson**, B148422, Canadian Infantry Corps, July 1943, friend of J. Henry McCauley, Albion Twp.

Frank Nelmes, Vaughan Twp.

Staff Sergeant, **Elgin McIntyre Nelson**, B2025, RCOC, July 27 1942, son of Hunter Nelson & Margaret Ann McIntyre, Caledon East

Regimental Sergeant Major, **Harry G. Nelson**, B94271, RCEME, Nov 1940, son of Louis Nelson & Eleana Margaret Pilson, Bolton

Leading Aircraftsman, **C. Louis Nelson**, R116420, RCAF, son of Louis Nelson & Eleana Margaret Pilson, Bolton

Gunner, **Orville Beatty Nelson**, B127981, RCA, Apr 9 1943, son of Hunter Nelson & Margaret Ann McIntyre, Caledon East

Roger E. Nelson, son of Louis Nelson & Eleana Margaret Pilson, Bolton

Leading Aircraftsman, **William J. Newlove**, R251093, RCAF, Mar 1943-June 1946, son of William A. Newlove & Pearl Astells, Albion Twp. He was the husband of Pearl Harvey, a long time teacher with the Bolton School Board and the Peel County Board of Education, forerunner of the Peel District School Board.

Walter Nichol, Sand Hill

Driver, **Joe Nicholson**, B32102, Oct 1941-Jan 26 1943, son of Joe Nicholson & Eliza Jane Parker, Bolton

John Giffen Nixon, son of Harvey Nixon and Gertrude Giffen, Mono Road

Russell Alexander Nixon, son of Harvey Nixon and Gertrude Giffen, Mono Road

Corporal, **William J. Northcott**, B60769, Royal Hamilton Light Infantry, Sept 1939-Sept 1945, son of William Northcott & Lillian Hill, King Twp., Canadian Volunteer Service Medal, The 1939-1945 War Medal

Private, **Cherry Norton**, B41319, Brant & Haldimand Rifles, July 20 1940-1943, son of George A. Norton & Isabella Cherry, Bolton

Sergeant, **L.A. (Bill) Norton**, B51709, RCASC, June 1940, son of George A. Norton & Jean Devins, Bolton

Corporal, **George Oltsher**, RCAF, 1943-Oct 1945, son of Paul Oltsher & Hermaine Drolshagen, Paisley Ontario, husband of Dorothy Neelands, Caledon East

Able Seaman, **Patrick O'Neill**, V54526, RCNVR, born in Ireland, next of kin - Mrs. William Maw, Mono Road

Flying Officer, **Richard Herbert Orr**, J20704, RCAF, Mono Mills, son of Arthur Joseph & Bertha Jane Orr, Underwood Ontario was killed in action at age 27, Aug 28 1943. #78 Squadron (Nemo Non Paratus) Halifax aircraft # JD406 was shot down over Souilly during operations against Nuremburg, Germany. Flying Officer Pilot Orr is buried in the Churchyard at Souilly, Meuse, France, grave 3
(Quoted from book - *They Shall Grow Not Old*)

Private, **William Osburn**, Lorne Scots, employed by George Rawn, Caledon East - next of kin, Mr. Osburn, Orangeville

Sergeant, **James B. Palmer**, R175391, RCAF, 1942, son of D.H. Palmer, Dundalk and former teacher at Caledon East Continuation School

Leading Aircraftsman, **Norman J. H. Palmer**, R179973, RCAF, July 17 1942-Oct 15 1945, son of Harry Palmer & Martha Fleming, Albion Twp., General Service Badge

Nursing Sister, **Mary Parkinson**, RCAMC, 1944, daughter of Elisha Parkinson, Bolton

Private, **George Parks**, B168233, next of kin - George Samuel Clarke, Albion Twp.

Gunner, **George Edgar Patterson**, B72041, RCA, Aug 4 1942-Apr 1946, son of John Edgar Patterson & Mary Strath, Albion Twp.

Private, **Ernest Peer**, B103240, Jan 25 1944, next of kin - William Gray, Caledon East

Private, **John Albert Perdue**, B158149, Infantry Training Centre, Jan 1944, son of James M. Perdue & Hazel Faulkner, Caledon East

Squadron Leader, **John Wycliffe Perry**, DSO, DFC, R93139 and J9192, RCAF, Jan 1941-1946, son of William M. Perry & Ethel G. Hope, King Twp., Distinguished Service Order, Distinguished Flying Cross, The 1939-1945 Star, The Atlantic Star, The Air Crew Europe Star (& Germany on bar), The Defence Medal, Canadian Volunteer Service Medal (Maple Leaf on bar), The 1939-1945 War Medal.

Trooper, **William Irwin Perry**, RCAC, Tank Corps, 1940-1946, son of William M. Perry & Ethel G. Hope, King Twp., Canadian Volunteer Service Medal, The Defence Medal, The Defence of Great Britain Medal, The 1939-1945 Star, The France and Germany Star, The Normandy Medal

Private, **Glenn Phillips**, Army Headquarters, London, England, Oct 1942-Mar 1946, son of William Phillips & Pearl Stykes, Kleinburg

Private, **Louis C. Pilson**, B51717, Lorne Scots, Apr 8 1941-Jan 18 1946, son of Roger Pilson Sr. & Violet Smith, Bolton, Canadian Volunteer Service Medal, The Defence Medal, The 1939-1945 War Medal

Private, **Roger Pilson**, B136324, RCASC & RCAMC, Jan 26 1943-Jan 26 1946, son of Roger Pilson Sr. & Violet Smith, husband of Mary Stein, Bolton, Canadian Volunteer Service Medal, The Defence Medal, The 1939-1945 War Medal

Private, **Fred Piper**, B56095, RCASC, Sept 21 1942, husband of Wanda Watts, Bolton

Wilfred Piper, army, employed on various King Twp. farms

Sapper, **Lloyd George Pollard**, B92969, RCE, July 23 1944, Caledon East, brother of Mary Olive Cousins, Brampton

Lance Corporal, **Gordon Leslie Porter**, R56637, RCEME, July 17 1942-Jan 12 1946, son of Harland John Porter & Gladys Alma Keith, Caledon East and Bolton, Canadian Volunteer Service Medal with Clasp, The 1939-1945 Star, The 1939-1945 War Medal, The France and Germany Star, The Defence of Britain Medal

Sergeant, **Winnifred Alma Porter**, W22211, CWAC, Sept 22 1943-Nov 13 1945, daughter of Harland John Porter & Gladys Alma Keith, Caledon East and Bolton, Canadian Volunteer Service Medal, The 1939-1945 War Medal

Sergeant, **Frank Potter**, B56500, RCASC, Nov 26 1942, son of Percy Potter & Mildred A. Winger, Sand Hill

Captain, **Stanley Pringle**, B35235, Veterans' Home Guard, June 1940-Apr 1946, son of William Pringle & Hannah Armstrong, England, husband of Edna May Woolley, father of John, Edna & Bill, Nobleton, Canadian Volunteer Service Medal, The Defence Medal, The 1939-1945 War Medal

Flight Lieutenant, **Billy Proctor**, DFC, R153760 & J24138, RCAF, 601 Squadron, 1941-May 1945 son of James N. Proctor & Elizabeth Wright, Caledon East, Distinguished Flying Cross, Canadian Volunteer Service Medal with Clasp, The Defence Medal, The 1939-1945 Star, The Italy Star. Flight Lieutenant Proctor trained on Tiger Moth and Harvard aircraft and flew Spitfires in Egypt and Italy according to his son, Greg Proctor.

Major, **Charles E. Read**, MC, ADC, 48th Highlanders, 1941-1945, husband of Nancy Canfield, father of Dick, Tony, Mike & Peter, Bolton, Military Cross, Senior aide-de-camp. Major Read was the Commanding Officer for Military Cadets, District #2. According to his son Richard, Major Read was appointed the Senior aide-de-camp to The Honourable Ray Lawson, OBE, who was Lieutenant Governor of Ontario from December 26 1946 to February 18 1952. He also served as Senior aide de camp to The Honourable Louis Orville Breithaupt who was Lieutenant Governor of Ontario from February 18 1952 to December 30 1957.

Private, **Richard (Dick) Robert Reeves**, Dec 1 1940, employed by Henry Wilson, an Albion Township farmer north of Bolton on Highway 50

Signalman, **Angus Reid**, RCCS, Apr 1942, born in Scotland, lived in Toronto area, son of James Reid & Annie Campbell, King Twp.

Gunner, **David Reid**, Sept 1941, born in Scotland, lived in Toronto area, son of James Reid & Annie Campbell, King Twp

Sapper, **Earl Reid**, B119455, RCE, Nov 30 1943-Mar 18 1946, Palgrave, son of Andrew James Reid & Margaret Fields, Alliston, Canadian Volunteer Service Medal & Clasp, The 1939-1945 Star, The Italy Star

Private, **George Reid**, B75107, 48th Highlanders & Irish Regiment of Canada, Sept 1941, born in Scotland, lived in Campbell's Cross area, son of James Reid & Annie Campbell, King Twp., killed Dec 31 1944, grave I.H.20 Ancona War Cemetery, Italy

Gunner, **James Reid**, RCASC, Mar 1942, born in Scotland, lived in Toronto & Nobleton areas, son of James Reid & Annie Campbell, King Twp.

Robert John Edward Reid, B51920, Lorne Scots, husband of Bertha J. Reid, Mono Mills

Gunner, **John H. Reynar**, B9849, RCA, Nov 18 1941-Feb 19 1944, son of Hedley Reynar & Agnes Wallace, Palgrave

Corporal, **Arthur Richards**, B91805, RCASC, Jan 29 1942-Aug 18 1945, son of Albert Richards & Agnes Jamieson, King Twp., Canadian Volunteer Service Medal, The Defence Medal, The 1939-1945 Star, The France & Germany Star

Lance Corporal, **John Edward Richardson**, B93605, RCAMC, Sept 2 1939, son of William & Jeanette Richardson, Caledon East

Flight Lieutenant, **William Frederick Richardson**, RCAF, 1940-1945, son of Captain William Randall Richardson & Velvin M. Potter, Bolton, Canadian Volunteer Service Medal, The Defence of Britain Medal, The 1939-1945 Star, The 1939-1945 Victory Medal. After WW II Bill Richardson operated a Ford-Monarch car-truck dealership at the south west corner of Queen and Sterne Streets in Bolton. A vehicle repair and gas station business was previously owned and operated there by his uncle Elwyn Elliott, a World War I veteran. Prior to that, Elwyn Elliott's father, Thomas D. Elliott, hotelkeeper and liveryman, was the owner of the property which extended about half way to King Street.

Captain, **William Randall Richardson**, Royal Canadian Dental Corps, Apr 15 1942-Jan 16 1946, son of Dr. William Richardson & Ada Christina Hickling, Barrie, husband of Velvin M. Potter and father of William, Bolton. Dr. Richardson's dental practice and residence was located at 15 King Street West in Bolton before moving to Woodbridge.

Harold Ridell, son of Herb & Naomi Ridell, 8th line, King Twp.

Lillian Rivers, CWAC, daughter of Rev. George William Wesley Rivers & Lottie Mary Polley, Bolton

Sergeant, **Raymond P. Rivers**, B83431, RCEME, June 1940, son of Rev. George William Wesley Rivers & Lottie Mary Polley, Bolton

Leading Aircraftsman, **Donald Robb**, RCAF, son of Judge Walter T. Robb & Elizabeth S. Warner, Orangeville

Lieutenant, **Jack Robb**, son of Judge Walter T. Robb & Elizabeth S. Warner, Orangeville

Leading Aircraftsman, **Kenneth Duncan Robb**, R257094, aircraft electrician with Bomber Command, RCAF, May 1944-1947, son of Judge Walter T. Robb & Elizabeth S. Warner, Orangeville. After the war, Kenneth Robb became a successful lawyer in Brampton and received the appointment of Queen's Counsel.

Corporal, **Lloyd Robb**, B135631, RCIC, Nov 5 1942-Jan 9 1946, son of Leonard Robb & Elva McCallum, King Twp., Canadian Volunteer Service Medal, The Defence Medal, The 1939-1945 War Medal, The Italy Star

Flight Sergeant, **Reginald Francis Robb**, R72335, RCAF, son of Judge Walter T. Robb & Elizabeth S. Warner, Orangeville was killed at age 25, Feb 26 1942. #158 Squadron (Strength in Unity). Wellington aircraft #Z8536 was carrying bombs when it had the port engine fail on take off. The aircraft crashed two miles north of the aerodrome at Pocklington Yorkshire. Flight Sergeant Robb is buried in St. Catherine Churchyard, Barmby-on-the-Moor, Yorkshire England. Row E. Grave 5 (Quoted from the book- *They Shall Grow Not Old*)

Warrant Officer, **J. Bruce Robertson**, 403A, RCAF, 1940, son of Rev. David A. Robertson & Florence Wren, Bolton

Private, **David A. Robertson**, Royal Canadian Dragoons, son of Rev. David A. Robertson & Florence Wren, Bolton

Private, **Delbert Robertson**, C11643, RCASC, 1940, son of William Robertson & Eliza Jean White, Bolton

Corporal, **Ernest J. Robertson**, B51891, Lorne Scots, Jan 5 1941, son of William Robertson & Eliza Jean White, Bolton

Private, **Verner Robertson**, B51792, Lorne Scots, Apr 26 1941, son of William Robertson & Eliza Jean White, Bolton

Able Seaman, **Gerald Robinson**, V69271, RCNVR, Aug 24 1943-Oct 22 1945, son of George Robinson & Florence Graham, Palgrave

Leading Aircraftsman, **Jack Robinson**, R141181, RCAF, 1942, son of Walter Robinson & Jennie Warwick, Caledon East

Sub Lieutenant, **Kathleen Elizabeth Robinson**, WRCNS, June 22 1942-June 1943, daughter of Albert Robinson & Clara Mabel Nattress, Bolton. Kathleen Robinson married Lieutenant James Bicknell Keachie, RCNVR.

Lance Corporal, **Charles Roden**, B51756, Lorne Scots, Apr 25 1941- Sept 1945, son of George Roden & Jane Wright, husband of Alice Huson, father of Larry, Rosalie, Charlie, Jimmie & Ross, Bolton, Canadian Volunteer Service Medal, The Defence Medal

Leading Aircraftsman, **Howard Roduck**, R285715, RCAF, Oct 25 1943, and Private Howard Roduck, B24619, Canadian Infantry Corps, Dec 21 1944-Feb 9 1945, son of Roberts Roduck & Mabel Palmer, Bolton

Trooper, **Kenneth Roduck**, B145603, RCAC, Apr 7 1943-Mar 30 1946, son of Roberts Roduck & Mabel Palmer, Bolton, The 1939-1945 Star, The France and Germany Star, The Italy Star

Corporal, **(Bob) Oliver James Fleming Roe**, R220916, RCAF, May 20 1943, son of Thomas J. Roe & Laura E. Wray, Palgrave

Corporal, **Thomas Wray Roe**, B74328, 48th Highlanders, May 20 1940, son of Thomas J. Roe & Laura E. Wray, Palgrave

Private, **Kenneth Rolley**, B57205, Aug 26 1942-Sept 1943, son of Norman Rolley & Martha Henderson, Albion Twp.

Lance Corporal, **Milton Rolley**, B134358, Oct 15 1942, son of Norman Rolley & Martha Henderson, Albion Twp.

Private, **Ira Russell**, B45304, raised by Mr. & Mrs. Bartlett, Sand Hill

Lieutenant, **Henry Rutherford**, B6771, RCA, Jan 4 1941-Oct 17 1945, son of James H. Rutherford & Mary See, Albion Twp., Canadian Volunteer Service Medal & Clasp, The Defence Medal, The France and Germany Star, The 1939-1945 Star

Basil Samari, B74756, Central Ontario Regiment, Caledon East

Captain, **C. Graham Sanderson**, 22nd Armoured Regiment, Royal Canadian Medical Corps, son of Charles Rupert Sanderson & Sarah Ethel Marshall, Caledon East, killed in action Aug14 1944, grave XXIV.A.5., Bretteville-Sur-Laize Canadian War Cemetery, Calvados, France

Sub Lieutenant, **Dorothy Sanderson**, WRCNS, 1942, daughter of V.S. Sanderson, Caledon East

Private, **Art Sandford**, son of William John & Edith Alice Sandford, Palgrave

Sergeant, **Charles Edward Sandford**, R89718, Royal Air Force, May 1941, son of Charles W. & Eva Sandford, Nashville, served in India

Private, **Jesse Sandford**, son of William John & Edith Alice Sandford, Palgrave

Private, **Norman Edward Sandford**, B43342, 48th Highlanders, son of William John & Edith Alice Sandford, Palgrave, killed Dec 25 1943, grave III.H.3., Moro River Canadian War Cemetery, Italy

Corporal, **Alex Shaw**, Grenadier Guards Tank Corps, 1942-Feb 1946, son of Earl Shaw & Frances Shaw, Kleinburg

Lance Corporal, **Everard Bruce Shaw**, B131407, RCA, Aug 21 1942-Aug 1945, son of Everard James Shaw & Mabel Armstrong, Albion Twp.

Private, **Frank Shaw**, B241754, RCEME, Jan 1944-May 1946, son of Earl Shaw & Frances Shaw, Kleinburg

Craftsman (Cfmn), **Lorne Hewgill Sheardown**, B2490, RCOC, Sept 28 1942-Mar 19 1946, son of Colin Sheardown & Irene E. Hewgill, Bolton, Canadian Volunteer Service Medal & Clasp, The Defence Medal

Private, **Gordon Sherman**, B127966, Kent Regiment, Dec 1942, son of Ainslee E. Sherman & Helen Blanche Moore, Sand Hill

Private, **Osborne Howden Shields**, B18241, RCATC, May 21 1941, son of George S. Shields, Toronto, husband of Rena E. Oliphant, Caledon East

Private, **Clayton Smith**, B53046, Aug 27 1941, son of Earl Smith & Clara Walker, employed by Gordon Munro, Palgrave

Aircraftsman 2, **John Chester Smith**, R118987, RCAF, July 19 1941, son of John Elgin Smith & Clara Alberta Irwin, Caledon East

Sergeant, **Robert J. Smith**, R187986, RCAF, Aug 1942-1945, son of Dr. William John Smith & Priscilla Mae Rogers, Brampton, Canadian Volunteer Service Medal. After the war, Robert Smith, a pharmacist, became a partner in the Leggett & Smith Drug Store business in Bolton

Petty Officer, **Elmer (Al) Snider**, RCN, Nobleton, son of Roy Snider, Red Deer, Alberta

Sergeant, **James Charles Snider**, RCAF, June 1937, Nobleton, son of Roy Snider, Red Deer, Alberta Leroy Snider, Nobleton, from Red Deer, Alberta, a cousin to the aforementioned Elmer (Al) & James Charles Snider

Leroy Snider, Nobleton, from Red Deer, Alberta, a cousin to the aforementionied Elmer (Al) & James Charles Snide

Sergeant, **Harold Alexander Speers**, R175492, RCAF, July 2 1942, son of Archie Speers & Ida Martin, Caledon East

Corporal, **James Elwood Speers**, R156793, RCAF, Feb 23 1942, son of Archie Speers & Ida Martin, Caledon East

Private, **Raymond Robert Alexander Speers**, B46410, Argyle & Sutherland Highlanders, Sept 23 1940, son of Orville J. Speers & Mabel Arlow, Caledon East, killed in France Aug 28 1944, grave V.B.8., Bretteville-Sur-Laize Canadian War Cemetery, Calvados, France

Private, **Willis Henry Speers**, B135763, Queen's Own Rifles, Nov 10 1942, son of Vernet & Mabel Speers, Caledon East

Flying Officer, **Douglas McKenzie Speirs**, J21783, flying instructor of Harvard aircraft, RCAF, Oct 14 1941-1946, son of Peter Speirs & Euphemia McKenzie, Albion Twp., Canadian Volunteer Service Medal

Private, **Kenneth Steadman**, B78826, Irish Regiment

Corporal, **Byron Steele**, R156808, RCAF, Feb 24 1941, son of Harry Steele & Margaret Ewart, Bolton

Flying Officer, **James Murray Stevens**, RCAF, 1942-1945, son of Robert Stevens & Anna McKnight, Kleinburg. Flying Officer Stevens earned his Wings as a Pilot Officer at Hagersville in 1943 and was sent overseas. He was stationed at Uphaven in the south of England and Chipping Norton, near Rugby, as a Flying Instructor on Oxford twin engine trainers. He ended World War II as a Flying Officer. After several courses in science at Rehab School in Toronto, he entered the Ontario Veterinary College in Guelph and graduated in June 1950. He was appointed Regional Veterinarian for Eastern Ontario on the extension staff of Ontario Veterinary College. In 1954 he went into private practice in Stouffville but left the business in 1957 on the advice of his doctor. Dr. Stevens died of a massive coronary on August 31, 1958 in his 38th year. This information has been provided by Sinclair Stevens, a brother to James Murray Stevens.

Dan Stewart, B83925
RCASC, Caledon East

Sergeant, **Laura Stewart**, W311376, RCAF, Mar 1 1943-Nov 19 1946, daughter of Dill Stewart & Gladys Marshall, Albion Twp., Canadian Volunteer Service Medal, The 1939-1945 War Medal

Squadron Leader, **William Andrew Stewart**, RCAF, Feb 1940-1945, son of James A. Stewart & Edith Inkster, Indian Head, Saskatchewan, formerly Albion Twp., Canadian Volunteer Service Medal

Private, **John Stone**, B129598, Canadian Forestry Unit, Dec 18 1942-Mar 4 1945, son of George Stone & Lorna Crossley, King City, husband of Erma Watts, Bolton

Private, **William Peter Storey**, B127534, Canadian Fusiliers, July 17 1942, son of George & Maude Storey, Mono Mills, died July 22 1944, interred Plot 1. Sec.1. grave 3, St. John's Cemetery, Mono

Henry Stoutley, Caledon East

Leading Aircraftsman, **Charlie Strong**, R179736, RCAF, May 1942-Sept 1945, son of Wesley Strong & Olga May Copeman, husband of Audrey Bowes, Albion Twp., Castlederg

Sapper, **Frank J. Stubbs**, B130878, RCE, Sept 1942-Jan 1946, son of Albert Stubbs Sr. & Ida Booth, Bolton

Howard Lloyd Stubbs, Merchant Navy, Apr 26 1944-May 25 1944, son of Fred Stubbs & Lorna M. Gozalle, Bolton, husband of Hazel Packham, Toronto. The Merchant Navy played an integral part during the war by transporting desperately needed goods to the Allied Forces throughout the world.

Bandsman, **Lloyd Stubbs**, V59796, RCNVR, Apr 30 1943-1945, son of Sam Stubbs & Clara Heels, Bolton

Sergeant, **Joe Studholme**, B435102, Lorne Scots, 1939-1947, son of Robert Studholme & Annie Cooper, Bolton, Canadian Volunteer Service Medal & Clasp, Canadian Efficiency Medal, The Defence of Britain Medal, The Victory Medal, The France and Germany Star, The 1939-1945 Star

Sergeant, **Roy Studholme**, R250011C, RCAF, Oct 1941-Oct 1946, son of Robert Studholme & Annie Cooper, Bolton, Canadian Volunteer Service Medal & Clasp, Canadian Efficiency Medal, The Defence Medal, The Victory Medal

Dan Sullivan, son of Edward Sullivan & May Graham, King Twp.

Stoker 1, **Edgar Lorne Taylor**, V80137, RCNVR, son of Annie Taylor, Mono Mills

Captain, **Herbert L. Taylor**, RCAMC, 1942-1944, son of George Taylor & Leila Bentley, Toronto, husband of Ruth Fleming, father of Darlene, Deborah, Grover & Shelley, Bolton. Dr. Taylor was a popular physician and surgeon in Bolton following World War II and was active in various worthwhile causes in the village. His office and residence was located at 34 Temperance Street in Bolton which was previously occupied by two other soldier doctors namely: Captain John Graham and Major Charles Hunter Wilson.

Gunner, **Jeremiah H. Taylor**, B164251, RCA, Aug 18 1944, son of Leonard Taylor & Irene Hutchinson, Albion Twp.

Russell Taylor, son of Stanley Taylor & Cora Fagin, Albion Twp.

Gunner, **Albert George Terry**, B11249, RCA, 1940, son of William Terry, Waterdown, husband of Olga Reynar, Palgrave

Sergeant, **Arnold Thompson**, B94281, RCOC, Nov 24 1939-Oct 12 1944, son of Alfred Thompson & Sarah Gould, husband of Marion Elizabeth Ruston, father of Verda, Douglas, Whilliamein, Doreen & Robert, Bolton, Canadian Volunteer Service Medal with Clasp, Defence Medal, The 1939-1945 War Medal, The 1939-1945 Star, The Italy Star

Gunner, **Clarence J. Thompson**, B17886, RCA, Jan 6 1942, son of A.C. Thompson, Palgrave

Private, **Robert H. Townrow**, B57230, RCOC, Aug 28 1942, son of Harry Townrow & Mary Robinson, Bolton

Lieutenant **Bruce Train**, army, son of Leonard Train & Reta Kaake, King Twp., Nobleton

Cyril Trainor, army, son of James Trainor, King Twp.

Lawrence Turner, son of Richard Turner, Tullamore area

Corporal, **Jesse Turton**, BEM, Signal Reinforcement Unit, Mar 1941-Oct 1945, son of Roy Turton & Hannah Harvey, Nobleton, British Empire Medal

Flying Officer, **John Harold Brimley Veals**, B183576, RCAF, Aug 4 1942, son of Rev. John Spurgeon Veals & Lena Brimley, Caledon East

Lance Corporal, **William Venning**, B26754, RCE & RCOC, Sept 21 1942-Feb 14 1946, son of Albert J. Venning & Mammie Hanson, Toronto, husband of Versile Stephenson, Bolton, Canadian Volunteer Service Medal, The Defence Medal, King George Active Service Medal

Private **Sid Vicer**y, army, employed by Stan Cain, King Twp. farmer

Private, **Frederick Wagstaff**, B16165, Veterans' Home Guard, 1940, son of Sarah (Hayes) Wagstaff, step-son of Henry James Everett, Bolton

Driver, **Albert George Walker**, B87436, RCASC, Nov 7 1941, son of Wesley Walker & Ida Helen Campsall, Palgrave

Private, **Gordon Elmer Clifford Walker**, B87168, RCASC, Jan 6 1942, son of Wesley Walker & Ida Helen Campsall, Palgrave, died in England Dec 26 1943, grave 47.J.8., Brookwood Military Cemetery, Surrey, United Kingdom

Surgeon Lieutenant, **George Rutherford Walker**, RCNVR, 1942, son of Dr. Robertson R. Walker, Bolton

Hubert Walker, raised by Mr. & Mrs. Sullivan, 3rd line, Albion Twp.

Private, **Adam Wallace**, DCM, MM & Bar, B36177, Veterans' Home Guard, June 1940-Aug 1945, son of Robert J. Wallace Sr. & Mary Jane McGee, husband of Olga Moon, father of Verna, Keith, Robert, Cyril, Harvey, Doreen, Olga Marie and foster daughter Isabel Hepburn, Bolton, Distinguished Conduct Medal, Military Medal and Bar, The Great War for Civilization Medal 1914-1919, The War Service Medal 1914-1918

Leading Aircraftsman, **Charles Henry Wallace**, B193990, RCAF, 1942, son of Harry Wallace, Caledon East

Sergeant, **H.E. Wallace**, B94215, RCOC

Driver, **William Gordon Walton**, B81000, RCASC, Aug 1 1942-1945, son of William Walton & Irene Jackson, Albion Twp.

Private, **Graham Ward**, B122549, RCIC, Mar 10 1945-Sept 18 1945, son of James Campbell Ward & Florence Edna Neelands, Caledon East

Sergeant, **Jean Ward**, W20419, CWAC, Oct 24 1942-Feb 4 1946, daughter of James Campbell Ward & Florence Edna Neelands, Caledon East, Canadian Volunteer Service Medal, The Defence Medal

Bandsman, **Joe Waterer**, Palgrave

Wren, **Alice Watson**, W6372, WRCNS, Dec 1943-Apr 1945, daughter of William Wesley Watson & Winnifred Player, Caledon Twp., Canadian Volunteer Service Medal

Private, **Bert (Herbert N.) Watts**, B138678, RCASC, Jan 12 1943, transferred to RCAF Dec 29 1943, transferred to RCNVR Jan 26 1945, son of John Watts & Lodilla Robinson, Bolton

Ernest Waye, Nobleton - King Twp.

Thomas Allison Weir, Royal Canadian Artillery, son of Thomas Weir & Martha Blair, Caledon East

Sapper, **Wesley Odell Weir**, B25463, RCE, Feb 8 1941, born in Orangeville, employed by Oswald Potter, Caledon East

Pilot Officer, **Frank Westlake**, R102811, RCAF, May 3 1941, son of John Westlake & Mary Jane Horsley, Albion Twp.

Corporal, **David J. Whistance-Smith**, B113069, RCA, Apr 20 1942, son of Thomas Whistance-Smith & Adelaide Carnew, Mount Dennis, husband of Elizabeth Pearson, Palgrave

Trooper, **T. William Whistance-Smith**, B74775, Canadian Tank Regiment, July 1 1940, son of Thomas Whistance-Smith & Adelaide Carnew, Mount Dennis, lived in Palgrave & Bolton

Corporal, **John Whitbread**, B51798, Lorne Scots, Apr 29 1941-Nov 1945, son of William Whitbread & Lillian Osborne, Toronto, husband of Sarah Stubbs, father of Bill, Bolton

Private, **William White**, B80913, CAO, raised by Mr. & Mrs. Elwyn Searle (Irene Carey), Vaughan Twp.

Ordinary Seaman, **William Kenneth Whitlam**, V52132, RCNVR, 1943, son of Jack Whitlam & Hazel Cunnington, Caledon East

Private, **Cora Elizabeth Williams**, W22449, CWAC, Feb 7 1944, daughter of Sarah Martha Williams, Mono Mills

Lance Corporal, **Louis Oscar Williams**, B12361, Royal Canadian Artillery, son of Sarah Martha Williams, Mono Mills

Warrant Officer, **Harry Ward Williamson**, R71602, RCAF, son of Russell Williamson & Florence Ward, King Twp. killed July 16 1942. #158 Squadron (Strength In Unity). Halifax aircraft #BB203 crashed at Manor Farm, Cornborough, Yorkshire. Pilot Officer J.F. Withy (RAF) and three other RAF members of the crew were also killed. Warrant Officer Class II Pilot Williamson is buried at All Saints Churchyard, Newton-upon-Ouse, Yorkshire, England. grave 9, Row T (Quoted from book - *They Shall Grow Not Old*)

Major, **Charles Hunter Wilson**, RCAMC, son of John Condie Wilson & Amelia Jane Hass, St. George Ontario, husband of Grace Mitchell, father of Paul & Peggy, Bolton. Major Wilson was a special medical advisor in New Brunswick to the Department of National Defence during World War II. After the war, Major Wilson purchased the Dr. John Graham medical practice and residence at 34 Temperance Street in Bolton. He continued in this profession until his sudden death on June 8 1947. The June 13 1947 edition of the *Bolton Enterprise* states - "He was a particularly keen baseball player. Throughout his lifetime he maintained this interest in sports being a lawn bowling and curling enthusiast. For a couple of seasons he coached Ontario Hockey Association hockey teams in Bolton and maintained a live interest in other branches of community activities."

Rifleman, **Edward John (E. J.) Wilson**, B65773, Queen's Own Rifles & 48th Highlanders, July 2 1942-Nov 19 1945, son of Edward Wilson & Emma Barry, Bolton, Canadian Volunteer Service Medal & Clasp, The 1939-1945 Star, The France & Germany Star, The Italy Star

Private, **Everett Barry Wilson**, B158457, Irish Regiment, July 23 1944, son of Edward Wilson & Emma Barry, Bolton

Private, **George A. Wilson**, B112600, Royal Canadian Ordnance Corps, May 2 1942, son of William Wilson, husband of Jeane Younge, Mono Mills

Corporal, **Grant Ira Wilson**, B136518, Lincoln & Welland Regiment, Nov 23 1942-Mar 21 1946, son of Edward Wilson & Emma Barry, Bolton, Canadian Volunteer Service Medal & Clasp, The 1939-1945 Star, The France and Germany Star

Private, **Laude Wilson**, B37462, Royal Hamilton Light Infantry, 1940-1945, adopted son of George A. Wilson & Maybelle Leadbetter, Bolton, prisoner of war for three years

Private, **Thomas Oliver Wilson**, B132868, RCA, Sept 12 1942-Nov 30 1945, son of Edward Wilson & Emma Barry, Bolton, Canadian Volunteer Service Medal & Clasp, The 1939-1945 Star, The France and Germany Star, The Italy Star

Sergeant, **Alfred Tom Wolfenden**, B89126, RCASC, July 1940, born in England, husband of Jessie M. Beaton, father of Fred, Roy & Victor, Bolton

Sergeant, **Stanley Albert Wood**, R51027, RCAF, son of Albert & Elizabeth Wood, Palgrave, died Oct 20 1943, grave Lot GE.34. Coll., St. Donat Roman Catholic Cemetery, Quebec

Anne Woods, CWAC, daughter of George Bolton, formerly of Bolton

Private, **Lesley Young**, B56270, Veterans' Home Guard, Oct 16 1942, friend of Harold Ewart, Albion Twp.

Thomas Young, Vaughan Twp.

Flying Officer, **Norman Zimmerman**, R257993, J48754, RCAF, Aug 30 1943-Oct 1945, son of John Zimmerman & Lillian McGuire, Palgrave, Canadian Volunteer Service Medal, The 1939-1945 War Medal

≪≪ Chapter Sixteen ≫≫
They Live on in Our Memories

"Not for a better world, nor glory for my country, but for my home and family is my will to fight."
Private Robert McAllister, Lorne Scots (1941-1946)

For Those Who Served pays tribute to the men and women from this area who fought in the two world wars, and presents information that might otherwise have been lost in the shifting sands of time. Many details connected with these two Allied military accomplishments were written in letters by servicemen and women, some of which have been used here to illustrate a part of the lives lived by these courageous Canadians. While Canada has never sought conflict, it has always stood ready to defend the precious freedoms which were established across this land many years ago. Even though we are a peace-loving nation, it was necessary to engage in warfare on these occasions. This book helps to emphasize some of the qualities in Canadians that make us unique.

Keeping Our History Alive

The Commonwealth War Graves Commission was established by Royal Charter in 1917. Its duties are to mark and maintain the graves of the members of the forces of the Commonwealth who were killed in the two world wars. It is also charged with building memorials to those who have no known grave and to keep records and registers, including, after the Second World War, a record of the civilian war dead.

It was the energy of Sir Fabian Ware, the Commission's founder, which established the principles upon which the work of the Commission was built. Those principles, which have remained unaltered, are:

- each of the dead should be commemorated individually by name on headstone or memorial
- headstones and memorials should be permanent
- headstones should be uniform
- there should be no distinction made on account of military or civil rank, race or creed

1.7 million men and women of the Commonwealth forces died in the two world wars. Of these, the remains of barely more than half, 925,000, have been found. A personally dedicated headstone marks each of their graves. Where the remains of an individual have not been found, that person's name is commemorated on a memorial wall in one of the many Commonwealth cemeteries. There are war graves in some 150 countries, mostly in the 2,500 war cemeteries and plots constructed by the Commission.

There are also war graves in many civil cemeteries and churchyards throughout the world. The Commission employs craftsmen to maintain the architectural features of its cemeteries and memorials, and embellishes its sites with attractive landscaping to give fitting and peaceful commemoration to those who died.

The forward march by Canada's armed forces, and their contributions to worldwide peace have been somewhat overlooked over the years. Canadian men and women of the navy, army and air force risked their lives during various conflicts. Many died in the effort; others were left with permanent physical damage; still others were spiritually wounded. Our servicemen and women have served with distinction and courage in the truly unique, Canadian style - without fanfare.

Recently, however, two major steps have been taken to keep alive in our memories, the sacrifices this special group of Canadians made, along with the history that was written by their actions.

The Return of the Vimy Red Ensign

The Red Ensign flag carried up Vimy Ridge by Canadians in 1917 has been in the possession of the Imperial War Museum in London, England since the end of World War I. This flag displays the emblems of Canada's four original provinces, Ontario, Quebec, Nova Scotia and New Brunswick. Now, after many denied requests throughout the years, the Museum has agreed to lend the flag to Canada for two years. Approval was finally obtained through the diligent efforts of Duane Daly of the Canadian Legion. The Vimy Ensign will be the centre-piece for a new Canadian War Museum opening in Ottawa in 2005, and it holds great significance because, in the eyes of many people, Canada became a nation at Vimy Ridge. It is absolutely amazing that this flag survived the battle in good condition. It is also indeed gratifying to know that it is being placed in the hands of Canadians who will treasure it. They will do so because they possess a feeling towards it unlike any other people. Many Canadians lost their lives at Vimy Ridge, accomplishing what other armies could not. This victory symbolized the courage of a nation and the Red Ensign carried into battle by the 5th Saskatchewan Battalion symbolized Canada. Allowing the flag to come to Canada is therefore a fitting gesture on the part of the Imperial War Museum.

Commemorating the Juno Beach Landing in Normandy

A building called The Juno Beach Centre, "A Learning Centre and Tribute to Canadians" is scheduled to open at Courseulles-sur-Mer in Normandy, France on June 6, 2003. The concept was developed by a group of World War II veterans who participated in the D-Day landings on June 6, 1944 and other battles in Normandy and Western Europe. They recognized the need to preserve the memory, and to describe the facts of Canada's military and civilian contributions and efforts during the Second World War. Canadian participation in all war theatres will be featured. It will be an educational facility designed for all ages and built through donations from interested individuals, groups, corporations and government. The Department of Veterans Affairs is contributing one million dollars towards the undertaking as well as coordinating efforts to develop the project.

More than 120 Canadian warships took part in the landings at Normandy in 1944 as 15,000 Canadians soldiers made their way to shore at Juno Beach under the command of Major General R.F.L. Keller. While the USA-led invasions on Omaha and Utah Beaches and the British ones at Sword and Gold Beaches are celebrated loudly, the significant Canadian achievement at Juno Beach is sometimes overshadowed. On the night of June 6, Canadian troops were farther inland than any others. The Juno Beach Centre will thus be a fitting memorial to mark this historic event in our history.

Peacekeeping Role Continues

After the Second World War, Canada's role in peacekeeping operations has been impressive, taking men and women to the site of many conflicts. They include Korea, Lebanon, Congo, Cyprus, South Vietnam, Syria, Iran-Iraq, Haiti, Bosnia, Cambodia, Somalia, and Rwanda. Following the terrorist attack on the World Trade Centre in New York City on September 11,

2001, Canada re-entered the field of combat by sending troops to Afghanistan. When the need arises, Canada has always shown its courage and determination to do what is required. Men and women, like the ones mentioned in this book, in all branches of the armed forces have risen to the occasion without hesitation and contributed with great force and spirit.

While it is not our intent to promote war, we do want to keep alive the stories of those who sacrificed themselves so that we may live in peace. *For Those Who Served* is dedicated to those men and women and is an effort to help succeeding generations to understand the significance of these events in the development of Canada's history.

◇

"The people in both countries will suffer for a time after the war is over. It is much easier to go on fighting knowing that we will find our homes to return to, but many of the French and Belgium soldiers will have no homes to return to if they do get through safely."

Pte. Thomas Mills, Ypres, May 1915

"The Canadians got a severe setback as to casualties, but they held firm and did not lose any ground and even retook part of the French lost ground when they were forced to retire owing to the terrible suffocating gas used by the Germans."

F. S. Rutherford, Canadian Engineers in France, May 1915

"A year ago we were on top of Vimy Ridge, having secured it from the enemy on the 9th. Terrible weather then, rain followed by snow and as cold as ice."

Private Adam Wallace, France, April 1918

"About mid-day all except one machine of our Squadron returned. Warwick was the first one to land on the drome, and as I watched him taxi in I noticed that no observer was visible and I realized what it meant. I shall never forget the feeling I had when I realized this, and for a while I must confess that my spirits were dampened by the horror of the whole thing."

Lieutenant Joseph Gordon Dennis, France, August 1918

"I look back on four years service in the Canadian Army with pride and with joy. I never fired a shot in anger nor was I ever shot at. So my contribution at best was very peripheral. But it was a worthwhile effort just the same and an experience I am very glad I had."

Doris Evans (Porter), CWAC, 1945

"Four sailors went down in the ship and the rest were plucked from the icy cold waters. They were suffering terribly from frozen limbs and we gave them our blankets and rations of rum and then got them back to Halifax and waiting ambulances."

Gerald Robinson, Royal Canadian Navy, December 1944

"Squadron Leader John Perry is a highly efficient Pilot and Captain who has now completed two tours of operations. He is an outstanding organizer and leader whose personal example of fearlessness and extreme devotion to duty has had a most inspiring effect on all aircrew in the Squadron."

Squadron Leader Perry's Citation for the Award of the Distinguished Service Order, 1945

◄◄◄ Index ►►►